AGRARIAN UNREST
IN SOUTHEAST ASIA

ERICH H. JACOBY

Agrarian Unrest
in Southeast Asia

1949

New York · COLUMBIA UNIVERSITY PRESS

PUBLISHED IN GREAT BRITAIN AND INDIA BY GEOFFREY CUMBERLEGE
OXFORD UNIVERSITY PRESS, LONDON AND BOMBAY

To Lotte

Foreword

AGRARIAN UNREST in Southeast Asia is not a new phenomenon; but it has new and vast implications. In the following chapters Mr. E. H. Jacoby has made a survey of the difficulties and discontents of the peasant peoples on the mainland of subtropical Asia and in the tropical archipelagoes. Their troubles have recently erupted into the headlines; but they have been accumulating over long years. Mr. Jacoby has not attempted to extend his survey to the greater and better-known continental areas of China and India; but much of his analysis is pertinent to their great populations also. Behind the political unrest flaring into sporadic violence and rebellion, lies the tremendous fact that Europe is losing its grip over its colonial possessions in Asia. There is in process a retraction of empire—not only of the British imperial rule, but of the French and Dutch.

It is significant, however, that agrarian unrest is widespread in the areas of independent sovereignty—the Philippines and Siam as well as China. It has deeper roots than political subordination, and is in fact a phase of the economic dislocation caused by the breakdown of the nineteenth century world trading system. The economic consequences of two world wars have extended far beyond the main European battlefields. The welfare of half the world's population—the thousand million people who live in Asia—is gravely affected. One of the major conclusions to be drawn from Mr. Jacoby's survey is that there is a common cause of economic dislocation underlying the various forms of local agrarian discontents throughout Southeast Asia.

The magnitude of this fact is not easy to grasp. We commonly underestimate the role that Asia has played in European conflicts for centuries past, just as we tend to forget that the European peoples have not always been the dominant, organizing leaders of world production and trade. The legend of the gorgeous east is one of the essential clues to an understanding of European expansion from the sixteenth century onwards. It has colored the poetry as it inflamed the adventurous and aggressive economic enterprise of all the western European nations. The first of the empires on which "the sun never set" was that which resulted from the consolidation of Spanish and Portuguese conquests after 1580. The Dutch, French and British fought the Spaniards not so much for territory and dominion as for trading opportunities. Out of three centuries of practically continuous warfare the British emerged in 1815 not only with the greatest empire, but with sea supremacy; but, like the Ancient Mariner, they and the other colonial powers carried with their conquests the responsibility for shooting.

During the Pax Britannica of the nineteenth century a vast empire of trade was built up to feed the workshops of western Europe. This was a century of economic development and progress. In the western world the continuous increase in man's command over natural energy enabled the western European peoples to increase their numbers and at the same time to raise their levels of living to undreamed of heights. In the countries of European settlement overseas both the numerical increase and the advance in living levels were even more marked. In the colonial and semi-colonial Asiatic countries there was a great increase of productivity, constantly swallowed up by increasing numbers. When the century began Java had four and a half million people. Now it must support 42 millions. Bengal had six and a half, but must now support 65 millions.

The cycles of population increase thus initiated have far from run their course. Modern sanitation and hygiene have contributed something to the declining death rates which are the chief cause of increase; but the main reason for these declining death rates has been more abundant food enabling greater numbers to survive. In part the increasing productivity was the result of improved plantation methods, better soil management, improved varieties of seeds and better merchandising; but in part also it was the result of settled government, honest administration and impartial justice. A large proportion of the profits went to Europe, but sufficient remained in the eastern countries to support far larger populations and free them from the recurrent famines that always threaten poorly organized countries.

This, however, is a continuous cycle. The population of South-east Asia is now greater than it has ever been, but it is destined to be greater still. The babies are already born who in the next generation will become the parents of even greater numbers. Greater productivity still will be needed to support these increasing numbers; but the whole region is in the throes of political and economic changes, the outcome of which no one can as yet foresee. These empires were lightly held. Yet even the skeleton forces necessary for police and punitive purposes are now a heavy drain on the weakened European powers. The white man has lost in Asia the face that was his greatest asset. His bluff has been called. He cannot any longer maintain a facade of empire and he lacks the resources for repressive government. Meantime highly vocal minority groups press the cause of independence and repeat in many languages the slogans of European nationalism.

The great masses of the population in southeast Asia, however, have as little understanding of what is happening to them as the natives removed from Bikini had of radio-activity. The peasant-producer, with no market for his labor and insufficient resources for subsistence farming, may assent to nationalist slogans; but he is more apt to find an outlet for his discontent nearer home. The village merchant, moneylender, or landlord or the officials charged with execution of the law that affects the villager directly are more visibly the causes of his distress. By a natural trend the merchant is apt to be also the moneylender and ultimately the landlord. He is often an alien. More and more the focus of attack is the Indian in Burma or the Chinese in Java. Asia for the Asiatics is not a very effective slogan, but Burma for the Burmese may well be.

If the European governments are driven out, or make a compact with local national leaders, will it be possible either to attract foreign capital or to organize under the leadership of the nationals of these countries the economic enterprise and services that in the past have made it possible for population to increase? Here is a vast region that missed the scientific and industrial training on which the industrial revolution rested. To that revolution the Asiatic peoples contributed their resources and their labor; but from it they failed to get the skills that enriched the western world. Wherever, as in India, there are large groups of highly skilled people constituting exceptions to this general rule, there is at least a chance that effective organization of economic activity may not be too long delayed. But this is the crux of any power-change.

Mr. Jacoby's survey of agrarian unrest in southeastern Asia does not pretend to do more than reveal and document what is essentially a revolutionary situation. The economic as well as the political organization within which the increasing numbers of these patient peoples have struggled to win a precarious livelihood is now far advanced in disintegration. What can be put in its place? Can it be hoped that responsible national governments will receive aid and encouragement from the Western world? Or must there ensue another of those times of troubles of which the long history of Asia affords so many examples—times of civil war and famine, with increasing misery until some strong ruler emerges to impose subordination upon the contending factions? In the past such rulers have been military adventurers. In the future they may possibly be the exponents of a revolutionary creed.

The United States is vitally concerned with this whole area. It is in process of advancing its defensive outposts right up to the borders of southeast Asia. Yet the economic welfare and political stability of these, our good neighbors to the west, are drawn to our attention only when they lapse into disorder and violence. It is in the belief that they deserve more than such casual notice that Mr. Jacoby's study has been undertaken. The questions which it raises may well give Americans pause. The historical tradition of opposition to all forms of territorial imperialism is one of the most deeply-rooted policies of the United States. There is a natural tendency to sympathize with the aspirations of all peoples who are striving to free themselves from alien rule and domination. Yet this is in fact a negative attitude. If these peoples are to remain free, and still more clearly if they are to escape the miseries of economic disorganization, positive policies are needed. They need help to acquire the skills without which they cannot provide subsistence for their growing numbers. They need to get from more developed countries the equipment with which to modernize their economic activities. The only way in which they can get this equipment is by exporting the raw materials demanded by the western world. They cannot solve their political and economic problems except in a world of expanding trade and investment. Their difficulties are not of their own creation; but are the consequences of centuries of development within the European-dominated trading world. The solution of these difficulties is beyond the capacity of the Asiatic peoples themselves and failure to achieve solutions will have repercussions far beyond southeastern Asia. Americans may well give thought to the part they may be called upon to play in the coming struggle for the soul of Asia. The Carnegie Endowment for International Peace presents Mr. Jacoby's carefully documented survey as a material contribution to one of the greatest questions likely to confront American policy for decades to come.

J. B. CONDLIFFE
*Associate-Director, Division of Economics
and History
Carnegie Endowment for International Peace*

*New York
Summer, 1948*

Preface

DURING a four-year stay in the Philippines I had the opportunity to study agrarian conditions in the Islands in peace and war. This led to an interest in the problems of the farming population through Southeast Asia and resulted, through the generosity of the Carnegie Endowment for International Peace, in the present study.

In the following pages I have tried to analyze the multiple effects of economic dependence in the populous colonial and semi-colonial areas of Southeast Asia and to emphasize the vicious circle established by the interaction of cause and effect. The imminent mechanization of colonial agriculture is sure to bring about the gradual dislocation of a considerable part of the peasant population and thereby accentuate the lack of economic diversification that is almost inseparable from colonial dependence. As far as the national movements in Southeast Asia are concerned, I have tried to show that, to a considerable degree, they are movements for land and for the reasonable use of land.

In this connection I wish to stress that the present study is based largely on previously published material and that I am deeply indebted to all those who have worked in the field and have analyzed thoroughly the conditions in the various countries of the area. In this place I can mention only a few—Rupert Emerson, L. S. Furnivall, J. Van Gelderen (who died during the recent war), Pierre Gourou, Karl Pelzer, and Virginia Thompson. But especially I wish to acknowledge my indebtedness to Russell Andrus who placed at my disposal his manuscript on Burma, which has since been published by Stanford University Press, Palo Alto, California, under the title *Burmese Economic Life*.

I owe sincere gratitude to the Carnegie Endowment for International Peace, and also to Professors James T. Shotwell of Columbia University and J. B. Condliffe of the University of California, who followed my work with keen interest and who time and again gave me valuable advice and, finally, their critical assistance in editing the manuscript.

To my wife, Lotte Jacoby, who was with me in the Philippines during the war years, I am deeply indebted for her never tiring support and cooperation, for her encouragement and constructive criticism.

Finally, I extend my thanks to the U.S. Office of War Information in San Francisco for providing me with useful material, to the American Geographical Society, and especially to Mr. Charles B. Hitchcock for making possible the use of the maps for this study, to the staff of the Library of the University of California, Berkeley, for their most cooperative assistance, and to Matilda L. Berg of Columbia University Press for her conscientious editing of the manuscript.

Although this book is published under the auspices of the Carnegie Endowment for International Peace I must emphasize that I alone am responsible for the statements and opinions expressed.

E. H. JACOBY

New York
November, 1948

Contents

CONTENTS

Maps

AGRARIAN UNREST
IN SOUTHEAST ASIA

1
General Survey

INTRODUCTION   For the past sixty years, Southeast Asia has played
an important role in international politics. Immense economic enterprises and speculative adventures have been carried out in the
area; its population has constituted the labor force for steadily increasing production, and its exports have been an important factor
in the international balance of payments. But the people who live
there rank very low among the world's consumers.

The boom favored the few and almost by-passed the common
people of these countries; the slump was a disaster for both. Depression is particularly hard in regions like Southeast Asia, where a
one-sided economy produces raw materials for a few highly sensitive key industries in Europe and the United States, and where
manufacturing industries based on indigenous purchasing power
are lacking.

Until the beginning of this century the Western world was conscious of the glamor and splendor of the decaying native political
systems and the colorful personalities of their rulers but had little
knowledge of the sad condition of the population. In recent years,
however, the people of this area have emerged from the shadows of
the political backstage and have frankly exhibited their misery.
Their protests against the existing order have ranged from passive
resistance to active rebellion, from dignified demonstrations to mob
riots. Today, the entire area displays a movement for freedom unparalleled in its history, a history traditionally rich in emperors and
kings, wars and intrigues, but poor in mass movements beyond the
sphere of religion.

In the West, reaction to these dramatic developments has been
confused and uncertain. Economic interests, political and strategic

considerations, prestige and honest disappointment interfere with deep sympathy for the people in Asia who struggle for liberty and independence.

Recent painful experiences, however, have taught the Western world the basic lesson that political and economic developments are connected all over the world and that prosperity and poverty are as indivisible as peace and war. This simple political wisdom, for which a generation has paid with heavy sacrifices, marks today the Western approach to fundamental economic and political problems. Franklin D. Roosevelt's words "poverty anywhere constitutes danger to prosperity everywhere" have almost become a commonplace. The certainty that political and economic complications, wherever they may occur in this narrow world, will be felt all over the world, may promote a feeling of collective responsibility for finding collective solutions.

The problem of the dependent areas has now entered the stage of collective attention. Certainly, power politics is still important, but it is significant that today it has to be justified by appeal to the protecting terms of a world order which has not yet been fully organized.

The countries of Southeast Asia have an outstanding position among the dependent areas of the world. Geographically, economically, and culturally, Southeast Asia is part of the Far East. Its main territories are the Malay Archipelago, the Malay Peninsula, Burma, Siam, Indo-China, and the Philippines, the two latter flanking the China Sea. This large area, a center of civilization from time immemorial and an ancient battleground for recurring waves of immigration, is today inhabited by 150 million people. Since these people are engaged mainly in agriculture, and only to a small extent in industries, and then mostly in processing and extracting, the agrarian problem is fundamental all over the area.

Since the beginning of this century, Southeast Asia has been the main producer and exporter of two primary raw materials for modern industry: rubber and tin, for which the United States has been the main market. In 1940, 75 percent of the entire rubber exports from Malaya and 78 percent of its tin went to the United States. The United States, however, was also an important buyer of other products from Southeast Asia. Its share in the export from the Philip-

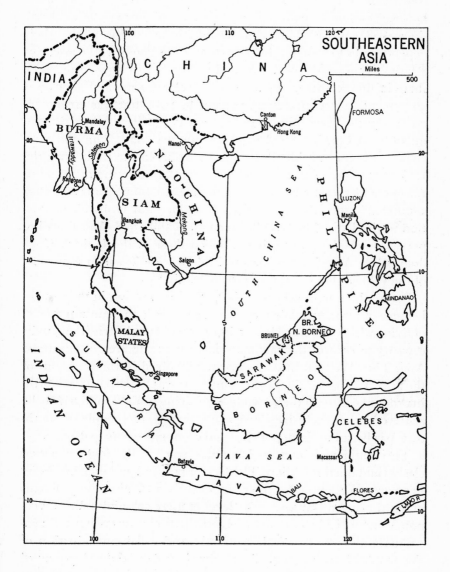

SOUTHEASTERN
ASIA

Miles

0   500

INDIA

CHINA

FORMOSA

BURMA

Mandalay

Canton

Hong Kong

Irrawaddy

Saween

Hanoi

INDO-CHINA

SIAM

Bangkok

Mekong

Saigon

SOUTH CHINA SEA

PHILIPPINES

LUZON

Manila

MINDANAO

MALAY
STATES

BR.
N. BORNEO

BRUNEI

SARAWAK

SUMATRA

Singapore

BORNEO

CELEBES

INDIAN OCEAN

Batavia

JAVA SEA

Macassar

JAVA

BALI

FLORES

TIMOR

pines, for example, was about 80 percent and for the other countries its market was second only to that of the respective "mother countries." Exports from the United States, in exchange, were, however, rather limited, as the respective "mother countries" have, since 1928, controlled and dominated the import business of their dependencies to an ever greater extent. Consequently, the area had a large export surplus to the United States.[1] In 1928, America's share in the exports of the area (aside from Burma and Siam) was 30 percent. It declined to 25 percent in 1938, but was greatly increased in the years immediately preceding the war, when rearmament created an increased need for raw materials. The dollar receipts from the considerable export surplus in the trade with the United States were in large measure transferred to the investors in Europe and thereby eased the exchange situation of the "mother countries," especially the United Kingdom and Holland, in relation to the United States.[2] Between 1926 and 1938, American imports from Malaya more than equaled those of the United Kingdom, while American exports to Malaya were less than 2 percent of the value of her exports to Great Britain.[3]

Before the war, Southeast Asia held a key position in the world's balance of payments. Western Europe was able to maintain a level of living which was based less on its own export industries than on its capacity to control the raw materials producing area of Southeast Asia. Thus Western interests became involved in the problems of the area. While the aim of these interests was to perpetuate control in order to maintain their own level of living, which could hardly be achieved by an exclusive European economy, the people of Southeast Asia began to claim political and economic emancipation.

This conflict of interests has today reached the stage of actual clashes and open rebellion. The lack of political and social stability in an area so essential for the peace of the world raises the problems of Southeast Asia far above the level of mere colonial politics. Economic and social reconstruction is only part of a far greater task: coordination of the political, economic, and social emancipation of the people of the East with the economic and social development of

---

1. *The Network of World Trade* (Geneva, 1942), pp. 59 ff.

2. Michael Greenberg, "Malaya, Britain's Dollar Arsenal," *Amerasia* (June, 1941), p. 147.

3. Kate L. Mitchell, *Industrialization of the Western Pacific* (New York, 1942), p. 188.

the world as a whole. It is not difficult to conceive that a historical
process of such dimensions may involve sacrifices by privileged countries and groups, and therefore may bring about important changes
in the Western countries concerned. Economic history, however,
proves that such developments bring compensations even for the immediate losers. Economic and social progress anywhere will finally
contribute to progress everywhere.

This book does not aim at a complete analysis of the economic
and social processes in this area. It is limited to an investigation of
the main causes responsible for the agrarian unrest and is consequently focused on the problems of land tenure, agricultural cultivation, and rural indebtedness. The present chapter summarizes the
subsequent studies of the individual countries in the area.

WESTERN PENETRATION   *General trends of dependent economy*—
When the countries of the Far East have finally achieved their emancipation, the history of Western penetration will be written and understood differently from today. Future historians will emphasize
the importance of the colonial administration which put an end to
the political and economic despotism of cruel archaic rulers and at
the same time disintegrated the tribal communities and thus prepared the way for regional consciousness. For it cannot be denied
that the political, administrative, and economic methods which the
West applied to its large territories in the East introduced there the
principles of nationhood and Western statehood, and thus gave
the people the spiritual and material incentive to seek a way out of
the colonial relationship. The colonial system, indeed, has regener-
ated the old decaying communities of the East, caught in backward
tyranny, caste system, and superstition. It has broken the bonds of
custom and forced the people into the realities of national consciousness and world contacts.

The penetration by the Western economy and Western ideas was
in no respect more disturbing than the incursions of earlier invaders
and of Hinduism and Mohammedanism.[4] There seems little doubt,
however, that the impact of the West was more valuable than that of
its predecessors, which perpetuated stagnation and blocked progress.

4. Rupert Emerson, *Malaysia, a Study in Direct and Indirect Rule* (New York, 1937),
p. 480.

Nevertheless, basic problems arose from the contact of different civilizations; economic and social engineering will have to solve these problems in order to help the native peoples adjust to the changed conditions of a modern world.

The actual process of Western penetration was by its very nature painful, and those affected by it were hardly able to recognize the progressive nature of the change.[5] The people of the East had suffered a brutal awakening at the hands of pirate traders and warriors, and their lot seemed little happier when mercantilist-minded government officials succeeded the pirate traders and supplanted casual exploitation by a tightened and highly efficient colonial administration. Certainly the advance of liberal ideas in the world influenced colonial administration and brought into effect welfare policies that not only were favorable to the growth of Western enterprises but also improved the living conditions of the native population. At the same time, however, the old village economy was brought to a slow death, as soon as a money economy penetrated the village and destroyed its self-sufficiency. The introduction of foreign trade and foreign ideas disturbed the established equilibria of social life with its traditional relationships.[6] Almost everywhere the native peasant turned from subsistence farming to the cultivation of cash crops and thus became involved in the price fluctuations of the world market and in the system of dependent economy. Naturally, the degree to which he became involved varied from country to country, but all the peoples of Southeast Asia were affected in some degree—even the native farmers who were still engaged in subsistence farming.[7]

In his triple capacity as producer, landowner, and worker, the individual native became the loser. Having no sources of cash income he was defenseless as the money economy speeded the process of disintegration, and he therefore became definitely tied to the lowest standard of living under the existing conditions of production. Certainly the colonial system improved the health and security of the population and thus greatly decreased the death rate. But it did not provide a correlative increase in economic opportunities. On the contrary, the large-scale elimination of handicrafts brought about

5. Solomon F. Bloom, *The World of Nations* (New York, 1941), "Backwardness and Empire," p. 52.
6. J. B. Condliffe, *China Today* (Boston, 1932), pp. 45, 46, 49.
7. Cf. Chapter IV, below.

by the import of superior ready-made goods reduced still further the material bases of living standards. The idleness of manpower, characteristic of the densely peopled East today, became one of the most striking features of the agricultural problem in Southeast Asia.

The development of the dependent areas was held within the limits and adjusted to the needs and general policy of colonial power.[8] Therefore the economic history of the dependencies reflects and emphasizes the general trends in the Western world. Under Western tutelage the colonies developed from territories mainly considered as sources of raw materials to centers of commercialized agriculture and extracting industries, while the establishment of manufacturing industries was prevented. At the same time, the colonies gained importance as markets and as factors in the movement of international payments. Economic penetration, however, was not always combined with complete political control. Different political systems were applied, ranging from direct to indirect rule. At times big power politics even favored the perpetuation of an independent political status, though the country economically was already on the verge of a colonial or semicolonial development.

Western penetration met with other forms of foreign enterprise in many areas of Southeast Asia. In some countries, as in Malaya, it encountered well-established Chinese interests. In other countries it had to cope with a gradual Chinese penetration which took advantage of the improved legal conditions and security guaranteed by the colonial administration. In hard competition with Western interests, Chinese business was able to win important positions in the economic system of Southeast Asia. In Lower Burma the Western powers even had to appeal for assistance as the colonial task seemed too immense. Indian bankers came in to help and became the financial pioneers of an unparalleled expansion of rice cultivation. As a result they are now in economic control of the entire area and of its native population, and constitute a serious political problem.

So far, however, these Asiatic penetrations of the Western colonial system have no life of their own. They are still dependent on the Western economy and exist as an auxiliary of its colonial eco-

8. Rupert Emerson, *Government and Nationalism in Southeast Asia* (New York, 1942), Part I, Introduction, pp. 8–9.

nomic organization, concentrated in the trading and banking sector. Therefore, the terms, "Western economy" and "Western penetration" will here be applied to the sum of economic activities connected with the colonization of a country, even though this total is partly infiltrated by Chinese and Indian interests.

The different political and economic, social and racial questions in Southeast Asia prove that the future problem is not only a political one to be solved by a mere declaration of independence, but that it is first of all a problem of economic and social adjustment which can be solved only on a very high level of political and economic reconstruction.

Indeed, the conditions in politically independent areas like Siam seem to indicate that it is not the political status but the mere fact of economic dependence which is the deciding factor in an area subject to foreign economic penetration. The absence of Western political responsibility in Siam even increased the economic weakness of the country and its lack of resistance in times of depression. Moreover, it is a fact that Siam lags behind the other countries in Southeast Asia in many respects, especially in the field of public health and public services.[9]

Students of the economy of Southeast Asia, especially Dutch students,[10] frequently use the term "plural economy." By this term they indicate that a balance could be obtained—at least in a limited field —between Western and native economy by the establishment of separate social orders with a minute sectional division of labor and by giving the native communities a chance of survival. The logic involved in the system of colonial economy, however, seems to exclude any possibility of coexistence, or of anything more than a temporary truce between the two systems. This is clear in the case of Java, where the conditions for coexistence seemed to be most favorable. A requisite for the development of Western economy is disintegration of the village economy. Coordination is therefore unrealistic and bound to result in failure. Actually the system of plural economy

9. See Chapter VII, below.

10. J. S. Furnivall, *Netherlands India; a Study of Plural Economy* (Cambridge, England, 1939), pp. 446 ff. He indicates that the "Dutch solution" of the problem of plural or dual society realized in Java has federal elements and may be called the federal solution conserving the native order and coordinating its interests with the other society (p. 468).

exists only to a very limited extent and is of a more or less transitional character. The expanding Western economy gains ground steadily at the expense of the decaying village economy. It is only logical that a conflict of interests will always be decided in favor of Western economy by the powerful combination of political, economic, and social forces—if not directly by law then at least by the interpretation or application of the law.

The fundamental characteristic of a dependent economy is its subsidiary relation to the economy of the colonial power. This relation is the basic principle, and differences of degree are of but minor importance. There is no example in colonial history of a dependent system with a well-rounded economy of its own and a normal social stratification.

Normally a nation's position in international trade is determined by a long process of economic and cultural growth; but a colonial economy creates an artificial world-market maturity without any relation to organic development and social consolidation. The weak native communities are brought into contact with world trade by connecting them to the most sensitive commodity markets. Consequently the effects of depression and slump were nowhere felt more keenly than in the villages of Java and on the plantations in Malaya.

Rupert Emerson describes the characteristic position of the dependent countries as follows: "Once the industrial demand elsewhere slackens as it did at a sickening pace from the beginning of the depression years, the one-sided character of their economic structure becomes desperately apparent and not only the economy but also the governmental apparatus which derives its revenues from the economy is brought to an abrupt crisis." [11] The sensitiveness of Southeast Asia to price fluctuations and thereby to the effects of depression is directly proportional to the degree of this dependence. Social dissatisfaction and agrarian unrest are also closely concerned, although other factors may be involved as well.

In the past the subsidiary character of the dependent economy prevented a solution of the fundamental problems of the native community, for instance, the use of the enormous reserves of idle manpower, which totals millions. The obstacles to the development of manufacturing industries and the lack of a diversified econ-

11. *Government and Nationalism in Southeast Asia*, Part I, Introduction, pp. 12–13.

omy is intimately related to the economic structure of the dependencies.

The trend and volume of economic activity in the dependencies have been decided by foreign interests which again are mainly decided by market calculations. Trade agreements and exchange regulations have been made primarily to serve the interest of the colonial power and only secondary that of the dependent country. The speed of colonization further increased the economic and social problems, especially the land and credit problem. It promoted the process of disintegration of the village community without granting space and time to eliminate disturbing factors such as usury and tenant misery.

It is true that a large-scale welfare administration became an integrating part of the dependent economy and that its influence has improved the general conditions over almost all of the area. But in spite of positive results in the first heroic years, the final effects of the well-intentioned welfare policy remained far behind expectations, because it proved inadequate to counteract the impact of unfavorable economic developments. To state these facts is not to blame the colonial powers who have generally tried to coordinate conflicting interests to the best of their ability. They could hardly be expected to carry out an economic policy which would alter the colonial status as such. The system of dependent economy is but a natural function of the colonial relation and involves therefore the maximal use of the resources of the dependency.

Another question which must be approached is the so-called "colonial drain," [12] which several students of the area have related to the colonial aspect of the trade balance and frequently refer to as the basic effect of colonial economy. The term has been defined in different ways; it has been erroneously equated to the surplus of colonial exports, as if the total amount of the surplus was transferred as profits to the investor countries. This ignores the not unimportant loss of capital during times of depression and the fact that part of the transfer must be considered as amortization. Frequently the whole problem has been given the very primitive formulation: profits

12. J. H. Boeke, *The Structure of the Netherlands Indian Economy* (New York, 1942), pp. 188 f.; Amry Vandenbosch, *The Dutch East Indies, Its Government, Problems, and Politics* (Berkeley, Calif., 1942), pp. 260–63; Rupert Emerson, *op. cit.*, pp. 10–11.

leaving the country—loss; profits remaining in the country—assets.

The export-import relation in the colonial countries is very un-balanced. J. R. Andrus gives a statistical illustration of the dispro-portional predominance of exports over imports which can be ex-plained by the large payments for "invisible" imports made by the countries of this area in the form of interest, dividends, remittances, pensions, and charges for insurance and shipping.[13]

PER CAPITA FOREIGN TRADE IN SOUTHEAST ASIA

(Annual average in U.S. dollars, in 1936–1939)

Country	Imports	Exports
British Malaya	63.00	72.55
Burma	5.60	12.65
Netherlands India	4.00	6.70
Thailand	3.55	5.10
French Indo-China	2.60	4.05

Source: J. R. Andrus, Basic Problems, p. 4.

Andrus asserts furthermore that cotton textiles and, in Malaya, rice constituted the only essential imports for the use of the native population; by far the greater part of the imports consisted of equip-ment, vehicles, and gasoline. But even this cannot be considered a basis for a clear-cut statement of economic profit and loss. It is diffi-cult to decide which imports might have been essential for the native population and which established services (invisible import) that might have been of value for the productive development of the whole country.

Considering the system of dependent economy as a whole, the question of the colonial drain loses actual importance. The different economic facts to which this term has been applied are all part of the dependent economic process. They can be explained satisfactorily as connected with the functions of a subsidiary economy, which natu-rally prevents any considerable accumulation of native capital.

This basic characteristic explains all the phenomena usually re-ferred to as "drain." The impossibility of any large-scale capital ac-cumulation by the natives explains fully the extreme poverty of the native communities and hence their difficulty in diversifying the co-lonial economy by means of their own. This condition perpetuates

13. *Basic Problems of Relief, Rehabilitation and Reconstruction in Southeast Asia,* Institute of Pacific Relations, 9th Conference, Secretariat Paper (New York, 1945), p. 4.

the traditional colonial relationship by enabling foreign capital to organize the manpower and control the natural resources of the dependent areas. It maintains the prevalence of a large-scale production of commercial crops and prevents at the same time social stratification within the native community. Finally it favors land concentration almost all over the area, thus eliminating the independent farming class where it exists, and blocking the way for its establishment where it could be developed.

Within the dependent economy the native producer, generally in need of cash, is automatically tied to the foreign entrepreneur who gives him contracts with advance payments, supplies on credit, or advances seeds. The dependence of the native economy as a whole is reproduced in innumerable individual relations between native peasants and alien landlords, plantation owners, shopkeepers, and rice dealers.

Population pressure.—The Western penetration of Southeast Asia brought about an unparalleled increase of population. The efficient work of the colonial administrations in the fields of public safety, public health, education in hygiene, and development of the transportation system, greatly reduced the death rate. Political security increased, and in some regions, even multiplied the crops available for food. This, in connection with improved transportation, became most essential in the fight against periodic famine. The people of the area responded quickly by multiplied population.[14] The importance of this connection can be recognized easily by comparing the population figures for Southeast Asia with those for China, where foreign administrative control hardly ever was established outside of limited areas and where the population increase was hampered by rebellions, civil strife, famine, and epidemics.

The tremendous growth of population during the last generation is solely a function of the decline of the death rate. As the birth rate is very high and nowhere shows any tendency to decline,[15] a steady increase of population is to be expected. A decline cannot be ex-

14. Warren S. Thompson, "Population Prospects for China and Southeastern Asia," in *World Population in Transition (Annals of the American Academy of Political and Social Science)*, Vol. 237, January, 1945, pp. 72 ff.

15. Thompson points out (*ibid.*, p. 76) that it can be shown by approved statistical methods that the birth rates in many countries, especially in the Philippines and Java, are far above the recorded rates (probably 45–50 per thousand) and that they are not declining.

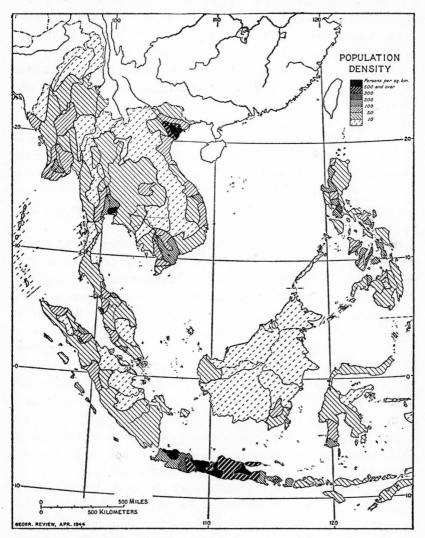

POPULATION
DENSITY

Persons per sq. km.
500 and over
300
200
100
50
10

500 MILES

500 KILOMETERS

GEOGR. REVIEW, APR. 1944

Source: J. O. M. Broek, "Diversity and Unity in Southeast Asia," *Geographical Review,* Vol. 34, New York, 1944.

pected until the area has reached a more advanced stage of "industrialization and urbanization." [16] This proves again how important it is to industrialize the dependent economy, since industrialization raises the level of living and slows down the rate of population increase. It is unreasonable to expect any appreciable decline of the birth rates in the countries of Southeast Asia much before the end of the present century. The growth during the next four to six decades will be determined exclusively by the trend of the death rate.[17] Warren S. Thompson has made an estimate of the future population of the region, assuming that the death rates on an average will re-

POPULATION FIGURES FOR SOUTHEAST
ASIA SINCE 1900 AND ESTIMATES FOR 1990

Year	Burma	Netherlands Indies	Indo-China	Malaya	Siam	Philippines
1903	..	..	..	..	..	7.6
1905	..	38.1	..	..	..	..
1906	..	..	16.1	..	..	..
1910	..	..	16.8	..	8.2	..
1911	12.1	..	..	2.7	..	..
1918	..	..	..	..	..	10.3
1920	..	49.4	18.9		9.2	..
1921	13.2	..	..	3.3	..	..
1930	..	60.7	21.5	..	11.5	..
1931	14.7	..	..	4.4	..	..
1939	..	..	23.7	..	..	16.0
1940	..	..	..	..	15.7	..
1941	16.8	71.5	..	5.5	..	..
1990	30.0	170.0	43.0	19.0	60.0	46.0

Source: Warren S. Thompson, "Population Prospects," p. 77.

16. Irene B. Taeuber and Edwin G. Beal, "The Demographic Heritage of the Japanese Empire." In *World Population in Transition*, pp. 64 ff. The authors indicate that in 1925, i.e., almost 60 years after Japan had begun its industrial transformation, the intrinsic birth rate was 37.58, and the intrinsic death rate 20.86. First in 1937 the intrinsic birth rate had decreased to 31.69, the intrinsic death rate to 17.38, and the intrinsic rate of national increase to 14.38. Carl L. Alsberg, in *Land Utilization Investigations and Their Bearing in International Relations* (New York, 1933), p. 19, indicates that native specialization in agriculture instead of subsistence farming would result in a higher level of living of the natives and thus in a slowing down of the rate of increase. Experience, however, does not seem to confirm this opinion. The birth rate in the commercialized areas of Siam and the Philippines is usually not lower than in Java, where the natives are largely concerned with subsistence farming.

17. Thompson, "Population Prospects," p. 76.

main as far below the birth rates as during the last few decades.[18]

The estimates for 1990 based on the facts and trends which have determined the population rates since 1900, demonstrate the seriousness of the problem. Southeast Asia is involved in a dynamic process which forces the economic problem of the area into a race between population increase and the expansion of economic productivity. Any general improvement of the level of living will first of all lead to a decline of the death rate, and thus to a still faster growth of population. Living levels can be maintained and defended only if economic productivity is increased at a still faster rate than the population. This is the real Malthusian dilemma. It is typical for densely populated countries in which the people live at or near a subsistence level and from which there is small chance of emigration. Warren S. Thompson says, "It should be clear that the care for an additional 700 million persons in this area (including the population increase in India and China) within 50 years or less is going to tax human ingenuity, and good will, to the utmost." [19]

It might seem doubtful whether human ingenuity can provide for a multiplied population within the frame of a colonial economy hitherto unable to procure sufficient economic possibilities for the growing population.[20] The population in Southeast Asia, however, is excessive only in relation to the present level of living within the dependent economy. Population pressure is closely connected with the scarcity of arable land and with the lack of productive application of the abundant manpower.

The problem is aggravated by the maldistribution of population all over Southeast Asia. Density is greatest in the lowlands, along the coasts, on intermountain plains, and in the big river valleys.[21] It is

18. Annual rates of increase: Burma 1921–41, 12.2 per thousand; Netherlands East Indies, 1920–41, 17.8; French Indo-China, 1920–39, 12.0; British Malaya, 1921–41, 25.5; Siam, 1920–40, 27.1; Philippines, 1903–39, 20.8.

19. "Population Prospects," p. 78. Thompson believes, however, that in Southeast Asia, contrary to China, wasteland reserves can take care of the increase for the next decades. But he seems to overestimate the possibilities for migration and underestimate the difficulties involved in an extension of land utilization under the present conditions.

20. Thompson concludes (ibid., p. 79) that a development of manpower in Southeast Asia comparable to that in western Europe and North America will necessarily endanger the colonial status.

21. Karl J. Pelzer, Pioneer Settlement in the Asiatic Tropics (New York, 1945), p. 81.

lowest in the mountainous sections and hilly areas, partly because of endemic malaria. With the growth of population the size of the individual farm decreases rapidly, especially when all suitable land, or rather, when all land which can be cultivated without great additional expense, has been taken up. But since intensification of agriculture cannot compensate in the long run for the smallness of the landholdings, a moment comes when the increased agrarian population can no longer gain subsistence from the land. This condition is today prevalent in large agricultural areas and is in addition, complicated by the continuous process of land concentration.

The excess population affects in various respects the status of land tenure in dependent areas. 1) It leads to a minute parceling of the land. 2) It consequently promotes the concentration of land in the long run, since the small landowners are generally unable to gain full subsistence from their plots and therefore become easy victims of land grabbers and moneylenders. 3) Finally it increases the army of share croppers. This is common in overpopulated Java where a small holder frequently will lease his land to another native on a share-cropper basis while he himself will look for additional income as artisan or laborer. This further increases the subdivision of the land, as the same plot must now support one household completely and one partly.[22]

It is one of the tragic features of colonial economy that the welfare policy, well intentioned as it was, contributed greatly to the agrarian crisis by spurring the rate of population increase. It saved the lives of millions but disturbed the natural equilibrium between population and production, balancing life and death without, however, establishing a new equilibrium.

Population pressure is one of the most dangerous aspects of the colonial problem. It speeds the process of economic and social disintegration and so far has frustrated any endeavor to relieve the situation. While the current level of living for the increasing population could be maintained in some areas even while it decreased elsewhere, the colonial system, generally speaking, has been unable to raise the level of living for the bulk of the people during the last generation.

Introduction of labor-saving equipment.—Just at a time when al-

22. Boeke, *op. cit.*, p. 47.

most the entire area is marked by excess population and shortage of productive opportunities, another dynamic factor related to Western penetration has entered the colonial field: the process of mechanization by labor-saving equipment. Before the recent war, human labor competed successfully not only with the tractor in every part of the area, but also in some countries, such as Indo-China, even with animal labor. The price of labor was generally so low that motorized equipment was unprofitable. The share-cropper family with one or two working animals, therefore, maintained a more or less uncontested monopoly. Considerable mechanizing was found only within the processing industries which already were close to the world market and mostly financed by foreigners.

There are several indications, however, that in recent years industry has succeeded in turning out equipment adjusted to tropical agriculture. Rice-field tractors have been designed for special use on soggy ground. Self-propelled harvester threshers are in use. Specially designed tractors supply dependable and economical service for every cane-growing operation and for speedy hauling during planting and harvesting. Cane equipment consisting of convenient and readily interchangeable tool units can be easily applied to the tractor. The labor-saving effect of this machinery is about to reach a point where cost calculation no longer is as favorable for native labor as before. Furthermore, progressive international regulations for the protection of labor are preventing or at least rendering difficult the traditional exploitation.

Mechanized production has the additional advantage of a more elastic adjustment to periods of depression and to any international restriction schemes. The relatively small amount of hired farm labor needed for the handling of modern equipment represents much less of a problem than tenant labor. Finally, the latent agrarian unrest in large areas of the Far East may induce the big plantation corporations to make themselves as independent as possible of human labor. These facts may enter the comparative cost calculation and definitely turn the decision in favor of labor-saving equipment.

On the other hand the introduction of mechanical power, to an increasing extent, may strongly influence the social situation and lead to an aggravation of the difficulties derived from the high population rate. The process of intensified colonization has already greatly reduced the economic participation of the native population and actually limited it to the labor sector, which has become the only native reservation. A large-scale introduction of labor-saving equipment will further aggravate the situation by economic displacement of large parts of the native population.

It is safe to say, however, that increased mechanization will mark the development in years to come, even if the tempo depends on various political and economic factors. If controlled, and adjusted to a gradual diversification of the colonial economy, this process can lead to improved levels of living based on increased production and to a more dignified position of human labor. It could thus contribute largely to the elimination of agricultural unrest.

If such adjustment does not take place, the result may be a period of chaotic unrest and the last and deciding step in antagonizing the native population. The uncontrolled introduction of labor-saving equipment would establish a new colonial economy with a maximum of capital investment and a minimum of participating native labor. This would constitute an additional source of agrarian unrest, in the form of technological unemployment manifest in two ways: the dislocation of hundreds of thousands of tenant families, and a structural mass unemployment of farm labor.

The dislocation of the tenant group will prove to be the greatest danger. Separation from the land (often the burial place of his ancestors) will hit the conservative peasant at his most sensitive spot and may change him into a dangerous rebel if no other adequate place in the economic and social pattern of his country is ready to receive him. On the other hand, modern techniques, if reasonably applied, will aid the peaceful growth of the dependent areas into economic and political statehood.

TYPICAL ECONOMIC AND SOCIAL FEATURES IN DEPENDENT COUNTRIES   A careful study of agrarian conditions will reveal some features and trends typical for the general economic and social pattern of Southeast Asia. Though we wish to avoid the mistake of generalizing and overemphasizing and we shall try to point out the different structures and problems of the individual countries, it can be said that the system of political and economic dependence has established, at least for a limited period, a more or less common economic background. The similarity of the problems and psychological reactions cannot be ignored. Substantial facts, such as excess population, land concentration, share-cropper systems, urgent credit needs, usury, indebtedness, and the generally low level of agricultural methods are typical features. They are interdependent, reacting upon one another partly as cause and partly as effect. They cannot be relieved by partial solutions. The history of these countries has proved more than once, that partial solutions are inadequate.

It will not be argued that the system of colonial economy is responsible for the entire complex of social and economic shortcomings in the dependent areas. Some of these are deeply rooted in Southeast Asia. But they have become part of the existing economies and have to be defined, valued, and critically considered in relation to the dependent system. Some of the most typical features will be discussed in the pages that follow.

The credit problem and its effects.—Any analysis of the economic situation in the countries of Southeast Asia will reveal the seriousness of the credit problem which is responsible for usury and indebtedness, malnutrition and despair. It is intimately related to the transition from subsistence farming to commercial agriculture and to the disintegration of village life. It cannot be considered in isolation from the general economic and social pattern of the native society, but only as one of its most essential characteristics.

The disintegration of the village economy, the withering away of native handicrafts under the competition of better and cheaper imported goods, the transition from food crops to commercial crops are the main factors responsible for the shortage of money and all that goes with it. The process of colonization favored money exchange at the expense of subsistence and barter economy, but did not provide the needed cash and reasonable credit facilities for the bulk of the people. The native was not accustomed to handle money and was therefore unable to transact a credit business—deliberately and cautiously. Consequently, when in need, he was driven to second and third-rate moneylenders, and ready to accept even the most usurious terms. Unreasonable credit caused hopeless indebtedness, loss of land, and decreased bargaining power in the marketing of produce, and inevitably led to an increased demand for new credit at a still more usurious rate.

This permanent bondage to the moneylender, has turned the farmer into a tenant and, often, the tenant into an agricultural laborer. At the same time the moneylenders, particularly in Burma, have developed into a powerful group of absentee landlords who calculate the rentability of their estates in terms of interest due from the tenants rather than in terms of agricultural productivity, and who are consequently uninterested in improving the land—one of the main reasons for the backward stage of agricultural cultivation. Of equal importance, however, is the fact that the tenant cultivator, demoralized and distressed, hesitates to apply additional labor, fertilizer, and implements himself and is fatalistic toward improvements in general. Furthermore, the lack of credit at reasonable terms stabilizes the bond between peasant cultivators and middle men. It paralyzes the effectiveness of government-owned or controlled institutions such as rice mills,[23] and prevents the establishment of an efficient marketing organization.

The unfortunate influence of the credit problem ranges from the sowing of the crop to the marketing of the produce. It reaches every phase of individual and public health. It degrades human labor and hinders the normal functioning of political institutions since indebted and dependent peasants are unable to act as citizens. The absence of reasonable credit institutions is mainly responsible for the improvidence and lack of any capacity to economize (even if the opportunity should arise) of the native population. Carl L. Alsberg [24] rightly emphasizes that "saving means present sacrifice and foregoing the satisfaction of a want or need with the expectation, thereby, of satisfying a need in the future," and continues, "The Malay, who with his family is never quite full fed, when through some good fortune he finds himself in possession of a few cents, can hardly be expected to lay by for a rainy day."

Speedy establishment of a colonial economy can hardly be consistent with an indigenous peasant proprietary without large-scale credit institutions. The basis for the rapid extension of the cultivated area is the transferability of land; this resulted almost everywhere in a large-scale transfer of native land holdings (partly to alien

23. V. D. Wickizer and M. K. Bennett, "The Rice Economy of Monsoon Asia," (Palo Alto, Calif., 1941), p. 169.
24. *Land Utilization Investigations*, p. 19.

nonagriculturalists as in Burma), whereas conditions unfavorable for transferability retarded the rate of extension considerably. "Rapidity of extension needs large capital advances and the only security for such advances in the majority of cases is the land actually extended. To permit such security is to jeopardize the possibility of the cultivator continuing to own his holding. It entails in a large number of instances the cultivator ultimately becoming the tenant of the land he has cleared with the capitalist as landlord." [25] The process of rapid colonization, without providing adequate credit facilities for the native farmer, has thus proved to be a large-scale liquidation of peasant property. This will continue until reasonable credit facilities are available in adequate proportion to the extension and intensification of agriculture.

Cooperative institutions have been far from successful. They were hampered partly by inadequate capital and partly by general conditions, which are unfavorable for their development. This is true of all types of cooperatives, but especially of the credit societies. Like all other government institutions these hardly ever reached the level of most urgent need, that of the tenant cultivator deeply indebted to the landlord, shopkeeper or rice trader, without securities to pledge, and unable to accumulate adequate savings for the refunding of loans. This proves again that the credit problem cannot be solved in isolation and that the principle of cooperative organization can be applied successfully only as an integral part of a thorough economic reorganization. In the future, these cooperatives must be a combination of marketing and credit societies which will regulate the credit accounts of the members from the returns of the marketing transactions and thus carry out an economic supervision of the peasant household.

The development of cooperative organization will be a natural part in the process of economic and political emancipation. It will advance gradually with the progress made in the solution of the urgent land problem. It will, however, be different from the cooperatives in the Western world, especially in the Scandinavian countries. Cooperative democracy can hardly be conceived before the peasant is tilling his own soil. As the native society in Southeast Asia has never experienced liberalism and free individual responsi-

25. *Census of India,* Vol. IX, 1911: *Burma,* Part I, Report (Rangoon, 1912), p. 313.

bility as has the Western agricultural communities, the demand for democratic rights by the individual member cannot be as strong as in Western organizations and the cooperative movement in Southeast Asia consequently might be somewhat more authoritative, perhaps even government controlled, at least for a transitional period. Generally speaking, the prospects are good. The social traditions of the native population show a primitive, natural form of spontaneous cooperation which is still manifest in their customs and ancient institutions, though this is less evident in countries such as the Philippines, which have been longest under Western rule.

The credit problem has not only an economic and social but also a racial aspect. The professional moneylenders, the shopkeepers and traders, are generally foreigners, mostly Chinese and Indians. They dominate the marketing and processing of the produce, and partly finance the agricultural production. They function as middle men, often completely isolated from the bulk of the population. The uninterrupted stream of considerable remittances to their home countries indicates that a great number of them still consider themselves foreigners in the area.

For the majority of the farming population the foreign middle man and moneylender is the representative of a hated economic system. His frequently doubtful activities and the high price of his services enrage the peasants and result in tension and riots. Consequently the middle man may be the first object of agrarian unrest, and where he is the representative of a racial minority, as in Burma, racial riots occur frequently. He is the immediate enemy, easier and less risky to attack than the white man or the native landlord. Smart political propaganda may make use of him as a scapegoat for the misery of the peasants, thereby diverting them from a demand for efficient agricultural reorganization to a fight against the foreign moneylender, though his existence is merely a function of the dependent system as such.

The class of foreign middle men, based economically on the absence of adequate credit and marketing institutions, has created a status of racial tension and conflict, previously unknown among the tolerant and hospitable Oriental peoples. Agrarian unrest in Southeast Asia thus gets a touch of racial warfare which endangers political understanding among the peoples of the Pacific area.

Low levels of education and cultivation.—From time immemorial Southeast Asia has been an agricultural region. Remnants of
primitive, but rather effective, irrigation systems can still be found
in many places. Shifting cultivation is still practiced in remote and
hilly regions, while intensive subsistence cultivation combined with
commercial crops is carried out in the central plains and along the
coastlines. Most of the work is still done by human labor. The different methods of land use, however, are not always adjusted to the
natural environment, and continuous misuse of the land still dis-
turbs the balance between soil formation and soil denudation. Shifting cultivation, resulting in deforestation and over-grazing, accel-
erates the denudation process to such a degree that soil erosion and
high floods are the final results.[26] The entire land use in the area
will have to be examined and reorganized after the relation between
crop (including double and secondary crops) and quality of soil
has been decided.

The average cultivator, however, has not reached an intellectual
and economic level which would enable him to obtain a maximum
yield at the lowest cost. He has not yet learned to take advantage of
active cooperation with advisers and agricultural institutions, and
the problem of education and training is therefore of utmost importance. It must be emphasized that the entire problem of education is intimately related to the general economic level. The low
evaluation of human labor is one of the greatest obstacles, and its
apparent futility is one of the main reasons for the fatalistic attitude
of the peasants to technical improvements and the introduction of
fertilizer and new crops. Time and again, the colonizing powers
experienced the futility of their well-intentioned educational and
training work, and many observers have been inclined to put the
blame on the stubbornness, lack of adaptability, and passive resistance of the farming class. They have not realized, however, that
agricultural education can show but meagre results when the
operator lacks the capacity for economic calculation and cannot see
the benefits of it.[27]

26. Karl J. Pelzer, *Population and Land Utilization:* 1941, pp. 78 ff., and especially
p. 83.
27. Alsberg, *Land Utilization Investigations,* p. 18: "The native is quite as quick to
see where he can make a profit as anyone else. Very generally, when he refuses to
change his way it is because he fails to see the benefit to him in such a change."

Western agricultural education has been carried out for almost a generation, through agricultural universities, training camps, and exhibitions. But in spite of this large-scale effort the level of native production has remained practically the same. While the introduction of agricultural machinery naturally was delayed by the competition of cheap labor, the same explanation does not hold true for the delay in application of new methods of agricultural chemistry and plant physiology. Cost is not always sufficient reason, though it has to be taken into account, especially in fertilizing. But also with regard to crop rotation, selection and breeding of seeds, and control of plant diseases and insect pests, agricultural advisers all over the area report at best only slight progress and, often, stagnation. The fact that outstanding success has been achieved on certain model farms and in selected villages does not greatly change the general pattern. Investigations made by agricultural schools confirm the common feature that even the most industrious students very seldom transfer the acquired knowledge to their villages after graduation. Many of them very soon tend to relapse to the customary agricultural methods.

These facts should not discourage cultural and educational work, but they prove that the optimism of the first decades of this century was an illusion. Agricultural education cannot have lasting success when applied in a social vacuum. A disintegrating native community with a very narrow margin for economic experiment is not the proper basis for progress. It is not necessary to appeal to terms like "Oriental mentality" in order to explain the partial failure of an educational work hampered by general economic and social conditions. Here too, we must emphasize the mutual causality of all the factors involved in the problem of a dependent economy. The low level of cultivation, partly a result of economic distress, further increased misery and poverty and, therewith, the deficiencies of the entire system, which in turn increased the obstacles for agricultural education. The agricultural level stabilized by poverty, and inadequate for the support of an increasing population, is in itself an important factor contributing to agrarian unrest.

Racial stratification.—The native society in the dependencies of Southeast Asia lacks any social stratification. A real middle class has never been established, partly because of the inferior position of la-

bor in the colonial economy. All over the area, 70 to 90 percent of
the population is found in agricultural communities tilling the
soil, mostly as tenants or agricultural workers, rarely as owners. But
even the owner cultivators are often deeply in debt and are therefore tenants in an economic sense.

Lack of sufficient and reliable statistical material makes it difficult
to obtain a clear picture of the general income situation. The distribution of income taxpayers in the Netherlands East Indies [28]
may indicate the general trend, especially since this is one of the
countries longest under Western rule and most efficiently administered. Though the population pressure on Java is stronger
than anywhere else in Southeast Asia and the land there is minutely
subdivided, the general social situation is not very different. This
is confirmed by surveys and reports from other countries.[29]

Seen as a whole, it may be said that about 80 percent of the native
population is underprivileged.[30] They are not actually starving,
but live near the border line of starvation. They have insufficient
food, bad clothing, inferior houses, and neither physical nor moral
resistance against the heavy, periodic, economic fluctuations inherent in the system of economic dependence. Most of the people
are excluded not by law but by economic status from the establishment of any position in society which involves responsibility, supervision, and leadership.[31]

Racial stratification is one of the peculiarities, indeed almost a
part of the political definition, of the dependencies. This does not
imply, however, exclusive Western influence. The economic management and control of the dependencies is generally in Western
or Chinese hands with Western influence predominant in banking,
shipping, mining, and plantations, and with Chinese influence
largely confined to trade and the processing industries. The great
Indian share in Burma and the strong position of the Spanish-

28. *Mededeelingen van het centraal kantoor voor de statistiek,* No. 69 (1929) and
Statistisch jaaroverzicht van Nederlandsch-Indië, 1928, Department van Landbouw,
Nijverheid en Handel (Weltevreden, 1929); see Chapter II, below.

29. Quoted in the individual chapters.

30. In 1925, 89.69% of the native taxpayers (number of assessments) in Java and
Madoera and 87.18% in the entire Netherlands East Indies were in income groups of
120–400 guilders per annum.

31. Emerson, *Malaysia,* p. 484, reports these conditions for Malaya and the Netherlands East Indies.

Filipino upper class in the Philippines are exceptions to the general pattern. The income derived from the dependent economies is distributed according to a racial stratification that assures the foreigners a level of living immensely above that of the natives and also far higher than the corresponding level in Western countries.[32] But practically no stratification has taken place within the native society, which has become the undifferentiated foundation for the social structure of the dependencies.

The process of colonization not only stabilizes this social order but also favors its extension. Land concentration further reduces the group of small landowners. International regulation schemes affect the native rubber holdings, and indebtedness generally is increasing. It is not laws and discriminating regulations that prevent the establishment of a native middle class, but the mechanism of the dependent economy as such. Rupert Emerson [33] states that for Malaya and the Netherlands East Indies there is nothing in official policy to prevent the outstanding native from raising himself in the economic scale as the Chinese have done; but he can count on very little, if any, official support in his fight against the terrific odds of an almost complete lack of capital and the inevitable opposition of large and deeply entrenched vested interests with huge capital resources behind them. This statement can be applied to the entire area. The political risk inherent in this situation is apparent. The identification of social and racial barriers builds up a dangerous degree of tension and prepares an emotional readiness for revolutionary movements.

Health and nutrition.—Except in Siam a vast health program has been carried out in Southeast Asia. The policy of the colonial powers was concentrated on improving drinking water, fighting epidemics, and instituting efficient antimalaria methods, along with general rural sanitation and the organization of preventive health services. This was supplemented by a general welfare program to increase security and to prevent natural catastrophes such as death-dealing famines, floods, and droughts. The decreasing death rate attests the success of the program. Official statistics and reports to

32. In 1926, according to *Mededeelingen van het centraal kantoor,* 38% of the European taxpayers in the Netherlands East Indies enjoyed an income of more than 5,000 guilders. In 1936, after the slump, the figure was still as high as 27%.

33. Emerson, *Malaysia,* p. 486.

the Health Organization of the League of Nations indicate, however, that continuous progress is hardly to be expected, as the problem now is "largely bound up with economic conditions." [34] Epidemics have been brought under control in most of the area, but
the general health conditions remain very poor.

The basic problem throughout the East is food; [35] chronic malnutrition marks the bulk of the people. Lack of the vigor, vitality, and
initiative necessary for productive work can be traced back to an
insufficient diet which results in the typical deficiency diseases, and
boosts the incidence of tuberculosis and infant mortality. Students
of the area agree that the shortcomings of native labor are largely
related to lack of adequate food. Naturally, customs and predilec-
tions influence the native diet, but the problem is mainly one of
quantity. As far as quality is concerned, especially in regard to the
insufficient protein intake, a more adequate diet of fish, vegetables,
meat, and eggs is beyond the buying capacity of the peasant family.
Improvement of diet, health conditions, working energy, and economic productivity are first of all dependent on a higher purchasing
power.

A system of mutual chain reactions works between health and
nutrition, economic productivity, and level of living. Under favorable conditions a public health program might have a temporarily
stabilizing effect, but it can scarcely prevent deterioration in the
long run. Western medicine and health policy have now come to a
standstill. They were effective as long as the general standards were
below the level attainable by the colonial administration, but they
are unable to offset the deficiencies inherent in the system itself. The
stagnation in the field of health and nutrition during recent decades
is due to the same factors which caused the stagnation in the field
of agricultural education and in other sectors of native life.

THE WAY OF POLITICAL PENETRATION   The colonial areas in
Southeast Asia are the final result of the mercantile ideology of the
seventeenth century. Commercial competition forced the East

34. League of Nations, Health Organization, *Intergovernmental Conference of Far
Eastern Countries on Rural Hygiene,* held in Badoeng (Java) Aug. 3–13, 1937
Report (Geneva, 1937), p. 67, Recommendation No. 1.

35. *War and Peace in the Pacific,* Preliminary Report of the Eighth Conference of
the Institute of Pacific Relations, Quebec, December, 1942 (New York, 1943), p. 105.

Indian companies to interfere in the native political life. Alliance with local rulers was generally the first step to a colonial administration. When Western governments succeeded the decaying trading companies, commercial influence grew necessarily into centralized political control.

Western political penetration has developed two types of administration. The way of "indirect rule" [36] characterized the trading companies in the seventeenth and eighteenth centuries. As the European traders lacked the technical means for a direct control of the vast, inaccessible and densely populated areas, they tried to gain influence by political means, mostly by intrigues. They gradually secured a stronger hold on native chiefs and princes whom they supported in conflicts with rival chieftains and who finally became dependent on foreign advice and support. Occasional presents and contributions, often combined with most realistic threats, were the normal means to keep the chiefs loyal and remind them of their obligations. Apart from these obligations, however, the chiefs were free to govern their territories by their own methods.

The intensified penetration of the nineteenth and early twentieth century necessitated a setup that would ensure continuous control and initiative. With the end of the mercantile expansion and the coming of the industrial age a change in the European attitude towards colonial areas became manifest. The form of indirect rule was no longer sufficient, as the development of Western capitalism and the technical progress in transportation and manufacturing industries demanded the real conquest and intensive development of the affected areas in the Far East. The new forces of liberalism felt the call to enlighten the people in the colonies and to carry through an "ethical policy" (as it was later called in the Netherlands East Indies). Thus economic considerations supported by liberal and humanitarian ideas paved the way for an intensive administration—"direct rule." But when the expansion of the empires continued and direct administration required larger expenditures and a huge staff of efficient men, both systems were combined, with the most intensive direct control over the centers of economic activity. The history of the administration of Malaya and Indo-China

36. Emerson, *Malaysia*, pp. 3–4 ff., gives a valuable analysis of the systems of direct and indirect rule.

and also of Java illustrates clearly the relation between intensified colonization and intensified administration, though it varies in appearance according to the given circumstances.

The character of indirect rule has changed greatly since the time of the trading companies. It has developed into a very expedient form of administration, using the services of the native rulers as an efficient link.[37] It is psychologically manipulated in order to combine a maximum of control with a minimum of political friction, thus disguising the actual political responsibilites. It had a real renaissance when it proved that it could be used successfully to minimize the feeling of political dependence in the ruling class, especially the landlord class.

No doubt the native population gained in individual security by the intensified colonization but had to sacrifice its traditions and customs to an ever-increasing extent. However, where indirect rule was applied preservation of the native mode of life might have softened the pressure of colonization to a certain extent but obviously could not change the basic facts of the colonial relation.

The progressing Western penetration decidedly affected the life of the native family. Very often the capitalistic organization of agriculture created a land problem even in areas which previously had been famous for their abundance of waste land; it favored the concentration of economic and political power in the hands of a limited group of native estate owners and officials. This group and hardly ever the bulk of the farming population shared in the honors and benefits of the political system. It was only logical—both from a political and economic point of view—that the ruling native group more and more identified itself with the Western groups whose economic influence was based or at least dependent, on estate economy. A certain type of partnership therefore developed between the two economic groups. Though it displayed different features in the various areas and was sometimes disturbed by diverging interests in other sectors of the ruling native group, the

37. *Ibid.*, p. 8: When imperialism was forced to find moral justification in a world whose conscience had been temporarily aroused, it came to its true glorification. . . . No longer a stopgap, indirect rule could lay claim to being the instrument by which a humbled Europe could lead the "backward" peoples to self-government, preserving the best of the old and integrating it with the best of the new. Colonies were in bad odor, but indirect rule could be invoked as itself a kind of mandate on behalf of humanity and of the peoples under Europe's generous tutelage.

increasing agrarian unrest and the desire to maintain the existing land-tenure system further intensified the alliance. The colonial administration, confronted with ever-growing native opposition and fearing the political vacuum, finally found the badly needed political hold in the cooperating landlord class. Economic cooperation thus developed into political alliance, and has frequently replaced cooperation with the native princes, who all over Southeast Asia are losing their glamor and the reverence of their people. The political cooperation with the landlords who became safely established in the ranks of administration, government, or council, is the last and most adjusted form of indirect rule.[38] However, political cooperation with the landlord class involves a considerable disadvantage. It deepens the political crisis within the colonial system as the bulk of the population begins to identify colonial rule with landlord rule.

It would be erroneous to assume that Western political and economic penetration introduced the agrarian problem. It has, however, emphasized it and enlarged it considerably. Since all kinds of political interests have now become involved in the problem, the unstable political and social status with its latent tension entails the risk of political intervention from abroad, summoned by an intimidated landlord class or distressed peasants and workers.[39]

In the present period of colonial rule the Western powers have to police the native societies which actually are in a status of rebellion. They are bound in a most pathetic way to maintain an order

38. The landlords, always in fear of agrarian revolution, were naturally the given political tool for the Japanese invader who, e.g., in the Philippines established a most efficient system of indirect rule based on the collaboration of the landlord group.

The establishment of the great landowners as a political ruling class, guaranteed by the colonial power, might in some countries in the area—not in Java where Dutch administration successfully prevented large-scale landownership—complicate the political problems after independence, as the semifeudal character of society blocks the way to democracy.

39. J. Russell Andrus, "Burma; an Experiment in Self-Government," *Foreign Policy Reports*, Dec. 15, 1945, p. 260. Andrus asserts that the political leaders of Burma toyed with Japanese connections even though they actually did not want Japanese control of Burma but merely wanted powerful foreign aid in the struggle for independence.

In the Philippines the landlords established the Executive Commission in January, 1942. It cooperated with Japanese Military Authorities in order to fight the tenant guerillas in the central provinces of Luzon who were a threat against the large estates. In 1943 the Commission was superseded by the Laurel puppet government.

contradictory to their own ideology and dangerous to the interests of peace.[40]

40. Former Undersecretary of State Sumner Welles said in a radio message on Feb. 18, 1946, that "the United Nations General Assembly must face squarely the demand of millions of Colonial peoples for freedom and self-government if it is to build a lasting peace." He continued, "It is impossible to conceive of a peaceful world, were the New World order to be founded upon a recognition of the right of a few nations of Western Europe to dominate almost three-quarters of a billion of human beings, many of whom are ready for self-government."

2

Java

INTRODUCTION   The Netherlands East Indies form a link between Asia and Australia and comprise the major part of the Malay Archipelago. The population in the Netherlands East Indies is today estimated at around 70 millions, of which around 50 millions live on Java. The last census of 1930 showed a total population of 60.7 millions, with 42 millions in Java and Madoera on an area of only 130,000 square km. Jan O. M. Broek,[1] estimated the average density on Java in 1941 at 950 inhabitants per square mile. According to another estimate,[2] the population on Java reached a nutrition density of 1,360 persons per square mile in 1939. Such density is outstanding among the agricultural areas in the world and is a significant fact in the study of the economic and social problems of the island.

The first contact of the Dutch with the people of the Malay Archipelago occurred more than three centuries ago (c. 1600). It was a contact of "wild trading" [3] which the vigorous merchants of the East India Company imposed on the people of the islands. In return for assistance in the many internal wars which wasted the riches of the islands and the lives of their inhabitants, the Dutch obtained valuable privileges from the grateful rulers who paid lavishly with the work and sweat of their people. During centuries of increased contact, the Company developed from the status of

1. Jan O. M. Broek, *Economic Development of the Netherlands Indies* (New York, 1942), p. 17.
2. Peter H. W. Sitsen, *The Industrial Development of the Netherlands Indies,* Institute of Pacific Relations, Netherlands East Indies Paper, No. 2 (New York, 1943), p. 1.
3. G. H. van der Kolff, "European Influence on Native Agriculture," in B. Schrieke, ed., *The Effect of Western Influence on Native Civilization in the Malay Archipelago* (Batavia, 1929), pp. 102 ff.

trader to that of territorial ruler. It steadily assumed greater administrative responsibilities when this proved to be the only practical way to exploit its monopoly. Taxes replaced trading profits, and force took the place of bargaining. The Company established its influence by means of indirect rule, dealing mainly with the princes and rulers who, as their contribution, organized a system of forced supply.

After the collapse of the Company at the end of the eighteenth century, the Netherlands East Indies came under Dutch Government control. There followed a period in which a highly efficient colonial system developed, with certain liberal tendencies. For the last eighty years, the economic interests of the native population have received increasing consideration. After the Agrarian Act of 1870 and to a still greater extent after the introduction of the so-called Ethical Policy (1901), the Dutch administration in the Netherlands Indies tried to promote colonial prosperity by conserving and developing the native economy and society, independent of the imposed Western economy. Although the colonial administration of the Dutch may have been politically less elastic than Britain's realistic policy in India,[4] nevertheless Dutch economic policy in Netherlands East Indies with its mixed Western and native economy has had some liberal aspects. Any study of conditions in the Netherlands East Indies, and especially in Java, must take account of both sectors of the colonial economy and consequently must be "a study of plural economy." [5]

The system of plural economy and plural society is best represented in Java, the most intensively colonized and most densely populated area in the East Indies. Western enterprise in Java and Madoera in 1939 occupied more than 1 million hectares for mass cultivation of valuable export crops. The native farmers, meanwhile, tilled mostly food crops on an area of 7.9 million hectares and thus continued an economic existence within the framework

4. G. H. Bousquet, *A French View of the Netherlands Indies* (London, 1940), pp. 32–33, asserts that the political intolerance of the Netherlands results from the fact that they lack the necessary material resources for an energetic colonial government which, like England, can employ a repressive system which consists in intervening only after it is too late, but intervening then with a vengeance. The Netherlands must necessarily practice a preventive policy.

5. This is the subtitle of the J. S. Furnivall's *Netherlands India*.

of a village economy which, however, even then had been shaken to its foundations. Java, less than one-fourteenth of a total area of the East Indies, holds a key position because of its large area of low plains, its fertility, the high development of its native community, and its central location. Around 70 percent of the population of the Archipelago live on Java and Madoera, an area which is only 7 percent of the total area of the Netherlands East Indies. The other islands, undeveloped and partly untouched by the colonial process, are called the "outer islands," corresponding to their secondary importance in the Dutch Empire. Consequently, this study will deal mainly with Java, which presents all the factors pertinent to an investigation of a rural native community under colonial rule. It was the outstanding feature of Dutch administration that it tried to coordinate the interests of the Western and native communities. A study of the effects of this policy, carried out for more than seventy years, will be valuable in determining future policy in dependent areas in general.

POPULATION PRESSURE AND LAND UTILIZATION   Though Java, in the world of today, certainly "affords the most remarkable example of the application of science to the development of the tropics," [6] its present productive capacity hardly meets the needs of its population. There is no other area in the world which supports as large a population with as great a rate of increase as Java. Dutch colonial policy has contributed equally to the growth of population and to the expansion of agricultural production. Between 1815 and 1945, the population on Java increased from 4.5 million to around 50 million; [7] the annual increase is now around 600,000. While this tenfold increase was taking place, the population continued to be predominantly rural. In fact, its agricultural activities were emphasized when modern traders imported Western manufactured commodities which displaced the native handicraft industries. Native agricultural production, mostly of food crops, was multi-

6. W. G. A. Ormsby-Gore, *Report on Malaya, Ceylon, and Java,* Parliamentary Papers, CMD 3235 (London, 1928), p. 110.

7. If no other source is mentioned, the figures are taken from official agricultural statistics and sources such as *Statistisch jaaroverzicht van Nederlandsch-Indië* (Statistical Abstract for the Netherlands East Indies), and *Statistisch zakboekje,* published annually by the Departement van ekonomische zaken. Centraal kantoor voor de statistiek (Batavia).

plied partly by clearing new ground and improving irrigation, partly by the enormous increase of the so-called secondary crops, and last but not least, by improved technical methods. However, the race between increase of population and expansion of production more and more approached the Malthusian limits. The margin of food dwindled from year to year, and today the critical point seems to have been reached—agriculture is expanded to marginal lands and intensification has reached its limit.

From 1929 to 1938 the native arable land in Java and Madoera rose from 7,600 thousand ha. to 7,781 thousand ha., or by 3.5 percent, only. The increase of population between 1930 and 1940 is estimated to be 15 percent. But of even greater importance is the fact that while the occupancy figure for annual crops in 1929 was 96 percent of the arable land, it increased in 1938 to 111.4 percent.[8] The increase in acreage was also largely due to greater intensification, which is undoubtedly a result of the cultivation of quickly growing secondary crops. This is a dangerous development because of the increased prospect for accelerated exhaustion of the soil. J. H. Boeke quotes the statement of one of the foremost colonial economists at a Congress of Netherlands East Indian Agricultural and Industrial Advisors in 1937: "We may well look with anxiety upon the fact that in Java the crop balance becomes negative with every crop failure of any dimension and that we are only two years ahead in the race between production and population." [9]

The limit for expansion of the agricultural area on Java at the expense of forest land is already past, as 30 percent of the area of Java should be forest-covered in order to protect the water supply vital to the wet rice lands.[10] The process of deforestation is already far advanced, and the forest area has decreased to 23 percent—a very dangerous point. That explains why an official commission in 1936–37 made an estimate that only an area of 300,000 ha. of arable land is still available in Java, an area which would be sufficient to support two-fifths of the annual population increase for seven years or of the total population increase for three and a half years.

The combined effects of population pressure and land scarcity have resulted in the minute subdivision of the cultivated area in

8. J. H. Boeke, *The Structure of Netherlands Indian Economy* (New York, 1942), p. 177.

9. *Ibid.*, p. 163.   10. Karl J. Pelzer, *Pioneer Settlement*, p. 162.

Java. In 1938 the average size of holdings, per taxpaying landowner, was only 0.86 ha., which includes 0.36 ha. of wet rice land *(sawah)* and 0.50 ha. of dry ground for every native owner—an area undoubtedly inadequate.

In contrast with other countries in the area, Java's agricultural development is far advanced in large-scale technical irrigation, intensive methods of land utilization, seed selection, and the like. Owing to the cultivation of secondary crops the Javanese are less idle than the population in some of the other areas, even though their working capacity is far from being fully employed.[11]

Java today is marked by an abundance of unused man hours, which is one of the most impressive arguments against the existing economic system. The productivity of the millions of lost working hours could be usefully applied to raising of the living standard of the population. This, however, would necessitate a change in the economic setup of the island. Today, the abundance of manpower largely resulting from the minute subdivision of the land is delaying the introduction of agricultural machinery outside of the large estates.

The Dutch Agricultural Advisory Service is of the opinion that the trend of intensification can still continue by the use of green manure, control of soil erosion, and so on, and that the application of improved methods could result in a considerable rise in the standard of living. It is difficult to determine whether this official opinion is correct or is merely an expression of wishful thinking or political expediency. Many serious students maintain that the limit has been reached and that there is no longer space for large new irrigation projects such as would make further intensification of agriculture possible.[12] As a matter of fact, Javanese agriculture today is characterized by extensive double cropping, by planting of dry season crops in addition to rice crops wherever possible. From 1926 to 1936 Java's crop area increased from 131 percent of the cultivated area to 142.4 percent. The effects of increased irrigation in the last 30 years, however, have been very poor, and were more or less offset by the population increase, though 190 million guilders were spent, and 124 of these millions since the beginning of World War I.[13] After 1.4 million ha. were irrigated, the official welfare

11. Boeke, *op. cit.*, p. 51.   12. Pelzer, *Pioneer Settlement,* p. 174.
13. Boeke, *op. cit.*, pp. 175 ff.

survey stated in 1924 that, on the average, the poorer agricultural population now gets a little more food than before the World War, but that the food is of rather inferior quality.

Though this narrow margin of cultivation might still be increased to a certain extent—surely not very much—the effect on the standard of living would not be great. In Java, as in other overpopulated districts of this area, the yield per acre is high, but the yield per farmer low. In other words, agriculture is too intensive in the use of labor. However, the fact that it is overmanned and, from a modern point of view, underequipped because of lack of capital is a result of the structure of Java's economy as a whole and can hardly be eliminated by mere administrative measures.

THE WESTERN EXPORT ECONOMY   Under Dutch rule the Netherlands East Indies, and especially Java, developed from a country of subsistence farming to one of the most important large-scale producers of agricultural raw materials for the world market.

The Dutch imposed on the islands a large-scale production of commercial crops. Thus the Netherlands East Indies were established as an important factor in world production and in the balance of international payments. Their share in the world export is: for tea, 19 percent; coffee, 4 percent; sugar, 6 percent; coconut, 27 percent; rubber, 37 percent; quinine, 90 percent; pepper, 86 percent; kapok, 63 percent; agava and sisal fiber, 33 percent; and tin, 18 percent.[14] The total export of the Netherlands East Indies before the depression of 1929 amounted to 1,446 million guilders, by 1933 it had shrunk to 470 million guilders. The corresponding figures for Java were 710 million guilders and 193 million guilders. In 1937 the export total of the Netherlands East Indies had recovered to 1,012 million guilders but for Java and Madoera only to 310 million guilders. The figures for 1939 were 787 million guilders for the Netherlands East Indies and only 287 for Java and Madoera. The figures show that Java and Madoera have never regained the share in the exports which they had before the depression.

The remarkable colonial economic development of the islands established a high degree of dependence on world markets and

14. Pocket edition of the *Statistical Abstract of the Netherlands East Indies* (Batavia, 1940), Table 126. The figures for quinine, kapok, and coffee are for 1938, the others for 1939.

tied prosperity in the East Indies to the movement of business cycles. It was only natural that this dependence was strongest in the case of Java, where the colonial development has been most intensive. As has been noted, the system of plural economy resulted in the large-scale cultivation of commercial crops on plantations financed and managed by western capital. This sector comprised more than 1 million ha., on which about a million natives worked for the production of commercial crops.

The development of this export production was rendered possible by large-scale foreign investments in the area, the greater part of which were made after 1900. The total amount of outside capital was estimated in 1937 as 5,657 million guilders or $2,263 million.[15]

Foreign investments in the Western sector of the Netherlands East Indies economy were estimated [16] in 1927 to be $1,411 million of which about $1,040 million—75 percent of the total amount— were Dutch; [17] $200 million were British, and $90 million were American. The rentier investment, consisting mainly of government bonds, was very high after the depression; it amounted to $852.5 million, of which the Dutch held the overwhelming majority. In addition to private initiative, the government's participation in the economy was very important. This can be easily explained by the historical background of Dutch colonization. It will be remembered that the government had to step in to continue the work of the bankrupt East India Company, and was forced to assume commercial as well as administrative functions. Its strong partnership in the economic life of the Netherlands East Indies made possible broad interference in the whole complex of economic relations which is so typical of Dutch colonial rule. Side by side with private business, the government has a dominating position as investor and owner of large-scale enterprises, mostly in the industrial, but also in the agricultural field.

The Dutch share in the production of agricultural export commodities is very differently estimated. The amount of Dutch invest-

15. Since the data relate to long-term investments, largely made before 1932, there is applied a rate of exchange of 1 guilder = 0.40 U.S. dollars.

16. Helmut G. Callis, *Foreign Capital in Southeast Asia* (New York, 1942), pp. 26 ff.

17. A. Vandenbosch, "The Netherlands Colonial Balance Sheet," *Southern Economic Journal* (1937), p. 329, estimates, however, the Dutch share to only ⅔ of the total.

ments in East Indies' agriculture was probably about 1,500 million guilders or $600 million before the war. While Callis, in agreement with Keller,[18] estimates the amount as around 1,500 million guilders, he mentions in a later article [19] an amount of approximately $800 million or around 2,000 million guilders. Sugar and rubber, in about equal parts, accounted for about two-thirds of the total investment in agriculture. Sugar production was predominantly Dutch, and rubber production was Western-controlled (mostly Dutch) to about 50 percent. Foreign investments likewise played a large part in tea and coffee production. The monopolistic production of quinine, however, was exclusively, and the palm olive industry predominantly, Dutch. The teak forests are state-owned, and the lumber industry is a government monopoly.[20] Before the depression of 1929, a large volume of interests and profits flowed from the plantations, mines, and other colonial businesses to Europe. The East India Company poured out in dividends, alone, 36 times its original capital of 6.5 million guilders or an average of 18.5 percent a year. The total gains to the Dutch people through the East India Company, including wages, salaries, remittances, and so on, have been estimated at two billion guilders.[21] The annual profits from the East Indies ran as high as 500 million guilders in the years before 1929, of which, always according to Vandenbosch, 250 million annually were remitted to the Netherlands. Of course, the slump eliminated a large amount of capital, and commercial and industrial profits disappeared almost completely. But a period of recovery followed, and in 1937 returns on Dutch business investments remitted to Europe were estimated at 62 million guilders.[22] A. S. Keller estimated in 1940 the average annual returns of the Dutch as 200 million guilders in direct profits and 120 millions in indirect gains (such as salaries, pensions, and wages paid in Europe for Dutch exports).[23]

18. A. S. Keller, "Netherlands India as a Paying Proposition," *Far Eastern Survey* (Jan. 17, 1940).
19. "Capital Investment in Southeast Asia and the Philippines," *Annals of the American Academy of Political and Social Science* (March, 1943), p. 27.
20. The Dutch hold also big interests in the mineral oil production and mining industry, where many important tin mines are government owned.
21. A. Vandenbosch, "The Netherlands Colonial Balance Sheet," p. 329.
22. *Quarterly Review* (Amsterdamsche Bank, October, 1938), p. 24, quoted from Vandenbosch, *The Dutch East Indies*, p. 223.
23. A. S. Keller, "Netherlands India as a Paying Proposition."

Indeed, the economic ties between the Netherlands and the East Indies have been very close. Every third Dutch family is in one way or another economically interested in the East Indian dependency. Vandenbosch reports that about 80,000 Dutch people are employed in Dutch industries exporting to the East Indies, and that 80,000 more people are employed in the consumption of the profits derived from the Indies.[24] According to him the retention of the East Indies is a bread-and-butter interest for about 400,000 Dutch. However, Vandenbosch's estimate seems to be rather low, if the interest of the Dutch merchant fleet, of Dutch shipbuilding, of the tens of thousands of pensioners of the Indian colonial service, and the large colonial business houses are considered. Callis is probably not far from the truth when he says that from one-tenth to one-fifth of the entire population of the Netherlands directly or indirectly depends on the commerce or the industry of the East Indies,[25] a fact which helps to understand the Dutch attitude to the Indonesian question.

Java's annual income was 2,500 million guilders.[26] European industries took 800 million guilders of this and the government and the professions took 200 million leaving as the native share about 1,500 million. In other words, the native population received only 60 percent of the total income, while 40 percent went to foreigners and to the colonial administration. The latter, totaling 1,000 million guilders, was further divided as follows: 450 millions left the country to pay for profits, interests, and capital goods; 300 millions went to Europeans and Eurasians in Java, and 250 millions to Chinese. However, the collapse of the sugar industry has greatly changed the situation in Java, and the decrease which marks the Javanese export balance can be largely explained by the strong contraction in this industry.

Naturally, foreign enterprises made a large contribution to the budget of the Netherlands East Indies. In the years before the depression this contribution was as much as 40 percent; government

24. A. Vandenbosch, *The Dutch East Indies, Its Government, Problems, and Politics.* (Berkeley, Calif., 1942), p. 223.

25. Helmut G. Callis, "Capital Investment in Southeast Asia and the Philippines," p. 27.

26. J. W. Meijer Ranneft, "The Economic Structure of Java," in B. Schrieke, ed., *The Effect of Western Influence on Native Civilization in the Malay Archipelago* (Batavia, 1929), p. 75.

industries supplied 20 percent, leaving the other 40 percent to be raised through taxation of the natives. The fact that the natives' share was relatively small was very often cited as proof of the beneficent attitude of the colonial administrators towards the population.

A new period of colonial economy had been initiated by the agrarian policy of 1870. This made enlarged economic activities possible by granting long-lease concessions to foreigners for periods up to 75 years. The victory of liberalism in Holland forced the Dutch Government to end the traditional colonial policy of shipping profits to the government treasury in The Hague, and gave instead broad opportunities for profits to individuals. At the beginning of this century, European capital poured into the Netherlands East Indies. It opened the Outer Islands, especially Sumatra, for colonization, and established there a large-scale plantation production, whose exports, by 1930, matched the export production of Java and Madoera, and in 1939 largely exceeded it.[27] It made possible the plantation economy of Java, especially the development of the sugar industry. The size of this flood of capital can be recognized from the accompanying statistics.

NETHERLANDS INDIES TOTAL INVESTMENTS 1900–1937

(In Millions of U.S. Dollars)

Year	Rentier	Entrepreneur	Total
1900	18	300	318
1914	68.4	675	743.3
1930	396.7	1,600	1,996.7
1937	852.5	1,411	2,263.5

Source: Helmut G. Callis, *Foreign Capital in Southeast Asia,* p. 36.

These predominantly European investments initiated in the Netherlands East Indies a process of construction and new economic development;[28] at the same time they caused disintegration and dissolution in the age-old sector of native economy and society, especially in Java. These effects went beyond the intention and plans of the conservatively minded Dutch colonial administrators, whose main aim was to give space for a prosperous capitalistic development. But they hoped none the less to maintain the native

27. Exports in 1939: Java and Madoera: 287 million guilders; Outer Islands: 500 million guilders.

28. From 1850–1935, the number of Europeans (including Eurasians) grew from 18 per 1,000 natives to 42 per 1,000.

sector of the Indies and to coordinate Western and native interests in a broad-minded welfare policy. Though the chief goal was to create the most favorable working conditions for Western capitalism by developing communications and public health, by improving legal security, and by giving at least a minimum of education, the colonial administration hoped to bring some improvement in the living standards of the native population. Frequently their efforts encountered the resistance of influential capitalist groups chiefly interested in cheap and obedient labor.[29] On the eve of World War II, Western enterprise in the Netherlands East Indies, and especially in Java, was progressing in spite of temporary drawbacks caused by business cycles and international crises. It was in complete control of the plantation agriculture, drawing upon the native population as the always available source of labor.

THE NATIVE COMMUNITY UNDER WESTERN INFLUENCE   The native sector in the economy of Java is not a homogeneous economic unit. Rather it represents an aggregate of separate village and family units, whose mutual contacts are limited. In critical periods, the native population shows a tendency to retreat to village economy as the last line of defense. De Kat Angelino gives an excellent picture of the economy of the eastern society, in the framework of which "the barter of commodities and of labor, supplemented by a restricted use of money for the acquisition of commercial produce, and for the payment of taxes, is sufficient for the slow rotation of goods within a limited circle." [30] Eastern society forms its members into an economic unity "free from the obsessing care for the future which continually oppresses the West." However, this age-old society, ruling human destiny from time immemorial, blocks social progress which is intimately related to the process of Western colonization. De Kat Angelino writes:

As soon as progress begins, the mechanical solidarity rooted in uniformity disappears to give place to organic solidarity born from the differentiation of western society. Both forms of solidarity are the cement of the community where they prevail. Both develop their own method of co-

29. Raymond Kennedy, *The Ageless Indies* (New York, 1942), pp. 177, 178.

30. A.D.A. de Kat Angelino, *Colonial Policy* (abridged translation from the Dutch by G. J. Renier, The Hague, 1931), p. 69.

operation, and sometimes there is little to distinguish them. The cooperative societies developed in the West according to modern ideas and those that exist in the East based upon custom and tradition, are similar in their outward appearance, and do not greatly differ in their functions and their aims. But their essence is very different, and they are separated by the same number of centuries as lie between customary law and modern legislation.[31]

Dutch colonial policy affected the village economy in different and rather contrary ways:

1. It inspired the agrarian legislation of 1870, which opened Java and the Outer Islands to large-scale plantation economy by permitting the government to make long-term concessions of unused land. But at the same time, it tried to secure and reserve the property rights of the population. The Agrarian Decree of 1870, part of the East Indian Government Act, represents a compromise between the interests of the Dutch entrepreneurs, asking for land suitable for a plantation economy, and the rights of the natives under customary law.

The principle of the legislation was to acquire for the public domain only such rights as remained after deduction of all native rights to the land. But the interpretation of the customary law was unfavorable to the native population, and promoted the interests of plantation capital. No doubt the legal problem was very complicated, as the native rights to the soil were of a collective nature and vested in the village or tribe, and not in the individual. The question of Indonesian property rights and their violation by the agrarian legislation is much discussed, and the dispute has been very heated for many years.[32] Official Dutch opinion holds to the State-domain principle and argues that Indonesian customary private law is to be recognized only so far as the legislator finds it unnecessary to limit it in the general interest—which most often happens to be the interest of the plantation capitalists.

This legal discussion of state ownership and Indonesian customary law is not as important as the actual economic development which resulted from the official interpretation of the law. In spite of a restrictive interpretation, the Agrarian Decree secured to the na-

31. *Ibid.*, p. 72.
32. A. Vandenbosch, *The Dutch East Indies*, pp. 244 ff., gives an excellent review of this discussion.

tive community a considerable area of land as a basic factor for the maintenance of the traditional village economy. It conserved this basis by not permitting foreigners to acquire this land. By preserving the foundations of the village economy, the Dutch policy prevented at the same time the concentration of land (with some exceptions in West Java) and thus the formation of a landlord class, such as we find in other parts of Southeast Asia. On the other hand, the restrictive interpretation of the law narrowed the margin for the continued existence of village economy, and contributed largely to the serious economic crisis which faces the native community today. Though Dutch colonial policy had guaranteed the existence of the native community to a certain extent, it had cornered it into a very limited sector of the Netherlands East Indian economy.

2. Far more deciding was, however, the steadily growing invasion of the village economy by money as the carrier of foreign commerce.[33] Money is needed to pay the land tax, to light the houses, to buy salt from the government monopoly, to buy fish and cigarettes, and many other things wanted by the natives when they have been influenced by Western civilization. The demand for cash was further increased by the partial elimination of native handicrafts caused by the import of superior foreign commodities. The amounts spent by the villagers are considerable. According to the excise tax, the inhabitants of Java and Madoera spend 7.8 million guilders on petroleum, more than 2 million on matches, and 18 million for tobacco. There is a natural tendency to increase contacts, to merge the separated economies as trade relations multiply. In this connection, Boeke rightly emphasizes that the advanced methods of food production have a similar effect,[34] for example, centralized rice milling has supplanted rice pounding in the villages. An increasing part of the crop is sent to the rice mill and what-

---

33. Boeke, *The Structure of Netherlands Indian Economy*, pp. 60–61, mentions the Chinese coins of small value which were already a curious phenomenon of Chinese trade in the days of the East India Co. Although very popular for all kinds of purposes, including religious ones, these coins had no connection with foreign commerce; they represented only a commodity of exchange, used, for example, by the Company to buy rice from the natives, but there was no opposite payment movement from the village to the outside. Bruno Lasker, "Southeast Asia Enters the Modern World," (Southeast Asia Institute Paper, New York, 1947), gives an interesting picture of the villagers first contact with modern commerce.

34. Boeke, *op. cit.*, p. 111.

JAVA 47

ever returns to the village for consumption has to be bought with colonial money. It is likely that the native farmer will already have spent the money earned in previous transactions for other obligations, such as taxes, and now has to face the most serious problem in which the process of colonization has involved him: the necessity of taking credit, which will be granted to him only at usurious rates of interest, or what is actually worse, as advance payment on the crop.

The native population of Java actually lives on credit, a fact which very often is erroneously blamed on the natural disposition of the populace, but is largely a result of the entire economic and social environment. In 1924, the amount of credit extended by government institutions in Java and Madoera was 241 million guilders, or 17 percent of the total income. The amount extended by private, mostly Chinese or Arabian, moneylenders is not known, but in some sections it is believed to have equaled the total income.[35] The private rates of interest are generally 10 to 15 percent monthly, especially high for workers who are not able to give any security to public credit institutions.

Aware that laws against usury are ineffective, since they cannot eliminate the cash needs of the rural population, the government established a pawn shop monopoly in 1900, and a popular credit system in 1904.[36] The credit system is worked largely by rice banks from which the peasants can borrow rice until harvesting. They repay the loan in kind, with interest, after the next harvest. The rice not loaned out is sold each year, and the surplus, less operation expenses, is placed in a reserve pool. The interest rate, however, in the early years was as high as 50 percent, and had by 1928 been reduced by 25 percent in nearly 60 percent of the banks. Certainly, rates of interest on such levels may be human in comparison to the moneylender rate, but it is difficult to conceive how they can strengthen the position of the farming population and contribute to native savings. Besides the rice banks, the popular credit system included village banks and popular credit banks.

35. *Verslag van den economischen toestand der inlandsche bevolking* (Batavia 1924), pp. 311–13, 325 ff.
36. Vandenbosch, *The Dutch East Indies*, p. 270 ff.
J. S. Furnivall, *Studies in the Social and Economic Development of the Netherlands East Indies, III; State and Private Money Lending* (Rangoon, 1935), especially, pp. 15 ff.

The number of rice banks reached its peak in 1917 with 11,000, but has declined to less than 6,000. In 1937 the reserves of the rice banks amounted to 8, 205, 000 guilders, and 1,326,000 piculs of rice. The village banks deal only in small short-term loans. Between 1919 and 1937 their number increased from 1,994 to 6,538. At the end of 1928 their combined capital was almost 13,000,000 guilders, of which about 9,000,000 was lent out in loans, whereas in 1937 the corresponding figures were only 9,000,000 and 3.5 million guilders. In 1928 the average loan in Java was 14 guilders. The interest rates have been reduced from 10 to 6.8 percent, and frequently to 5 percent.

The popular credit banks were intended to promote public welfare by providing opportunity for safe investment and the extension and improvement of industry. However, in 1929, they had only 75 million guilders outstanding in loans, with an average loan of c. 65 guilders in Java. In 1929 the interest rates, originally 18 percent, were reduced to 6 percent. The banks largely served as intermediaries for the village banks, from which they received 61 percent of their deposits.[37] However, even this system could not solve the credit problem of the native population, and its achievements were relatively unimportant. The best proof of its failure is the continued functioning of the private money market at rates from 10 to 15 percent monthly.

Nevertheless, the public credit system to some degree alleviated the misery of the natives. Its difficulties are intimately connected with the structure of Java's agricultural economy, which offered no opportunities for native saving and, consequently, hampered native credit operations. From the very beginning, therefore, it met with scant attention and slight interest from the Indonesians. To the great disappointment of the Dutch administration, the banks developed into predominantly official institutions thereby proving once again that it is not enough to establish a well-organized popular banking institution in a colonial environment. The experience of the postal savings bank reflects this fact in a very striking manner. From 1913 to 1932 Indonesian deposits in the postal savings banks increased from 2 million guilders to 8.6 million guilders. However,

37. For the last 20 years also cooperative credit institutions tried to operate in various sections. By 1937, only 90 cooperative societies, mostly credit societies, were registered. They are strongly nationalistic and against Chinese domination.

Vandenbosch comments on the record with these words: "Savings
in this form are not made by farmers but by the new indigenous
classes, such as functionaries, soldiers, clerks, and servants, who
have lost contact with the soil and are completely taken up in the
money economy." [38]

The failure of the public credit institutions is generally recognized. The Encyclopaedie van Nederlandsch-Indië gives a well-
rounded picture of the background for the problem:

Compared to the western world, native society is stagnant; the urge
toward advancement and improvement of welfare, which is accepted in
the West as a matter of course, is almost entirely lacking. The very small
farming industries (and approximately 80% of the population is engaged in agriculture) are directed at satisfying the needs of the family
and consequently are operated on a rational basis to only a slight degree.
. . . More than that, he [the native] is so tightly encompassed on all
sides by the village society, an overpowering administration, the economically stronger Chinese and the capital power of the large cultures,
that these external factors considerably strengthen his natural inclina-
tion to repose. Against that credit can do nothing.[39]

This explanation is fair enough and places the problem of inadequate credit facilities and government action in a correct relation
to the whole economic picture.

It is no wonder then, that in this atmosphere of chronic money
need, the native population is always seeking new opportunities to
get cash. The problem is greatest for those who hold only a share of
communal land which they are not entitled to mortgage. Pelzer
states that when in need of cash they will lease their land to a villager, to investor groups, or mostly to the rice trader, for a cash-rent
payment in advance. The lessee does not cultivate the land himself
but employs the owner and lessor as tenant (practically as subtenant) on a share-cropper basis and takes at least one-half, often up
to five-sevenths, of the crop. If the lessee is the rice merchant, he will,
in this way, assure himself of a very cheap supply of rice; if he is an
investor group (savings society of nonagriculturists), the group will
get a very high profit out of such a combined land-rent plus share-
cropping transaction. The pressing money situation forces the na-

38. Vandenbosch, *The Dutch East Indies*, p. 262.
39. *Encyclopaedie van Nederlandsch-Indië 1917-39*, Aanvullingen (Supplement),
p. 716.

tive landholder to become a subtenant on his own land receiving a rather low rent, because the transaction involves the considerable risk of buying in advance a share of a future crop.[40]

Finally, Western enterprise offers a very convenient outlet, namely, to lease the land to the plantation company. The Javanese peasant will often seize this opportunity to get badly needed cash, and he will, thus, find temporary relief. In this way, the urgent need for money resulting from Western penetration into the native community initiates a dynamic process which steadily promotes colonization.

The establishment of a trader group, largely racially different from and bridging the gap between native producer and the Western export trade, is intimately connected with the entire process of colonization and the shortage of money within the native community. Wholesale collectors, mostly Chinese, act as middle men and perform in the remote villages of Java a dangerous and very expensive combination of services. They act as brokers, warehousemen, processing producers, and also as bankers who finance the native crop production. As Java's native agriculture is not adapted to produce for the market, a whole series of middle men makes the connection with the market and takes care of all stages between the producer and the export trade. This group bridges the geographical and social distance between colonial export business and village production. It has, financially and technically, an immense superiority over the native producer, who is always in urgent need of money, often in real distress. When advance payment is given on the crop (the most expensive form of credit), the market price, generally unknown to the native producer, is no longer a standard and the transaction is made on the terms of the middleman.

There are no statistics available about the share of this group of middle men, and the combination of credit and sales transactions makes it particularly difficult to get a clear picture. However, it is not exaggerated to assume that the share of the middle men averages about 50 percent of the market price [41]—an extreme profit in re-

40. Pelzer, *Pioneer Settlement,* pp. 169 ff. He quotes a survey made in 1939 in the regency of Toeloengagoeng, eastern Java, which revealed that out of a total of 2,740 landholding peasants 74.2% had leased some of their land and 33.9% had leased all their land in order to obtain cash.

41. Boeke, *op. cit.,* p. 178.

lation to the services extended, even if the credit and storage risk in the transaction is considered. The lack of a properly organized market is one of the biggest failures of the existing economic system, and contributes much to the dissatisfaction and racial tension in Java. The nationalist movement has tried to counteract the Chinese trading domination by establishing cooperative consumer and marketing organizations [42] which, however, before the war were still in an early stage of development.

As a matter of fact, the serious marketing problem in Java can be solved only by the establishment of efficient cooperative credit institutions which will bridge the time between sowing and harvest and, by providing cooperative storage, financing, and marketing facilities, enable the native producer to decide for himself the timing of the sales transaction. However, it is very doubtful whether such an organization can be developed within the framework of Dutch colonial economy, with its powerful impact of superior economic and social influences on the native population. An efficient government-owned system of credit and marketing institutions has not been developed in any colonial area, not even in Java, where, as has been noted, a government-controlled credit system made a good start. The inadequacy of such institutions in colonial areas may result from the successful resistance of vested interests which resent this form of government interference as well as other "humanitarian" projects.[43] However, without an efficient marketing organization, the share of the native producer in the market price will remain so low that there is almost no possibility of higher living standards for him.

The effects of the colonial system has changed the age-old, unwritten, but still powerful constitution of the Javanese community where the rights to the land are primarily vested in the village community and the individual has only secondary rights to specified plots. However, the traditional rights of the village to the land has been impaired in recent generations, since land cleared by the individual generally remained his uncontested property. With the progress of agriculture from shifting to sedentary cultivation, individual landed property has become permanent.[44] The disintegra-

42. A. Vandenbosch, The Dutch East Indies, p. 277.
43. Raymond Kennedy, The Ageless Indies, pp. 177–78.   44. Boeke, op. cit., p. 24.

tion of the collective village economy by independent individual rights has changed its structure, promoted a smoother adjustment to outside developments and weakened consequently its character as a "closed" economy. All these economic and social conditions favor the Western plantation companies operating in the neighborhood of a village and interested in renting native land. The peasants, always in need of cash, become accustomed to leasing the land for cash in advance on terms set by the company. In the communities where communal landownership with periodic redistribution of *sawahs* (wet riceland) still was the rule (in 1932, 8.8 percent of all *sawahs,* especially in the sugar districts of Java, were still under this tenure), the plantation negotiated with the village officials who frequently gave away the village land very cheaply, even more cheaply than the individual peasant had done.[45] Very often the *lurah* (the head man in a Javanese village), highly commissioned by the plantation, sold his community out to the company and in this way put the time-honored Malay institution into the service of Western colonial enterprise. Nevertheless, it must also be recognized that the Dutch colonial administration has in many ways tried to protect the peasants against the abuses of plantation companies and village officials, for example, by setting minimum rentals for each class of *sawah,* and by limitation of the length of the lease; moreover, the plantation is allowed to occupy only one-third of the village land at a time, so that a minimum area is reserved for food crops. However, Pelzer concludes that, in spite of the government's balance policy, the Javanese peasant has regularly come out of the transaction at a disadvantage.

The indirect influences of a Western plantation, operated in the area of a crowded native community, can hardly be overestimated. They range from increased money income for the landless inhabitants, who in the traditional village community have no social standing, to the effects of newly established communications, of improved health conditions, modern irrigation, and so on. They result in better communications, in enforced public safety, and in experiences with advanced agricultural methods. To a certain extent these influences have contributed to social progress—they have also largely contributed to the increase of population. But simul-

45. Pelzer, *Pioneer Settlement,* p. 173.

taneously, intimate contact with Western enterprise is resulting in the disintegration of the village way of life. The greatly increased monetary circulation, the multiplied opportunities for contact and labor income, the whole change in the economic setup, and the invasion of new ideas and principles related to a new way of living threaten the time-honored village economy.

Both sociological and economic factors contributed to this development. The fact that landless natives came into the possession of colonial money revolutionized the social balance of a community where, on the one hand, only landownership gave rights, but on the other, the need of money became urgent. The process of dissolution is only natural and in accordance with the law of societal development which rules human destiny. Without denying the spiritual values of Oriental society, it is nevertheless true that the borders of the native village blocked the way to progress. But the new problem is how the native, socially and physically weakened and isolated from his decaying community, is to remain within a colonial system which he considers hostile and which he meets with hatred. How shall a renewed native community be balanced economically and socially while the village economy, which, after all, gave a minimum of material protection and a maximum of spiritual compensation, is withering away?

In Java there is found, besides the great concentration of foreign capital, an enormous surplus of labor, the only economic factor in abundance.[46] Consequently, in Java the West and the East have met head on. The island is also, therefore, the site of the most aggressive rebellion against the colonial system. One of the most outstanding Dutch colonial experts, J. Van Gelderen, emphasized already in 1929 before the depression, the growing pressure on the native community there:

The development has pressed back the elements of the higher developed home industries. The native export trade was destroyed and disappeared before the wave of cheap, mass-produced imports. The remnants of the native higher classes became civil servants in the state organizations ruled by the Westerner. It is true that unit of the life of the people, the *desa*,[47] was interfered with only to the extent necessary for the delivery

46. J. Van Gelderen, "Western Enterprise and the Density of Population in the Netherlands Indies," in B. Schriecke, *op. cit.*, p. 96.
47. Javanese village, which includes a number of classes based on landownership.

of produce. Politically and economically, this was a very great burden on the village.[48]

The people on Java and Madoera are, in the overwhelming majority, small farmers working on minute plots. According to the Census of 1930, about 8 millions were engaged in native agriculture, 960,000 were working on foreign estates, and 1.6 millions were engaged in industry, that is, largely in home production, mostly women. Only 120,000 worked in large factories. The foreign Asiatic population is mainly represented by a Chinese community of 600,000, which, as usual in this area, largely monopolizes the retail trade, but is also engaged in wholesale trade.

The expansion of large-scale industry after the depression and especially in the period immediately before the Japanese invasion has not decisively influenced the typical structure of the native population. As a result of the conservative colonial administration, the masses of the people have remained farmers but have frequently become subsidiary workers on estates in the off-season. The possibility of getting extra paid work on the Western estates has counteracted the tendencies to urbanization of the population which is so typical in other countries of this area.

Ranneft illustrates clearly in the following table the percentage of the heads of families in different occupations.

OCCUPATION OF HEAD OF FAMILIES

	Percent
Officials	2
Workers in Western industry	5
Native trade and industry	8
Better situated farms	3
Farmers with own land	47
Casual laborers who for the greater part are employed in the native agriculture	35
	100

Source: Ranneft, "The Economic Structure of Java," pp. 78 ff., 81. This table was published in 1929, but conditions did not change considerably in the last decade before the war.

Ranneft mentions that there is socially little difference between the last two groups. The landless are closely connected with the small

48. Van Gelderen, op. cit., p. 99.

landowners through personal relationships and are largely economically dependent on them.

As a matter of fact the social differentiation of the native population is very limited. The small farmers, combined with the groups
of casual labor and regular labor in the Western industries, form
about 87 percent of the population. They represent the broad foundation on which the pyramid of colonial economy is constructed.

As the crop area of the native population of Java and Madoera
in 1937 amounted to 6,431,369 ha. or 0.16 ha. per capita, the subdivision is very minute and results in an average size of the native
holdings of 0.86 ha.[49] The main crop is rice (occupying 45.1 percent
of the crop area), with corn (22.9 percent) ranking next, chiefly as
a secondary crop. The yield is high per hectare, low per capita.
Further intensification and improvement of methods may increase
the yield to a certain extent, but not provide sufficient food for a
population increasing at the rate of 600,000 per year. Without the
additional extra pay of the Western enterprises, the Javanese small
owners as a class would already have reached almost a level of starvation.

Since the direct share of the farming population in export production is unimportant, the masses of the people do not participate
greatly in the blessings of the boom, but vegetate in their narrowed
sector of the colonial economy. The crowded population, lacking
capital, can cultivate only for its own use; it must produce food
crops if it is to survive. Therefore, though the number of peasants
in Java and Madoera is about twice as large as in the Outer
Islands, on an average the latter receive from the export of their
crops twice as much money as do those of Java. But if we consider
the number of peasants working for themselves, the whole picture
becomes still clearer. In 1930 the share of the peasants on Java in
the export trade was 8.8 guilders against 46.3 guilders on the Outer
Islands. The corresponding figures for 1935 were 4.0 guilders and
17.5 guilders. The cultivation of rice instead of export crops has
weakened the effects of the depression on the population to a certain
extent and, generally speaking, somewhat reduces their economic
dependence. Nevertheless, the food production of the native economy remains inadequate. With the exception of 1936, Java and the

49. Karl J. Pelzer, "Population and Land Utilization," pp. 148–49, 154.

Outer Islands were dependent on rice imports. In 1938 the volume of rice imports to the Netherlands Indies was as much as 335,000 tons, costing 22 million guilders (in 1939, 280,000 tons costing 18.6 million guilders). The shortage of rice production is serious enough to have a disastrous effect on the food supply, whenever a crop failure shortens the yield or whenever an unfavorable business cycle causes a contraction of the plantation areas accompanied by reduced wage payments, reduced land rentals, and generally decreased contacts and transactions with the Western sector of the economy.

Java, overcrowded and economically disorganized, exports labor to the Outer Islands, just as south India provides Malaya with cheap labor. The planters on Sumatra import the main body of their labor from Java, where the level of living is much lower. At the end of 1934, about 204,000 Javanese laborers were registered in the estates of the Outer Islands (excluding south and east Borneo). The majority worked on the rubber, tobacco, and tea plantations of eastern Sumatra, from which, during the depression, shiploads of useless manpower were returned to the overcrowded and distressed home island.[50]

THE SUGAR INDUSTRY AND ITS INFLUENCE ON THE NATIVE POPULATION   In 1939 there were on Java 1,187 estates with a total area of about 1,100,000 ha. (of which 600,000 were planted with export crops).[51] Sugar cane was by far predominant. The sugar area grew until the beginning of the slump almost without interruption, reaching in 1931 about 200,000 ha. The depression reduced it to 28,000 ha., although shortly before the war it was again about 100,000 ha.[52]

The native population suffered terrible losses. From 1931 to 1935, the ground rent dropped from 25 million guilders to 3.8 million guilders. In the same period wage payments decreased from 83,978,000 guilders to 7,270,000 guilders. The volume and effect of this catastrophe for the native community of Java, physically,

50. Rupert Emerson, *Malaysia*, p. 45.
51. The corresponding figures for the entire Netherlands East Indies for 1938 are, 2,402 estates with an area of 2,500,000 ha. (planted, 1,200,000 ha.).
52. Also the cultivation of other estate crops like tea and cinchona was contracted to a great extent after the depression that inflicted great losses on the native population.

spiritually, and socially, revealed its hopeless situation within the framework of Dutch colonial economy.[53] In later years, production again expanded considerably, but there still remain effects that may counteract an expansion of the Java sugar production to the levels prevailing before the slump.[54] The market is in the Far Eastern countries—India, China, and Japan—areas which, after the slump, started sugar production of their own. While Java in 1927 and 1928 produced 18.7 percent of the world's cane sugar and 11.9 percent of beet and cane sugar, its share fell to 7.5 percent and 4.8 percent, respectively, in 1940. The inevitable contraction to a much lower level, possibly to around 50 percent of the peak before the slump, cannot be counteracted within the framework of the existing economic system. A new balance could be established only by a diversification that would change the entire economic and social structure.

The area of sugar production has for decades been the classical stage for social unrest. It is the center of social pressure, latent resistance, and open clashes. In the social pattern of Java, the sugar plantations, though operating only on rented lands, take the place of large-scale land concentrations in other countries of this area.[55] J. Van Gelderen asserts that the sugar industry has penetrated the native community far more deeply than all other industries.[56] He continues:

It used, periodically, the natives' ground in many districts in Mid-East Java and also hundreds of thousands of laborers, thereby increasing the popular income to a large extent. On the other hand, it exercises a considerable pressure on the Javanese villages, and the government was obliged to resort to drastic laws. It is no accident that the most backward forms of agricultural property rights in Java are encountered in this territory. It is undoubtedly a deterrent to a more prosperous farmer class.

The Dutch literature about Java recognizes the direct and far-reaching effects of the long-lease sugar estates. J. Van Gelderen and

53. *Berichten aan de leden der centrale organisaties van de suikerindustrie in Nederlandsch-Indië*, No. 33 (1939), p. 110.
54. Pelzer, "Population and Land Utilization," p. 156.
55. However, Boeke, p. 44, mentions a new type of land accumulation, also in Java, carried through by moneylenders of no social standing who took advantage of the money scarcity after the depression.
56. *Op. cit.*, p. 99.

G. H. van der Kolff [57] emphasize that the influence of this industry has reached a very serious point, affecting the rotation of crops by the preference for sugar in alternation with rice. The management of a sugar factory dominates the whole economy of its district, because the rice and other crops are coordinated in a large-scale agricultural program drawn up by the sugar company. Frequently, the village authorities are practically under the control of the plantation. Such an arrangement can affect water division and land rents to the serious disadvantage of the native.[58]

Where sugar plantations have been operated in the territories of Javanese principalities—the *Vorstenlanden*—the pressure on the population has been of a dual nature: exactions made not only by their rulers but also by the plantation operators, who have made full use of the rulers' sovereign proprietorship of the whole land. Certainly, far-reaching reforms have been introduced also here, but their effect has been hampered by the vested European interests and by the difficulties involved in exterritoriality.[59]

Concerning the influence on the individual native peasant, van der Kolff states as a dominating fact that the sugar industry does not promote the development of a strong farmer class within its sphere of influence. In fact, it has stood distinctly in the way of that development.

The sugar industry, for the sake of a cheap and assured production, benefits by a dense rural population, with a small and scattered land property, by preference consisting of periodically changing shares in the communal fields, so that it shows practically no attachment to its lands and feels dependent on the work opportunity which the estate offers.[60]

Moreover, the total area occupied yearly by sugar cane, about 200,000 ha. in 1931 and about 100,000 ha. in 1941, does not render a basis for a precise judgment concerning the impact of the sugar industry on the native agriculture. Van der Kolff [61] estimates the sphere of influence of the sugar industry in connection with the rotation of crops at about four times the area of the yearly plantings. Taking the area planted with sugar in 1941 as a basis, we come

57. Van der Kolff, "European Influence on Native Agriculture," in B. Schrieke, *op. cit.*, pp. 122 ff.
58. Vandenbosch, *The Dutch East Indies*, p. 259.
59. Rupert Emerson, *Malaysia*, pp. 460 ff.
60. Van der Kolff, in B. Schrieke, *op. cit.*, pp. 122 ff.   61. *Ibid.*, pp. 124–25

to the conclusion that no prospect exists for the development of a strong farmer class over an area of about 400,000 ha. This is equal to 10–12 percent of the total rice-field area of 3.5 million ha. Unfortunately, the sugar cane fields are the most fertile and the best irrigated areas in the districts concerned and would have given the best chances for the development of a strong native farmer class, while actually the native community within the sphere of a sugar factory is being reduced to the state of a coolie colony.

Van der Kolff had an excellent opportunity to study the social conditions on Java in his capacity as Acting Government Adviser for the largest official credit institution in the Netherlands East Indies. He comes to the following conclusion: In a region like Java where "the disturbing element of a too rapidly penetrating money economy in an agrarian community . . . causes a temporary loss of balance and discomfort," the best counterweight against revolutionary currents is a satisfied community of substantial farmers. But the present shape of the sugar industry of Java, he asserts, is the strongest factor in preventing such a fortunate development.

This powerful industry is based on lands voluntarily rented to the plantations by the native owners who later, as a rule, become laborers on their own land or in the sugar factories, after they have spent the advance payment for rent. Boeke asserts that the amount of rent does not depend on the fertility of the soil but on the scarcity of money in the region concerned, on how badly the landowners suffer from the increasing shortage of cash, and on how urgently the Western enterprises need land.[62] But these factors which determine the minimum claim of the native landowner are not met with a businesslike calculation of the marginal productivity of the land. On the contrary; the plantation takes over on its own terms, undeterred by free competition, since it enjoys a monopoly in its own sector of operation. Its strong position in the land market naturally influences the minimum rentals of the government and determines, in fact, the general rental level. The government's function is mainly as a police against abuses; it is not a factor in price decisions. Thus, powerful economic and administrative forces, which are intimately related to the whole system of colonial economy, fix the share of the native owner in the colonial export business at a very

62. Boeke, *op. cit.*, p. 127.

low level, though he provides the deciding factor for the production, namely, the native soil.

The position of the Javanese small holder as worker on the sugar estate is equally unfavorable. The Outer Islands, where there is a chronic scarcity of labor, have established intensive hygienic care and a scheme of protective regulations (until the thirties combined with a system of penalty-enforced contract labor); [63] whereas the abundant labor on Java enjoys scarcely any social protection. J. van Gelderen refers in this connection to "a system of coolies working on piece work and engaged by middle men" for field work, coolies who generally have no further contact with the estate.[64] The legislation for the sugar industry, unlike the tobacco industry, centers on the subject of the hire of native land and neglects native labor. Even the wage level is much lower in Java than in the Outer Islands.[65]

The sugar plantations can draw for manpower on the masses of the landless (around 40 percent of the population) and on the small owners who have leased their plots to the company. According to the census of 1930, 529,000 workers were employed on the sugar estates.[66] However, the number of regular laborers was very small; in 1930, it was only about 32,000 and that of semiregular seasonal workers (men and women) about 82,000. The majority of the workers, irregularly employed, are not included in the statistics. Since only the wages of regular and semiregular workers, a negligible minority, are recorded, we are, in fact, devoid of any statistical data for a judgment of the social conditions of the sugar workers in general. However, the population pressure and the great number of landless people guarantees an inexhaustible and cheap labor supply to the sugar plantations. As Rupert Emerson says: "The expansion of the sugar plantations . . . has brought great wealth to the investors, but to the Javanese it has meant only increasing

63. This kind of contract labor was practically eliminated on account of the Blaine Amendment to the U.S. Tariff Law of 1930, prohibiting the entrance of the products of convict, forced, or indentured labor under penal sanctions, unless such products could not be produced in the United States in quantities sufficient to meet American needs. Because the Sumatra tobacco plantations wanted an American market they have since 1931 employed only free labor.

64. Op. cit., p. 100.

65. Harold B. Butler, Problems of Industry in the East (Geneva, 1938), p. 56.

66. Boeke, p. 133, considers this number too small. His estimate is 800,000.

labor at a bare living wage with the general standard of living even declining at times." [67]

Western enterprises have done away with the ancient walls of isolation and stagnation in Java and have made room for some social progress. However, no new balance of economic and social forces has appeared. On the contrary, strong forces in the Western economic penetration, as in the sugar industry, attack the native peasant in his role as a member of the village community and as landowner and worker. They have moved him about and used him without providing adequate economic or social compensation, thereby changing him into a rebel—he who was once one of the most conservative types ever to be found in rural society.

SOCIAL STRATIFICATION AND LEVEL OF LIVING The social stratification in Java is along racial lines. Enormous differences in income contribute to racial and social tension throughout the Netherlands East Indies. Especially is this true in Java, where the contrasts are greatest and in closest proximity. The Central Bureau of Statistics of the Netherlands East Indies [68] has published an analysis of the total income and the way in which it is distributed among the population. The investigation is based on the statistics of the income tax of 1926, a comparatively favorable year for Java. This official material clearly illustrates the racially decided social stratification. According to these statistics almost 90 percent of the native taxpayers in Java in 1926 had an income of less than 400 guilders; almost 80 percent of the group made less than 200 guilders, and 50 percent less than 150. But even these statistics do not give a really true picture, as only 3.4 percent of the native population had taxable incomes. The Central Bureau of Statistics explains that there are "a great number of persons receiving an income below the minimum limit fixed at 120 guilders." [69]

But in the same year (1926), almost 50 percent of the European assessments were on incomes between 1,200 and 5,000 guilders, of which almost half were above 3,000 guilders. Incomes between

67. *Malaysia,* p. 44.
68. *Statistisch jaaroverzicht van Nederlandsch—Indië,* 1928, *Department* van Landbouw, Nijverheid en Handel (Weltevreden, 1929).
69. Mededeelingen van het centraal kantoor voor de statistiek No. 69, Departement van Landbouw, Nijverheid en Handel (Weltevreden, 1929), p. 25.

RACIAL DISTRIBUTION OF INCOME TAXPAYERS IN JAVA AND MADOERA
IN 1926

Income (in Guilders)	Europeans	Foreign Asiatics	Natives	Total
120–150	157	8,000	568,000	576,157
150–200	279	7,300	222,000	229,579
200–250	294	6,100	117,000	123,394
250–300	257	4,300	63,000	67,557
300–400	880	11,500	78,000	90,380
Total:	1,867	37,200	1,048,000	1,087,067
400–1,200	7,400	69,500	104,000	180,900
1,200–5,000	29,700	19,600	19,000	68,300
5,000–10,000	15,500	2,400	899	18,799
10,000–25,000	6,700	807	154	7,661
25,000–100,000	1,100	211	13	1,324
100,000–200,000	97	8	1	106
200,000–500,000	18	3	–	21
Total:	60,515	92,529	124,067	277,111
Grand Total:	62,382	129,729	1,172,067	1,364,178

Source: Compiled from figures given in *Statisch jaaroverzicht van Nederlandsch-Indië*, 1928, Table No. 106, pp. 146 ff.

5,000 and 25,000 guilders were enjoyed by 33 percent of the European taxpayers, of whom almost one half had more than 8,000 guilders; 77 percent of the taxable Europeans were assessed for income tax. The group of foreign Asiatics, mostly Chinese, represented the middle class; almost 55 percent of them had incomes between 400 and 1,200 guilders and of those over 50 percent earned more than 600 guilders. In the aggregate, the Europeans had an assessable income of 348 million guilders; the foreign Asiatics, 135 million; and the natives, 297 million (1925).[70]

The relationship between the number and the amount of assessments by races reflects even more strongly, if possible, the social stratification along racial lines. The Europeans, representing only 4.5 percent of the number of taxpayers, paid almost 45 percent of the total assessment; the natives paid around 37 percent, in spite of the fact that they comprised 86 percent of the taxpayers. In 1925,

70. As the European incomes in the Indies are largely assessed in Java, the proportion is somewhat different for the entire Archipelago.

the Europeans paid 25 million guilders in income taxes, the foreign
Asiatics 9 million, and the natives 14.5 million in the whole of the
Netherlands East Indies. (No special data are available for Java
and Madoera.)

The slump increased the concentration of income along racial
lines. The statistics for 1933 reveal that the number of natives
assessed for an income of 120 guilders or more fell from 3.5 million
in 1929 to 2.4 million in 1933, of which more than 2 million were
reported as having incomes of 300 guilders or less.[71] Unfortunately,
the comparison cannot be made for later years, as a reform in 1934
exempted incomes in both wages and other income up to 900
guilders.[72] Therefore, incomes below that amount do not appear
in recent statistics, but, nevertheless, the general trend is clearly
illustrated. In 1938, 70,000 Europeans in the Netherlands East
Indies paid taxes on a total income of 337 million guilders, 47,000
Chinese and other nonindigenous Asiatics on 124 million, while
36,000 natives out of a population of around 66 million paid taxes
on a total income of only 69 million guilders. Though the Europeans represented less than 0.5 percent of the entire population,
they accounted for almost 65 percent of the total income subject
to income tax. The foreign Asiatic group, 2 percent of the population, made almost 25 percent, while the native population, 97.5
percent accounted for only 13 percent of the assessable income.[73]

It is a significant fact that the bulk of the Javanese population
has less than 200 guilders per family. Around 90 percent are underprivileged and only 10 percent have a modest middle class existence;
foreigners, on the other hand, constitute the middle class almost
exclusively and the high income groups completely.

These enormous differences have decidedly contributed to the
tensions in the Netherlands East Indies, and especially in Java.
Unfortunately, the continued concentration of foreign capital and
the great reduction in the share of the native population as a result
of the depression have widened the gulf in recent years.[74] In contrast

71. Emerson, *Malaysia*, p. 489.

72. From Jan. 1, 1935, the number of persons assessed under an income of 900
guilders per annum were covered by a special wages tax.

73. *Statistical Abstract of the Netherlands East Indies, 1940.* Table 195.

74. Ranneft, *op. cit.*, p. 81, says that there are in fact no educated natives employed
in the European large-scale industries.

to Western development, the income share of the native population, be it as native producers, ground renters or workers, is steadily
decreasing,[75] and the level of living is more and more reduced. Lacking any accurate statistics about the development of the level of
living of the Javanese population, we are dependent on estimates
which, in conformity with the general economic development on
the islands, agree almost without exception, that a considerable
decline has taken place in the last generation.[76] This judgment is
confirmed by the decline in rice consumption. The diet of the
people of Java has definitely diminished in food value, though not
in actual volume, in the course of the last generation. The rice
quantity available per head decreased from 102 kg. in 1913, to 87
kg. in 1940, and is by no means compensated by the increase in the
consumption of cassava and maize in the same years from 71 to
159 kg. and from 29 to 37 kg., respectively.[77]

The different social development of the foreign and native community has eliminated the possibility—still prevailing thirty years
ago—of a separate but peaceful coexistence of the two groups.
Instead, both sides have erected rigid social and racial barriers. As
a result of local conditions of production and communication and
also of economic isolation, important differences exist, on the welfare and social levels, in the various provinces, sections, and villages.
However, these differences are of relative importance only and have
no essential influence on the social level in general, which remains
unsatisfactory and shows a tendency to further decline.

Even the well-organized health service of the Dutch was limited
in its effect by the low standards of living which reached a level of
starvation in many regions during the depression. For the last
twenty years the death rate in Java has been more or less stable.
It fluctuates around 20 per thousand. Public health reforms cannot compensate for the lowered resistance of a population which is
chronically undernourished, and where consequently the rate of
tuberculosis is alarmingly high. Boeke [78] reports that paid laborers,

75. Boeke, p. 165.
76. Butler, *op. cit.*, pp. 51–52; Boeke, *op. cit.*, p. 89; Pelzer, *Pioneer Settlements*, p. 174, and Table, p. 258.
77. A. M. P. A. Scheltema, *The Food Consumption of the Native Inhabitants of Java and Madura* (Batavia, 1936), p. 16; Pelzer, *Pioneer Settlement*, p. 174, Table XXX.
78. Boeke, *op. cit.*, p. 96. League of Nations Health Organization, Intergovernmental Conference of Far Eastern Countries on Rural Hygiene, Preparatory Papers, Report

needed for strenuous work, must be built up physically before they are able to undertake it.

CONCLUSIONS Without doubt, future prospects for the Dutch in Java are gloomy. Though it must be recognized that Dutch rule, from an economic angle, was not indifferent to the interests of the native population, that it was the only colonial rule which effectively avoided speculation in land by a policy of strong regulations and has tried (but far less effectively) to guard the income of the native community, the final results are rather depressing. Even Vandenbosch, whose excellent book on the Dutch East Indies is most positive as to the merits of Dutch colonial rule, summarizes that "at all events, the economic benefits of Dutch rule have not gone into higher standards of living but have been neutralized by an increase of population." [79] It could be argued whether the failure of the colonial system is due to population pressure alone, when considering the entire lack of economic and social balance and the almost monopolistic position of foreign enterprises privileged by a combination of legal rules, administrative practices, and plain economic facts. The population pressure has only enhanced and perhaps overemphasized a logical development which indicates the difficulties, perhaps the impossibility, of emancipating a native population economically and socially by a colonial system. The pressure of complete economic dependence, and of all that goes with it, is in the long run the deciding factor responsible for the negative result. Even a well-constructed system of plural economy, such as the Javanese, with its subtle scheme of division of labor, cannot block the disintegration and dissolution within the native community caused by its increasing economic dependence.

It is necessary to understand this serious background for the Javanese problem in order to avoid wrong conclusions and especially over-estimation of the population pressure. There is no possibility of solving the Javanese problem by a mere resettlement, since even the best-organized migration will scarcely be able to cope with the annual population increase of 600,000. In the best circumstances, it may delay the crisis and smooth the tension. It will

---

of the Netherlands Indies (Geneva, 1937), pp. 132 ff., asserts that beri-beri has increased in the rubber regions.

79. Vandenbosch, *op. cit.*, p. 15.

hardly be more than local relief, though it certainly could be of value as one contributing factor among others more important, as, for example, industrialization. Van der Kolff[80] asserts that an annual emigration of 120,000 families, consisting of father, mother, and child (the age of the parents between 15 and 24 years), to the Outer Islands would be possible and sufficient to stabilize the population on Java, with the result that the total population in the year 2000 (by a permanent birth surplus of 1.5 percent) will not exceed 57 million, instead of 116 million without emigration. However, the calculation of van der Kolff rather seems to prove the inadequacy of emigration as a general remedy for the Javanese problem. The history of emigration from Java is not a very happy one,[81] and nothing seems to indicate that a large-scale emigration is possible.[82] But even an emigration system of the proportion suggested by van der Kolff, if it were not coordinated with other measures, would merely stabilize the present status of overpopulation. Finally it should be borne in mind that even the efficient Dutch policy of public health and the well-organized attack of the government on rural indebtedness by public bank institutions could not effect a social development that was doomed to failure by the contradictions involved.[83]

80. "Colonization and the Population of Java," in *The Far Eastern Review* (1938), p. 465.

81. An emigration movement between 1900 and 1905, encouraged and supported by the government, has given only meager results. Including contract labor, which cannot be considered as resettlement, the total number of the Javanese in the Outer Islands amounted only to about 650,000 in 1936. After the depression, especially after the establishment of a central commission for the emigration and colonization of natives (1937), the number of colonists in the Outer Islands increased with financial support of the government. The figures were: *1936*, 13,152; *1937*, 19,700; *1938*, 33,399; *1939*, 45,339. For 1940 an emigration of 55,000 was planned.

82. Van Gelderen, p. 97, emphasizes that an individualistic unorganized settlement of the Javanese is impossible. The Javanese is no pioneer. Further he mentions the difficulties of the strange surroundings and the necessity to change from intensive to extensive agriculture. Vandenbosch, pp. 226 ff. and Boeke, p. 175, are also very skeptical. Vandenbosch speaks only about emigration as a relief measure which could be important after the emigration had reached 100,000 annually. Pelzer, however, in *Pioneer Settlements*, p. 175, sees favorable aspects for emigration, of course, in connection with other measures such as industrialization.

83. R. Emerson, *Malaysia*, pp. 492 ff., "I can myself conceive, although there are many who cannot, the colonial governments adopting an essentially neutral attitude toward a gradual and peaceful change in the economic structure which would bring the natives into predominance . . . ; but I cannot conceive the colonial governments taking the initiative in such changes nor giving them any strong, consistent, and overt backing. Under the system of imperialist control the natives of any country are

After the catastrophe of the slump, the Dutch administration tried finally to adjust the economic structure to some extent by promoting a program of diversification within modest limits. By 1939 a considerable expansion of native handicraft industry and a very limited development of modern light industries had taken place.[84] But the Netherlands East Indies, and especially Java, remained predominantly a typical colonial area, entirely dependent upon foreign capital and foreign markets for the sale of its raw material production. Nevertheless, Java showed a limited trend towards the development of an industrial center for the archipelago and increased its industrial export to the Outer Islands from 34 million guilders in 1935 to 58.6 millions in 1939—certainly progress, though a very limited one. Under the pressure of war, the trend to industrialization increased, especially after the German occupation of the Netherlands, and the first real effort was made to establish large-scale manufacturing on Java, an effort very important for the planned defense of the Indies. Java was no longer considered a colonial area but the center of the Dutch Empire, politically, and also financially. Therefore, this last period of industrialization, which for the first time, began to establish large-scale manufactures, must be considered as being outside the framework of traditional colonial economy.[85]

But even an industrialization of Java within the colonial framework may not change matters very much with regard to social tension and turbulent dissatisfaction. It may merely serve to emphasize further the differentiation along racial lines, since the owners and managers of the new industries would be almost exclusively of foreign origin while the workers would come from the distressed agricultural areas, mostly landless people displaced by the advancing Western penetration into native agriculture. An

denied the effective and positive support in the economic sphere which it would be the first thought of any autonomous locally rooted government to give them."

84. Kate L. Mitchell, *Industrialization of the Western Pacific* (New York, 1942), p. 274. Broek, *op. cit.*, pp. 76 ff.

85. Peter H. W. Sitsen, *The Industrial Development of the Netherlands Indies*, p. 5, made an investigation on the basis of the census of 1930 and of very rough test counts, 'held in 1939, and of available industrial statistics concerned with industrial employment. He concludes that 22 million persons were employed around 1940–1941 in the Netherlands Indies, of which 14 million were in agriculture, 2.5 million in light industry, 300,000 in machine industry (both secondary), 600,000 in mining, and 4.6 million in commerce, transport, and profession.

awakened nationalism will attack Western enterprise in the industrial field no less vehemently than in the agricultural, because it wants the social differentiation to be within the native society. From the angle of social dynamics, the basis of unrest will merely be enlarged and spread from the field of agriculture to the industrial field. Prudent Dutch students like de Kat Angelino, van Gelderen, Boeke, and van der Kolff saw the difficulties very clearly and hoped for a development which would grant the native population a just share in the economic and social life.

The time for concessions, however, has passed. The national movement in Java has grown fast and has risen above the mere colonial level. The change is in process from trusteeship to partnership. From the war in the Pacific the most representative and successful national movement in Southeast Asia has emerged in Java. It was able to establish the Indonesian Republic which received "de facto recognition" both by the Dutch Government and by the United States except with regard to foreign and economic affairs.

In April, 1947, the Indonesian Republic announced a ten-year plan for the liquidation of the colonial character of her economy by means of diversification and the guiding of a larger share of the proceeds of industrial and agricultural production into Indonesian hands. The plan provides compensation for the present owners, if utilities, now in private hands, are transferred into public ownership. This is also to be the case for industries and estates now belonging to the Netherlands East Indies government. The cooperative movement will be given an outstanding place in the reorganization of Indonesian economy.

The international status of the Indonesian Republic, however, is not yet stabilized. The present relation between the Netherlands and Indonesia is formulated in the so-called Linggadjati Agreement (November 15, 1946), the controversial interpretation of which led to war. According to Dutch interpretation the agreement is "not a constitution, but rather a program of principle . . . not a juridical, but a political document." It has, however, clearly recognized the government of the Republic of Indonesia as exercising de facto authority over Java, Madoera, and Sumatra and the obligation of the Netherlands and the Indonesian Republic to cooperate in the rapid formation of a sovereign democratic state on a federal basis, comprising the Republic and all other territories of Indonesia, to be called The United States of Indonesia. The agreement further provides that in order "to promote the joint interests of the Netherlands and Indonesia" a Netherlands-Indonesian Union shall be established, comprising the United States of Indonesia and the Netherlands, Surinam, and Curaçao.

The agreement of Linggadjati was outruled by war but was again recognized as a basis for the relationship between the Netherlands and the Indonesian Republic in a truce agreement mediated by the Security Council of the United Nations (January, 1948). According to this agreement the people of Java, Sumatra, and Madoera shall decide in a plebiscite whether they will join the Indonesian Republic or some other state within the planned United States of Indonesia. Soon after the truce, however, the tension between the Indonesian Republic and the Netherlands increased again, since the Republic accused the Dutch government of continuing a disguised colonial administration.[86]

The Linggadjati Agreement has never been more than a transitional compromise in the historic struggle between the Indonesian national movement and Dutch colonial rule. It reflects, however, irrevocably the trend of a development which alone can lead to the termination of colonial economy in Java.

In this connection it must be emphasized again that Java is one of the few areas in Southeast Asia and in the entire Far East which is not marked by disproportionate land concentration and the existence of a landlord class, dangerous for the economic, social, and political development of the country, because the Dutch Administration has conserved the native soil as the national heritage of the Indonesian people. It can, therefore, be said with some degree of certainty that the future political and economic development of the Javanese people might be more peaceful, more democratic, and more fortunate that in other comparable areas, when the traditional colonial system is giving way to a new and not dependent economy.

86. The Dutch Governor-General van Mook established a temporary Federal government consisting of representatives of Netherlands East and West Borneo, West Java, and other regions politically dependent on the Netherlands. The Indonesian Republic refused to join this provisoric government and protested officially against it (March, 1948).

3

Burma

INTRODUCTION   The economic development of Burma has been different in many respects from that of Java. While the Dutch administration in Java protected the natives' property rights to the soil, the British in Burma observed a policy of laissez-faire that finally resulted in an unparalleled land concentration. Increasing population pressure has marked Java's development, but Burma is still a country with vast areas of agricultural waste land. Political and economic dependence has created in Burma the typical colonial conflict, with its social and racial aspects. Conditions became further complicated by tension between the native population and immigrants from India who were urged by the British Administration to participate in the development of the fertile plains of Lower Burma.

A century ago, the British administration took over the lower part of Burma (partly in 1824, partly in 1852). In contrast to densely populated Upper Burma, with its highly complex, though not rigid, social organization, the greater part of Lower Burma then consisted of large areas of sparsely settled waste land. As a result of a series of devastating wars in the middle of the eighteenth century, only limited groups found it possible to cultivate cotton in the jungle, and this only as shifting cultivators, in small, scattered clearings.[1]

The revolutionizing factor in the development of Burma was not British rule as such, but rather the opening of the Suez Canal in 1869, which made it possible to sell tropical surpluses on the Western market. British rule established the needed political and economic conditions for the exploitation of this new trading oppor-

1. J. S. Furnivall, *An Introduction to the Political Economy of Burma* (Rangoon, 1931), p. 40.

tunity, and thus the basis for Burma's adjustment to the expanding world economy. In the years following the opening of the Suez Canal, large-scale rice production was developed in the delta region of Lower Burma, also called the Delta land. Long before the British finally took over Upper Burma (1886), a stream of individual immigrants had gone from there to settle in the Delta land. Later there followed well-organized Indian immigration on a large scale.

Contact with Western economy strongly influenced the social organization in the Delta land, disintegrating the traditional economic and social life of the people much faster and more intensely than was the case in Java, where Western penetration had been more restricted. Whereas the old economic life of Burma had been mainly feudal and based on the tradition of the village economy, the new economic setup in the Delta land became individualistic, exalting freedom of contract and freedom of enterprise.[2] The British school of economic liberalism applied its principles to this remote part of the world. Individual property displaced family property, and imports of superior manufactured commodities displaced the original local handicrafts. Land became a commodity[3] and credit arrangements conquered first the people and later the soil. J. Russell Andrus points out that the new immigrant villages in Lower Burma were composed of individuals and no longer of clans and groups, and that the head man of each village had jurisdiction over all its residents. Thus, the principle of geographically based administration displaced the ancient tribal administration, a fact which has contributed in large measure to social rootlessness and confusion, during a period in which a new and stable social system could not be developed.

It cannot be denied that British rule was highly successful in opening Burma to world trade. Burma (until 1937 an integrated part of India) has become the world's main exporter of rice (with an annual average of 3 million tons) and an important exporter of timber (teak), petroleum, and valuable metals. An efficient flood control was established in the Delta land, and in three generations vast jungle areas were cleared, thereby increasing the rice acreage of Lower Burma from 1 to 10 million acres and developing it into one

2. J. Russell Andrus, *Burmese Economic Life* (Stanford, Calif., 1947), p. 15.
3. Furnivall, *An Introduction*, p. 58, quotes a saying "that land in Lower Burma changes hands almost as frequently as securities in a stock exchange."

of the most productive rice areas in the world. Seen from a purely technical point of view, this colonial penetration and development of Burma's economic resources was a first-rate performance. However, it lacked the somewhat more liberal-minded social considerations characteristic of the Dutch administration in the Netherlands East Indies.[4]

Foreign investments (partly in agriculture and partly in oil, mining, and lumber) decided the colonial development of Burma.[5] Before the war they were estimated at approximately 50 million English pounds, roughly three times as much as in 1914. Dividends averaged 20 percent or more on stocks outstanding, and the remittances of commercial profits were as high as 10 to 12 million pounds annually. Ninety percent of the total investments were British controlled. However, the estimate of the foreign investments does not include the large investments by the Chettyars [6] and other Indian moneylenders, who have financed the expansion of the rice economy in the Delta land and who have been considered "foreigners" in Burma since the separation from British India in 1937. Their investments are of particular interest to this study. According to an estimate of the Provincial Banking Inquiry Committee in 1930, the loans of the Chettyars on security of agricultural land alone amounted to Rs. 500 million, or $190 million.[7]

Colonial development is concentrated in the Delta lands, where agriculture has become largely commercialized and has taken on the

4. Helmut G. Callis, *Foreign Capital in Southeast Asia*, pp. 80 ff. See also Helmut G. Callis, "Capital Investment in Southeast Asia and the Philippines," pp. 22 ff. However, Callis's estimate of the foreign investments in Burma is not complete. J. R. Andrus, "Burma, an Experiment in Self-Government," *Foreign Policy Reports* (Dec. 15, 1945), pp. 264 ff., estimates them to be, including Chettyar investments and government debts, £150,000,000.

5. See note 4.

6. The Chettyars are a caste of hereditary moneylenders in South India (Madras). They are famous for their alertness, shrewdness, and charity. They are intimately acquainted with the English banking system and cooperate with British banks in India. Their strong organization and almost unlimited credit, thanks to their longstanding connections with British banks and their firsthand knowledge of local conditions, completely exclude any native competition. They work through an organization of subagents in the large villages, thus monopolizing the banking business. See Furnivall, *An Introduction*, pp. 119 ff., and L. C. Jain's *Indigenous Banking in India* (London, 1929), p. 30.

7. The normal exchange value of the rupee was 1s. 6d., or 36.5 American cents. The range was 24–37 cents during the decade 1930–40. As of October, 1940, the rupee was valued at 29.85 cents.

typical industrial characteristics of large-scale production and minute division of labor.[8] An almost unlimited supply of land, security of rainfall, and the practice of concentrating on a single crop have permitted a division of labor by alloting each process to a different man. Large-scale production has been made possible by an abundant supply of cheap labor flowing into the area from Upper Burma and crowded South India. It has been financially supported by easily borrowed capital. Consequently, Lower Burma's land ownership is represented by stocks and shares.[9]

Today the agricultural wealth of rice-producing Burma is concentrated in the lands around the deltas of the Irrawaddy, Sittang, and lower Salween rivers. These areas, together with the Arakan region, comprise Lower Burma. It differs greatly from Upper Burma, where a stable population continues cultivation under more traditional conditions, and which is characterized by less dependable rainfall, less fertile soil, and frequent crop failures. The Chettyar moneylenders, who have provided most of the capital for developing the Delta lands, fear the risks of farming in Upper Burma and prefer the fertile plains in the south, where the rice crop is more regular. Upper Burma owes to its relatively unfavorable natural conditions its more stable social development, free from the disturbances of an unbalanced commercial economy. It is today a country of small independent holdings yielding a variety of crops (rice, red millets, sesamum, cotton, beans, ground nut) that insures the farmer in a problematical climate against a total crop failure. In fact, only one-seventh of the land in Upper Burma is controlled by nonagriculturists, in contrast with one-half in Lower Burma. Since this study, however, is primarily concerned with areas having a typically colonial economy, it will deal mainly with the economic and social conditions in the Delta lands.

In Burma, as in other dependent areas, there is almost no manufacturing, and only some processing and extracting. Large imports of cheap consumer goods cripple native handicrafts and practically eliminate the possibilities for development of any native industry.

8. Furnivall, *An Introduction*, pp. 44 ff. Andrus *op. cit.*, p. 16, recognizes that the rapidity of the development and the degree of division of labor are uncommon features in agricultural communities, but indicates that conditions are still far different from those in a large factory.
9. Furnivall, *op. cit.*, p. 45.

The dependence on the Indian market for rice exports (one million tons) prevents the imposition of protective tariffs against cheap Indian-made consumer goods, a fact which Burma's nationalistic leaders deeply resent.[10]

For the last decades Burma has been one of the most problematic of Western possessions in Southeast Asia. The war not only damaged its economy severely but at the same time shattered its entire political and social system. However, the great economic problems with which Burma is confronted today have a new basis for solution in the political agreement signed in London between Great Britain and Burma on January 27, 1947. Displaying superior British statesmanship in acknowledging political facts, the agreement contains the procedures enabling Burma to achieve, in the near future, self-government with the option of remaining in the Commonwealth.[11] Burma decided, however, to leave the British Commonwealth, and on January 3, 1948, proclaimed its independence. The Republic of Burma is the first state to separate from the British Empire since the American colonies did so in the year 1776. Independent Burma will now have to find the right solution for the numerous difficulties that accumulated during a period of unparalleled economic expansion terminated by a war of disintegrating effect upon the economy of the country.

POPULATION AND LAND UTILIZATION   The Census of 1931 [12] reported a population of 14,700,000, of which more than 50 percent lived in the Delta land, 30 percent in Upper Burma and the remainder in the Shan States in the east, or in other tribal territories on the western, northwestern, and northeastern frontiers.[13] The 1941 Census, which had not been analyzed before the Japanese invasion, reports a population of about 16.8 million; today, the population may have passed the 18 million mark, thereby reaching that of the Philippines.

10. Kate L. Mitchell, *Industrialization of the Western Pacific*, pp. 194–95.

11. Clarence Hendershot, "Burma Compromise," *Far Eastern Survey*, Vol. XVI, No. 12 (June 18, 1947).

12. Here and elsewhere in this chapter is referred to the Census of India, 1931, Vol. XI, Part I, Report on Burma. All figures mentioned in this chapter are based on official material.

13. Institute of Pacific Relations, "Problems of the Post-War Settlement in the Far East" (United Kingdom Paper. Eighth Conference, Quebec, 1942), p. 2.

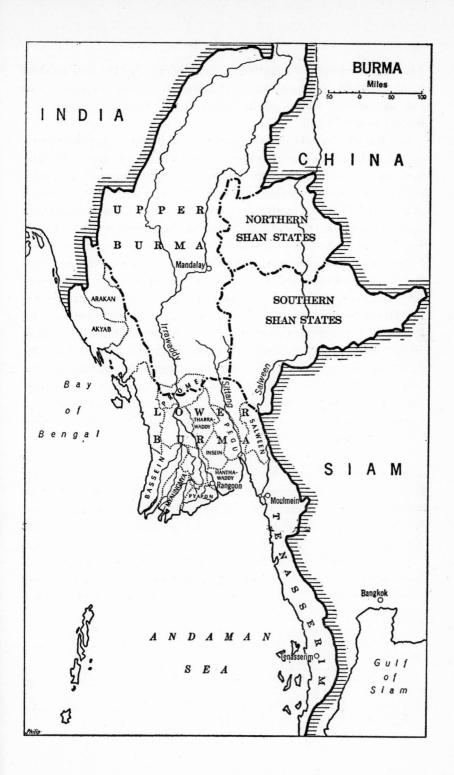

BURMA

Miles

50   0   50   100

INDIA

CHINA

UPPER

BURMA

Mandalay

NORTHERN
SHAN STATES

SOUTHERN
SHAN STATES

ARAKAN

AKYAB

Bay

of

Bengal

Irrawaddy

Sittang

Salween

KYOME

LOWER

THARRA-
WADDY

PEGU

SALWEEN

BURMA

INSEIN

BASSEIN

MAUBGMYA

HANTHA-
WADDY

Rangoon

PYAPON

Moulmein

SIAM

TENASSERIM

Bangkok

ANDAMAN

SEA

Tenasserim

Gulf
of
Siam

Philip

About 70 percent of the gainfully employed work at agriculture, while fewer than 100,000 work in factories, chiefly for extracting and processing.[14] One million Indians and 200,000 Chinese lived in Burma before World War II,[15] the Indians mostly as unskilled workers, agricultural laborers, and traders; the Chinese largely as traders, unskilled workers, craftsmen, and landowners. Thirty thousand Europeans (0.2 percent of the population), mostly British, held the key economic and administrative positions.[16]

The area of Burma is about 250,000 square miles, of which some 100,000 are within the tribal territories. The density of the population is, generally speaking, not considerable and is lower than in the neighboring countries. About 55 percent of the population lives in areas with a density of less than 150 per square mile; 35 percent in areas with a density between 150 and 300 per square mile. The Delta area and the plains along the rivers are, for the most part, densely populated. The center of the commercialized rice cultivation, the Pegu Division and the Irrawaddy delta (one-eighth of the total area of the country) is occupied by one-third of the population. In 1940–41, 21.5 million acres were cultivated; that is, more than 20 percent of the total reported area. An additional 20 percent was reserved for forests. The area of agricultural land still waiting for cultivation approximately equals the cultivated area, but large expenditures will be needed for its cultivation.[17] The remainder— 40 percent of the total area—is not suitable for cultivation. Only about 1.5 million acres are irrigated; most of this acreage is in Upper Burma, where rainfall is not as dependable as in the Delta land.

In 1940-41, two-thirds of the cultivated area was planted with

14. Mitchell, *op. cit.*, p. 191.
15. The Indian immigration, starting in 1876, increased with every year and reached a peak in 1927 with a total number of more than 400,000 immigrants, of whom 350,000 remained in Burma.
16. Callis, *Foreign Capital*, p. 95.
17. The waste lands are partly located in the fertile Irrawaddy delta. John Leroy Christian, *Burma and the Japanese Invader* (Bombay, 1945), p. 11, asserts that Burma has now no large cultivated areas that are not under rice. This statement does not agree with the statistical data published in the *Season and Crop Report for the Year Ending June 30, 1941* (Burma, Department of Land Records and Agriculture, Rangoon, 1941). Andrus, *op. cit.*, p. 44, asserts that it is doubtful if there can be found a comparable area in Asia with as much potentially excellent rice land not in cultivation. This is especially the case with the Irrawaddy delta land, which could give excellent crops if the necessary work could be done to protect the lands from floods and clear off the dense jungle.

rice. Ten million acres were in Lower Burma, 7 million of which were in the Pegu division and the Irawaddy delta alone, rice being almost a monoculture there. During the year 1940–41, a very good rice year, the total yield was around 8 million tons, a million more than the average for the preceding five years. More than 6.7 million tons were harvested on the plains of Lower Burma, where the average yield per acre in normal years is more than 1,600 lbs.[18]

The particular type of colonization in the Delta land has greatly influenced the system of land tenure and has eliminated independent peasant proprietorship in most of the commercialized area. Therefore, land concentration, with all its consequences, becomes the central agrarian problem, though the greater part of Burma's rice is still produced on small holdings, the cultivator being a tenant or small proprietor.[19] In the older, less commercialized districts north of the Delta, in the Tenasserim and Arakan division, small colonies of peasant proprietors can still be found. As a result of subdivision by inheritance, their holdings, however, are often extremely small (frequently less than an acre) and hardly produce a satisfactory subsistence for a family. [20]

THE LEVEL OF AGRICULTURAL CULTIVATION   Levels of cultivation in Lower Burma are not higher than those generally prevailing in Southeast Asia. The Delta land is endowed with good climate and soil and is easily cultivated. There is no problem of irrigation, since the rainfall is dependable and crop failures are almost unknown. Consequently, the cultivator is very reluctant to introduce new varieties, improve implements, or to use artificial fertilizer, in spite of considerable urging by the Agricultural Department. In less-privileged Upper Burma, however, the farmer is more progressive and has accepted wholeheartedly the introduction of certain new crops, such as the groundnut.[21]

In all Burma, only an area of 1.2 million acres was sowed more

18. *Season and Crop Report, 1941.* Andrus, *ibid.,* asserts that all areas aside from the main river valleys, and the Divisions of Arakan and Tenasserim are either barely self-sufficient in rice or have to import it from other parts of the country.

19. Markets Section Survey, No. 9, "Rice" (Burma, Department of Land Records and Agriculture, Rangoon, 1941), p. 15.

20. Furnivall, *An Introduction,* pp. 64–65. However, it is to be remembered that Furnivall's book was published before the slump, and that the trend to land concentration in the meantime also largely has affected this area.

21. *Ibid.,* pp. 98 ff. O. H. Spate, "Beginnings of Industrialization in Burma," *Economic Geography* (1941–42), p. 84, asserts that government activities have not been

than once.[22] In the Delta land as in almost all of Southeast Asia, millions of working hours are lost by lack of diversification. The cultivation of rice requires only about six months, from June to January, and the handicrafts are no longer a source of gainful occupation.

Cattle and water buffalo are still the working animals in the Delta, and the introduction of labor-saving equipment proved to be a failure. Andrus reports [23] that by 1932, 60 tractors had been imported, but bogged down in the swampy ricelands during the rains. Fuel and spare parts were too expensive, and the cultivators lacked the needed technical skill to make repairs. However, more adaptable machinery may have a chance under the new progressive government in post-war Burma, as the war has reduced the cattle and buffalo population considerably.

Artificial fertilizer is not used to any great extent, but the land is flooded annually, and the silt carried by the floods is deposited on the land, helping to restore its fertility. The farmer has yet to learn to distribute the silt, which is unevenly deposited and does not reach the center of the plot. This could be achieved by digging channels for the silt-laden water.[24] The Burmese farmer, however, may be ready now for a rapid introduction of modern techniques as a result of being shaken out of his traditional conservatism by war and national revolution.[25]

INDEBTEDNESS AND LAND CONCENTRATION—TENANCY All over Southeast Asia we encounter a very urgent credit and indebtedness problem, intimately related to the structure of colonial agriculture. It is the natural result of Western economic penetration, of the elimination or crippling of native handicraft, and the lack of diversification. But in the case of Burma it developed far beyond the general economic and social limits. The mechanism of colonial expan-

---

adequate. They lack coordination and are not sufficiently in touch with the masses of cultivators. "Machinery and drive seem to be concentrated on agricultural shows." At best, "the cultivator appears to treat them as opportunity for convivial celebration."

22. *Season and Crop Report*, 1941.   23. *Op. cit.*, p. 53.

24. Furnivall, *op. cit.*, pp. 18–19. Furnivall prefers fertilizing in this way to the spreading of cattle manure, as the rich new soil of the Delta land does not need manure. Andrus, p. 60, states, however, that cowdung now is in extensive use in the paddy nurseries.

25. See Chapter VIII below.

sion operated here more or less undisturbed by governmental interference. The consequence was that the people were forced either to
part from their land or become heavily indebted to a foreign
moneylender group.

The Delta land was not developed by the traditional imposition
of a colonial economy upon an existing native economic system, but
was, rather, the actual organization *de novo* of a pioneer colonial
economy. Taking this into consideration, certain features in the
picture may be more easily understood. The British colonial administration had to deal mainly with immigrants, and not with a
stable population. Its task was to achieve "the blending, harmonious or otherwise, of three distinct economic systems, the original
Burmese economy, the economy of the Chettyar moneylenders, and
the increasingly important capitalist economy of Western nations."[26] The immigrants from Upper Burma and south India
lacked the needed capital to develop the Delta area in a manner
commensurate with the opportunities presented by an expanding
world trade. This brought about the unique combination of British administration and Indian moneylenders, mainly represented
by the Chettyars. British law guaranteed the Chettyars that the loan
secured by mortgage (an instrument unknown to native custom)
would be honored and protected by the British courts. Now the
Chettyars could come to the rescue of the immigrant peasant,
gradually expanding their credit system over the entire Delta land,
following, and even ahead of, the expanding cultivation. Confident
in the law and order of British rule, and anticipating the economic
prospects of Lower Burma, within two generations the Chettyars
loaned out an estimated Rs. 750 million (equal to $U.S. 270 mil-
lion), two-thirds of it on the security of agricultural land.[27] The result was that by 1936 the Chettyars owned two and a half of Lower
Burma's ten million acres of rice land, and had heavy mortgages on
an additional 10 and 20 percent.[28]

As the Chettyars are professional moneylenders and not agricul-

26. J. Russell Andrus, "Three Economic Systems Clashed in Burma," *Review of Economic Studies* (London, February 1936), pp. 140 ff.
27. Burma Provincial Banking Inquiry Committee, *Report* (Rangoon, 1930); Chris-
tian, *op. cit.*, p. 120, points out that land foreclosures since 1930 have reduced the
Chettyar loans on Burma land to about Rs. 100 million.
28. Andrus, p. 68.

turalists, they have taken full advantage of the unprepared and easy-going native population. Their rates of interest have been between 15 and 36 percent annually, averaging 25 percent; this was often lower than that of indigenous moneylenders, but it was extremely high considering the first-class security covering the loan and the normal profit rate of the native cultivator.

In spite of the tremendous amounts involved, the Chettyar credit system was far from being economically efficient. Furnivall [29] gives excellent reasons for the inability of the Chettyars to solve satisfactorily the problem of agricultural finance in Burma. While subagents in all large villages combined access to large credit capital with local knowledge, the custom of changing personnel every three years—probably necessary on account of technical banking considerations—was prejudicial to agricultural efficiency. Long-term loans were rarely granted, and loans which should have been extended over periods of from ten to twenty years (considering the backward economic development of the area) were granted for a term of only three years. The inexperienced native farmer almost inevitably was forced to default on his debt and to lose his property.

As the Chettyar agents could not possibly acquire a satisfactory knowledge of their clients within only three years, they covered the risks involved by charging a higher rate of interest. Furnivall [30] estimates the consequent additional cost to Lower Burma, in 1931, at Rs. 7.5 millions (1 percent of the capital). The Chettyar thus makes his calculations exclusively with regard to the amount of security at hand and not with regard to the increase of agricultural productivity. Consequently, the cultivator frequently finds his credit exhausted just when the land is about to repay the initial expenditures made for developing it.

Too much lending, rather than too little, is generally the greatest drawback to the Chettyar credit system. The temporary agent is seldom interested in a stable, prospering clientele which he hopes to develop economically, as does a Western banker. He, as a mere moneylender, is concerned only with securities and interest. He seldom cares about the economic use of the money; frequently he encourages his clients to continue to borrow as long as they can give additional security. It is estimated that less than 10 percent of the

29. Furnivall, *op. cit.*, pp. 121 ff.   30. *Ibid.*, p. 123.

money lent on Burmese rice lands was actually used to improve the land or to purchase additional holdings [31]—an estimate, which, however, seems to be exaggerated.

This system has been detrimental for a new country like the Delta, cultivated by people unaccustomed to dealing with large sums of money and inexperienced in the use of credit. Consequently, the most recently cultivated lands were usually the first ones to pass out of the control of the original owners.[32] Some students emphasize that the strict religion of the people does not encourage the accumulation of wealth and that this is no less responsible than the Chettyars for the losses of the cultivators. No doubt, the fact that religious Burmese Buddhists are prohibited from making legally valid wills has brought about a minute division of family property, which naturally has not favored the accumulation of wealth. The elaborate spending of money for pagodas in order to accumulate credit for the next transmigration neither favors the establishment of a capitalist class nor does it foster sound economic thinking. Thus, the Burmese were completely unprepared for the new problems of a money economy.

The boom times at the beginning of the century, when the price of rice increased by 50 percent within only eight years, made the population still more adaptable to the credit system of the Chettyars.[33] The mere fact, however, that this system was able to operate unrestricted and uncontrolled in an area like the Delta land must be considered the main reason for the present situation. Other factors may have prepared or emphasized the development, but these are too remote to be causal. It is true that the Chettyars are not actually land grabbers, but prefer straight, profitable accounts to the trouble of taking over the land. Andrus [34] asserts that they are often more lenient than native creditors, in order to avoid foreclosures. However, the logic inherent in such a credit system ultimately leads to the most unfavorable consequences.

Although the British administration emphasized that it favored peasant proprietorship rather than large estates, the trend toward the elimination of native ownership was already apparent at the beginning of the century. Some legislative acts, such as the Land

31. Christian, *op. cit.*, p. 118.   32. *Ibid.*, p. 119.
33. O. H. Spate, *op. cit.*, pp. 74 ff.   34. Andrus, p. 67.

82   BURMA

Improvement Loans Act of 1883, the Agricultural Loans Act of 1884,[35] and the Debt Conciliation Act of 1905, stressed the graveness of the situation, but brought little actual financial relief. After serious rebellions, the government proposed in a press communiqué, May 19, 1931, "to re-examine the very difficult question of agrarian legislation, but that it will be some time before they can come to any conclusions on this controversial matter."[36] Not until shortly before the Japanese invasion in 1941 was legislation passed on land alienation, tenancy and land purchase. It came too late, however, since the process of land concentration in the hands of nonagriculturists was so far advanced that a mere legal measure was of little consequence.[37]

Statistically, the history of the colonization of Lower Burma shows an almost uninterrupted loss of land by native farmers. The periods of high rice prices at the beginning of the century, and during and after World War I, did not stop this trend. Land con-

35. The Acts of 1883 and 1884 made possible small loans at low rates of interest, but the administration was hampered by much red tape, which, in turn, caused many inconveniences for the cultivators. In the years 1919 to 1929, the total amount loaned by the government under the Acts averaged less than Rs. 2,000,000 per year, while the average agricultural borrowing from the Chettyars was Rs. 500,000,000 per year. According to the Land Revenue Report of 1938–1939, the over-all picture showed for loan and interest a figure of only Rs. 1.5 million. See also Furnivall, op. cit., p. 126.

36. Published in the CMD Papers, 3900, XII, 1 (London, 1931), 16.

37. This legislation was based on the Report of Land and Agriculture Committee, Part I, Tenancy; Part II, Land Alienation; Part III, Agricultural Finance, Colonization, Land Purchase, Burma, Dept. of Land Records and Agriculture (Rangoon, 1938), The Land Alienation Act (1941) was designed to prevent land from coming into the hands of nonagriculturists. The creditor can only retain it for 15 years, after which it has to be returned to the original owner without further payment. But, in fact, ever since the slump, the Chettyars had ceased to loan to any but their own tenants. Furthermore, mortgages already existing at the time the law was passed were accepted and should be respected. The Act was without much actual importance, as, by 1941 (according to an estimate of Andrus, p. 81) the land of Lower Burma owned by genuine agriculturists and not mortgaged amounted to only 15 percent of the total.

The Tenancy Act (1939), designed to solve the rent problem, proved unworkable because the individual judgment of local officials decided what constituted a fair rent. It was replaced by a government communiqué which transferred outstanding cases for judicial settlement.

Only the Land Purchase Act (1941) might have been favorable for future agricultural reconstruction. This law deals with the purchase of Chettyar and other lands by the government, which has the alternative to sell it on long-term contracts with provision for very low rates of interest, or to lease it to tenants.

After the war, the Moneylenders Act of 1945, the Land Disputes Act of 1946, and the Agriculturists Debt Relief Act of 1947 were passed. They gave, however, only transient relief and did not affect the real problem.

centration has been almost exclusively in favor of foreigners, mostly
Chettyars and Chinese. From 1915 to 1930, native owners lost
1,300,000 acres in the Delta land because of indebtedness.[38] By the
end of June, 1931, one-third of the occupied area was in the hands
of nonagriculturists.[39] This detrimental development increased
during the depression. The collapse of the rice price caught the
Burmese farmers completely unprepared, and a wave of foreclosures swept over the country, leaving the foreign moneylenders
in control of the best part of the land. The thirteen principal rice-
growing districts of Lower Burma—that is, the area from Arakan to
the region of Moulmein, focusing around the Irrawaddy delta—
were the center of this serious development.

CLASSIFICATION OF OCCUPIERS OF AGRICULTURAL LAND IN
THIRTEEN PRINCIPAL RICE-GROWING DISTRICTS OF LOWER BURMA

Year	Total Agricultural Area	(In Thousands of Acres) Occupied by Non-Agri- culturists	Percent	Occupied by Chettyars	Percent
1930	9,249	2,943	19	570	6
1932	9,246	3,770	36	1,367	15
1934	9,335	4,460	47	2,100	22
1936	9,499	4,873	49	2,393	25
1937	9,650	4,924	50	2,446	25

Source: This table was computed by the Land and Agriculture Committee.

The share of the Chettyar in these districts increased within seven
years from 6 to 25 percent. However, it was still higher in certain
key areas of rice production. According to the Report of the Land
and Agriculture Committee, the titles to 275,000 acres alone in the
Myaungmya district have passed to the Chettyars. According to
the Pegu Settlement Report of 1932–34, the share of the Chettyars
was 36 percent; according to the Insein Report, 31 percent. In
1938–39, nonagriculturists occupied 47.7 percent of the agricultural area in Lower Burma (as against 14.2 percent in Upper
Burma), of which 38.6 percent was held by absentee landlords.

Andrus[40] asserts that these figures may still be too optimistic,
as many "statistical" agriculturists are, in reality, nonagriculturists,

38. Burma Provincial Banking Inquiry Committee, *Report* (Rangoon, 1930), I, 24.
39. *Census of India, 1931*, Vol. XI, Part I: Report on Burma, p. 130.
40. Andrus, p. 70.

and that it is likely that more than 50 percent of the agricultural area of the Delta land has passed to absentee landlords. This assumption gives the only valid interpretation of the fact that 59 percent of the land in Lower Burma in 1939 was let to tenants at fixed rents.[41]

These conditions did not change during the more prosperous years following the slump. The best and most fertile rice lands remained in the hands of nonagriculturists, who, according to Andrus, owned 70 percent of the agricultural land in the Hanthawaddy district, 68 percent in Insein, 67 percent in Pegu, and 71 percent in Pyapon in June, 1939. In this connection, Andrus quotes the estimate of an official who had "excellent opportunities" to study this problem, and according to whom the Lower Burma lands in the hands of nonagriculturists was worth between Rs. 540 and 672.5 million, while the total value would have been between Rs. 655 and 787.5 million. In the five years ending June 30, 1941,[42] 51 percent of the occupied area in the 13 main rice growing districts was reported to have been in the hands of nonagriculturists. Decrease of the Chettyar share in one particular locality was compensated by large increases in other districts. Of about 5 million acres held by nonagriculturists in this area, the Chettyars controlled about one-half.[43]

The wholesale liquidation of the stable Burma farming class was an integral part of the process of land concentration. Statistics taken from the Census of India, 1931 [44] show that within the period 1921 to 1931 the group of male tenant cultivators increased only from 512,000 to 578,000, a 13 percent increase, while the group of agricultural laborers increased from 622,000 to over 1 million, a 60 percent increase. The group of male owners decreased at the same time from 1,160,000 to 927,000, a 20 percent decrease, and female owners from 903,000 to 321,000, a 64 percent decrease. This very unfavorable development took place in a period of relative

41. The last published Report on the Administration of Burma (1935–36), p. 24, mentions that the area let to tenants in Burma amounted to more than 9 million acres, of which far more than 7 million were located in Lower Burma. The Census of India, 1931, p. 130, mentions a figure of 5,260,000 acres as leased to the tenants. The figure of 59 percent is quoted from Andrus, p. 70.

42. *Season and Crop Report, 1941*, p. 8.

43. The 1941 figure exceeds the 1937 figure by more than 100,000 acres.

44. Pp. 128 ff.

prosperity. However, no statistics are available for the years of the
slump, the period of most rapid land concentration. Furthermore,
the census figures for 1931 do not indicate how many of the owners
economically were little better than tenants in the sense that they
had to pay high rates of interest on loans which were covered by
security on their property.

Landlordism, in general unfavorable for agricultural and social
development, had particularly negative effects in the case of Burma.
In Lower Burma, landlordism is in fact absentee landlordism,
established by moneylending transactions. In some agricultural
centers, as in Hanthawaddy, in Pegu and Pyapon, 80 to 90 percent of the landlords are nonagriculturists, mostly moneylenders
without any agricultural interests, with little knowledge of the
land, but with greediness for high rents.[45] In addition, the unfavorable effects of such a tenure system were multiplied by the
competitive pressure of the Indian immigrants, whose lower living levels enabled them to rent land at higher prices than the
Burmese farmers. The pressure of Indian immigration is frequently
mentioned in official documents. As early as 1910, an increase
of Indian tenants is quoted.[46] In 1914, it is mentioned that "in
or near Rangoon the steady pressure of the Indian immigration
is slowly but surely ousting the Burman." [47] It is added that even
Burmese landlords prefer Indian tenants because they pay higher
rentals and are more obedient. However, seen as a whole, this was
of less consequence than the effect of Indian competition on the
scale of rents.[48]

Ever since the Labor Act of 1876, the British government and
British and Indian employer groups have favored immigration from
India, as cheap labor was urgently needed for the development of
the Delta land and the immigration from Upper Burma was not
rapid enough. But even when immigration no longer was supported
by government subventions, the number of immigrants remained
consistently high.

45. Report on the Administration of Burma, 1935–36, p. 23. The report quotes
the proportion of land occupied by nonagriculturists in Lower Burma at 47.51 percent, and the area held by nonresident nonagriculturalists at 38.76 percent of the
total. It can be assumed that these figures have increased within the last decade.
46. *Season and Crop Report of 1910*, p. 7.
47. *Season and Crop Report of 1914*, p. 8.
48. J. S. Furnivall, *op. cit.*, pp. 68 ff., 73.

Indian competition, strong on account of the considerably lower level of living, steadily increased contract rents. In the years before the war, parts of the Delta land were so heavily rented that the economic rent level was reached or often exceeded.[49] No doubt such conditions must be prejudicial to efficient cultivation. The tenants frequently leave their holdings immediately when their contract period of one year has expired, pressed by the burden of debt, or they are evicted after two or three years. According to the statistical tables of the Report of the Land and Agricultural Committee,[50] about 50 percent of the tenants in Pegu and Insein, the key districts of rice production, left their holdings contracted for in 1932–34 or 1933–35, after only one year's occupancy. In almost all other important districts, far more than 50 percent of the tenants who had contracted their holdings partly in the years 1930–33 and and partly in 1933–37 had left after only two years.[51] Therefore, a migrating tenant class without the protective background of a home is one of the most characteristic features in the Delta land and has influenced greatly the standard of land utilization. The migrating tenant will refrain from investing additional labor or care, expenditures for fertilizer, implements, and animals; even if he had the means to do so, he would hardly want to enrich the landlord to that extent and thus enable him to demand a higher rent from the next tenant.[52]

In very few countries is the relationship between land tenure and social and moral standards as evident as in Burma. At the beginning of the war in the Pacific "the typical rural Burman was a landless laborer, often drifting from village to village and contributing to a crime record that gave Burma proportionately the highest rate of murders of any country for which accurate statistics are available." [53] Criminal statistics for 1935–36 [54] record 7,699 serious offenses against persons (6,839 in 1925) and a heavy increase of

49. *Ibid.*, pp. 68 ff., 73.   50. Part I, Tenancy.
51. In Insein, 68 percent; in Pegu, 65 percent, Andrus, *op. cit.*, pp. 71–72, asserts that approximately half of the tenants change holdings every year, and "that an economy of this kind is not a satisfactory basis upon which to build a sound society."
52. Furnivall, *op. cit.*, p. 66, gives an excellent picture of the tenant situation in Lower Burma.
53. J. Russell Andrus, "Burma; an Experiment in Self-Government," p. 258.
54. Report on the Administration of Burma (1935–36) p. 31; Christian, *Burma and the Japanese Invaders*, pp. 158 ff.

minor offenses against property. Within that year, major crimes numbered about 1,500, a very high figure especially in comparison with India. The Tharrawaddy region is noted as a center of crime, whereas the noncommercialized Shan states and frontier areas are little troubled by it.[55] Since 1936, the number of major crimes has again shown a clear tendency to increase. Taking only the first six months of the year, the number of murders increased from 539 in 1936 to 743 in 1940. The latent racial tension, which since 1930 has resulted in a series of race riots, was an additional cause of the high rate.

The colonizing of Lower Burma gradually dissolved the village community, with its fixed moral standards, and replaced it by a migrating tenant class. The tenant in Lower Burma—in contrast, for instance, with the tenants in Upper Burma and the Philippines —is no longer in contact with his native community and is thus deprived of its controlling influence on his social behavior. Isolated from the social order, he has lost the normal restraints which mark life in a decent community.[56]

Land concentration has not resulted in large scale agriculture. The landlords have preferred to let out the land in parcels of 15 to 30 acres [57] to tenants whom they themselves have financed by loans at 1.75 to 2.50 percent interest per month.[58] Money lending "has, thus, in the Delta, become a corollary to land owning," and is frequently the main source of income for the landlord. He controls the tenant's disposal of the crop by almost invariably insisting that rice to the value of the debt is sold to him or through him. However, if the landlord has come to the limit of his lending capacity or readiness to lend, the tenant must resort to outsiders, and his last possibility is the ill-famed "Saba-pe" transaction.[59] Of course, the

55. Christian, op. cit., p. 158.   56. Furnivall, op. cit., pp. 66–67.

57. Andrus, Burmese Economic Life, p. 71, mentions this size as typical. Also, the Markets Section Survey No. 9, "Rice," p. 32, cites a holding of 25 acres as a typical average unit. However, Furnivall, op. cit., p. 58, indicates that the normal size of the agricultural holding has risen from the small patch of a few acres, such as is needed for subsistence cultivation, to larger holdings of 30 to 60 acres, or more, the size which will give the maximum yield in production to the costs.

58. Markets Section Survey, No. 9, "Rice," pp. 31 ff. The Chettyar rents are 1¼ and 1¾ respectively, monthly. Frequently the landlord has borrowed from the Chettyar part of the money he gives to the tenant and increases the Chettyar rate by one-half percent monthly.

59. The Sabe-pe loans are actually not loans but advance sales. For sales made and

services of outside agencies, such as traders and village shopkeepers are even more expensive and restrictive. Their rates are between 7 and 15 percent monthly.

The average cultivator, whether small owner or tenant, is forced to part with the bulk of his crop immediately after harvest and to meet his commitments directly from the thrashing floor. Consequently, the market is flooded with sellers, ready to sell at any price, for two or three months after the harvest. "With the very considerable produce rents which are due to landlords and with the loans taken, it is easy to see why the bulk of the paddy rice must follow certain recognized channels of assembly into the hands of the landowner and the village trader or the money lender, or be urgently disposed of from the thrashing floor to meet other debts." [60] If the cultivator is a tenant, he will have to pay rent amounting to from one-quarter to one-half of his produce; subsequently he must repay loans for cultivation expenses and borrowings for the support of his family, for the feeding and payment of laborers, food for cattle, and seed for sowing. In general, the tenant-cultivator is indebted to the landlord, while the owner-cultivator has borrowed from Chettyars or traders. In addition, capital and land taxes are due soon after harvesting time. Consequently, the cultivator is forced into a typical buyer's market and has to face an elaborate purchase organization of shrewd brokers and speculators, with no possibility of bargaining or resistance. Such an economic system hardly ever makes it possible for a tenant, however thrifty, to work his way up the social scale by saving enough capital either to acquire or lease land without being heavily indebted. This fact has largely contributed to the general agrarian dissatisfaction in Burma.

COOPERATIVE ORGANIZATIONS   In Burma, as in other colonial areas, cooperative organizations have been unable to give more than very limited local relief. After the complete collapse of the 4,000 societies, with about 100,000 members, during the slump, a very difficult period of reconstruction started. In 1940, a total of only 1,273 so-

money paid in June, August, and October, respectively, the price for delivery after the harvest is roughly 50, 60 and 70 percent of the price which rice commanded in the previous season. See Markets Section Survey, No. 9, "Rice," pp. 31 ff.

60. *Ibid.*, pp. 32–34.

BURMA 89

cieties were registered under the law.[61] According to records of the
Ba Maw puppet government, there were 2,051 cooperatives at the
outbreak of the war, of which 1,599 were agricultural credit societies with a membership of around 82,000 and a working capital of
1,600,000 Rs.—surely a negligible amount compared with the
capital of the Chettyars. But, in spite of the limited means at their
disposal, the reconstructed organizations performed an outstanding
service and achieved, though on a small scale, a redistribution of
land. They acquired the titles of foreclosed lands and resold them
to the former owners who were members of the organization, frequently at book losses for the central cooperative bank (and finally
for the government). In this way, they also restored their reputation
in those regions where they had been forced to foreclose many
properties in the years of the depression. The new agreements
provided for payment in rice (rather than money), so that the
cultivator had to turn over his entire crop to the society, which deducted payment for interest, land tax, part of the principal, and
so on, and returned the balance to the cultivator. This "rent purchase scheme" enabled thousands of cultivators to start buying back
the properties by rent-like payments.[62] Experience seems to have
proved that, even under such economic conditions as prevail in
Burma, rice can be assembled for sale on a cooperative basis. This
eliminates the broker, who actually stands between the producer
and the mill and whose service ultimately is paid for by the producer. The frequently quoted Markets Section Survey on rice [63]
asserts that cooperatives which are only working on the assembling
and grading of rice for quick sale have a good chance to get a better
price than the individual cultivators selling from the thrashing
floor. However, the Survey deprecates the speculative storing and

61. *Report on the Working of Co-operative Societies in Burma for the Year Ending June 30, 1940* (Burma, Dept. of Industries, Rangoon, 1941), p. 4. See also Andrus,
pp. 91 ff.
62. Andrus, *ibid.*, reports that the Ba Maw puppet government continued the
cooperative work, and that cooperative societies were working during the time of
the Japanese occupation.
In 1940–41, following the studies of the Land and Agriculture Committee, small
cooperative land mortgage banks started to work in Pegu, Prome, Hanzada, etc., to
lend money for long and intermediate periods to members of cooperative credit
societies, thus giving the societies the opportunity to concentrate on the seasonal
credit business.
63. Pp. 36 ff.

processing of rice because of the risks involved for the cooperative organizations. It mentions, however, correctly, as the main obstacle, the difficulty which members of the cooperatives encounter in raising money for their immediate needs after harvest, while waiting for their crops to be disposed of. In other words, rice assembly on a cooperative basis is possible only if and when the credit problem is solved. This is proved in the settlements along the Sittang river (Pegu Division), where selected colonists are cultivating about 350,000 acres of government-owned land and have an efficient cooperative credit and marketing organization at their disposal. They pay almost 100 percent of the rent due, and represent one of the few stable farmer groups in the country.[64]

The general atmosphere in Burma has not been favorable to expansion of the cooperative movement. The development in the Delta area favored an individualistic mentality rather than a cooperative spirit. The weight of this fully commercialized and high speculative agriculture hampered the still weak organizations which were beginning to develop, a situation directly contrary to the Danish development, where fully developed cooperative societies buttressed the commercial development of the national agriculture. Finally, the cooperatives have to contend with racial, social, and economic forces which are superior in experience, tradition, and political background.

LABOR The process of land concentration in Burma, which is unique in proportion, tempo, and structure, has turned a large part of cultivators into landless laborers. As long as Burma's economy, now almost a rice monoculture, is not diversified, these Burmese laborers will have no possibility of steady work during a considerable part of the year (at least four months). The number of agricultural workers has increased by more than 100 percent since 1920. Such a large increase has naturally resulted in tensions on the labor market, aggravated by the racial factor of Indian competition.

However, Indian immigration surpluses gradually decreased in

64. *Ibid.*, pp. 36–37. Andrus, *op. cit.*, p. 93, quotes some students who propose a manifold expansion of these government estates by large-scale government purchases of land from nonagriculturists.

later years, as the result of aggressive Burmese nationalism.[65] Between 1921 and 1931, the Indian immigrant population increased only by 7.9 percent, from 572,000 to 613,000. The net immigration (mostly Indian), which in 1927 amounted to 67,000, was in 1937 only about 12,000. But as late as 1939, the port of Rangoon still reported a surplus of 44,000 Indian immigrants,[66] partly compensated by a net emigration from other places. In contrast to Malaya, where the Indian and Chinese immigration is constantly pressing back the native population and has already reduced it to a national minority, the Indian immigration to Burma was far more than made up for by the Burmese rate of population increase.

The Indians have entered Burma partly by crossing the land frontier. This explains the high percentage of Indian labor in Arakan during the harvest season. Before the recent war, 20,000 to 40,000 Indian coolies entered Akyab annually from Chettagonia, most of them only as transitory laborers for the rice harvest. The residents of the district could not compete with this cheap labor force and resented its arrival. However, the concentration of Indian labor in Akyab is exceptional; in the rest of the country it does not exceed 2.7 percent.[67] According to the Census of 1931,[68] only 51 out of 1,000 agricultural workers were Indian immigrants, while 675 were Burmese. The gradual replacement of Indian by Burmese labor might involve somewhat increased costs, but it will in turn reduce the racial tension.[69] For unrestricted immigration has been

65. *Report on Indian Immigration* (the *Baxter Report*) (Rangoon, 1940), p. 3. While the Indian population of Lower Burma rose from 5 to 11 percent of the total population within 60 years, the rate of increase slackened in the '20s and in the following decade actually declined.

66. Virginia Thompson, *Notes on Labor Problems in Burma and Thailand* (Institute of Pacific Relations, Secretariat Paper No. 8), p. 14; Census of India, 1931, Vol. XI: Part I, Report on Burma, pp. 60–61.

67. Census of India, *loc cit.*, p. 135.   68. *Ibid.*, p. 155.

69. According to the Baxter Report and the Census of India, 1931, p. 34, the productive capacity of the Burmese laborer has considerably improved (because otherwise he could not make a living) and is now not much below the Indian level. According to the same Census, pp. 155, 454 out of 1,000 unskilled laborers were Indians, while only 382 were Burmese. This proportion may have changed somewhat in favor of the Burmese during the last decade.

Andrus, *op. cit.*, pp. 270 ff., asserts that immigrant labor is not needed for industry unless a large unexpected industrialization takes place. The Burmese are highly capable of handling machinery, "Thus, the substitution of machinery for degrading and backbreaking work, such as carrying 200-pound bags of rice from boat to shore on the back of a 135-pound man, should be possible without large-scale importation of foreign labor." (p. 281.)

generally recognized as one of the major causes of racial unrest. Strike movements shortly before the war were permeated by racial tension. Even though they were industrial conflicts, their effect reached the most remote villages where Indian workers competed with Burmese.

For years the Burmese Nationalist movement has claimed with increasing vigor the legislative restriction of Indian immigration as protection for Burmese labor. But no restrictions could be applied before the separation from India in 1937, and, thereafter, interference with free immigration was prohibited for three years. Finally, however, an agreement was reached, and Indian immigration to Burma was put on an annual quota basis. Neither party, however, was satisfied, and the war in the Pacific started before the agreement was put into operation.

In accordance with the large-scale production and the minute division of labor, all operations involved in rice cultivation are specialized and the cultivator looks for the cheapest man in the village to do the single job. It is here that the Burmese landless worker encounters the cheaper Indian competition. Some decades ago, labor conditions were quite good because labor was in demand and, therefore, in a good bargaining position. Land was always available, and everybody who had saved or borrowed enough to live on for a year was able to clear a plot in the jungle and raise his crop. A laborer was generally hired for 10 months and could earn 100 to 140 baskets of paddy [70] a year and, in addition, receive free board and lodging for the entire 10 months.[71] But with advancing commercialization, the position of the laborer became weaker. He was hired only for the plowing season of four months and the harvest season of three months. With increased specialization, he was employed only for the separate operations of reaping and thrashing and no longer received free board and lodging for the three months of harvest, but for only two. Today, even the best agricultural laborers, who are employed throughout the entire process from plowing to thrashing, receive free board and lodging for only six months instead of for ten as before.[72] It is questionable whether

70. Paddy is unmilled rice; a basket contains 46 pounds of paddy and is slightly more than a bushel.

71. Furnivall, *op. cit.*, pp. 76–77.

72. *Ibid.* However, Andrus, *Burmese Economic Life*, p. 263, asserts that agri-

it still holds true that an efficient laborer in Burma is better off than a tenant.

Long periods of unemployment have contributed much to the agrarian tension in Burma for the last fifteen years. Furnivall is of the opinion that there probably has been some drop in wages; in 1931 he estimated the decline at 20 percent within the preceding sixty years, certainly enough to greatly reduce the laborer's capacity for saving. The wages for Burmese agricultural labor were slightly higher than for Indian labor, the women, however, getting only three-fourths of the wages for men. Unfortunately, the so-called "maistry" system is widespread. In this system, the employer deals with a labor contractor who supplies the needed laborers for a lump sum, out of which he pays their wages. He claims a commission on their earnings and has the additional function of moneylender. This system is also responsible for the very bad housing conditions of the laborers.[73]

Agricultural labor, both Burmese and Indian, was but slightly organized before the war. However, different political groups, propagating plans for redistribution of the land, found a considerable response among the agricultural laborers, who, in the overwhelming majority, had lost their land during the last decade and considered themselves more as landless farmers than as agricultural laborers.

GENERAL LEVELS OF LIVING—HEALTH CONDITIONS   It is very difficult to give a well-founded judgment on the general levels of living of the Burmese population, beyond the generalities which can be gathered from the recorded facts. There is no doubt that the level of living in Burma is higher than in China or India, though the general trend is declining. When considering the effects of land concentration, the transformation of farmers into tenants and agricultural workers, and the heavy reduction of their incomes, as reported by Furnivall and others, it is difficult to agree with Andrus [74] that "all in all, a rather high standard of living was maintained—almost certainly much higher than that in pre-British Burma."

---

cultural workers taken for the whole season receive seven months' free board and lodging.

73. Andrus, *op. cit.*, p. 264.   74. *Ibid.*, p. 334.

Certainly there has never been any real shortage of food in
Burma. Between 1920–21 and 1930–31, the occupied agricultural
area increased by more than 3 million acres, or more than 15 percent, and the exportable surplus increased by almost a million tons.
However, the Burmese did not participate adequately in this development; their share in national production decreased in direct
proportion to the social changes from owner to tenant and from
tenant to working class.

The death rate in the Delta, was 20.42 per 1,000 in 1935, considerably lower than the average in the period between 1911 and
1920 (27.69). The 1931 Census of India [75] traces the decrease after
1921 partly to inferior registration methods and partly to the fact
that there were no epidemics after 1920 similar in severity to the
influenza epidemic of 1918–19. The British administration has
improved health conditions considerably by extended health
services and rural reconstruction work, by better water supply,
hygienic propaganda, and so on. But the respiratory death rate
hardly decreased and was as high as 5.2 per thousand in 1932 (Bombay, 4.2).[76] In addition, the provincial rate for infant mortality in
1935 was 186.04 per 1,000 (rural, 176.55; urban, 255.82). In
1936, Prometown reported an infant mortality of 268 per 1,000,
and Basein, in the Irrawaddy delta, one of 283.36 per 1,000.[77] That
these tremendous rates could be reduced is proved by the fact that
infant mortality in Hlegu township (Insein Division), where a
health unit founded by the Rockefeller Foundation is operating,
is only 124.84, that is, one-third below the provincial rate. The
connection between tuberculosis mortality, high infant mortality,
and poor levels of living is well known and proves that public
health reforms can hardly counteract the effects of a deficient economic system.

"Poverty, isolation, disease, death, lack of education, and a sense
of inferiority to residents of the towns conspired to make the life
of the Burmese cultivator and his family anything but idyllic." [78]
This remark expresses the actual situation and may help to explain

75. Pp. 17 ff., and *Report on the Administration of Burma,* 1935–36, p. 110.
76. League of Nations Health Organization, Intergovernmental Conference of Far
Eastern Countries on Rural Hygiene, Preparatory Papers: Report of Burma, 1937,
pp. 47–48; *Report on the Administration of Burma,* pp. 111 ff.
77. *Ibid.*   78. Christian, *op. cit.,* pp. 117–18.

the lack of energy in the Burmese population, which so frequently is criticized. Only an improved living standard can give them renewed physical vitality and increase their working capacity.

REBELLION AND RIOTS Successive expropriation of the native farming class by the Chettyar credit economy, the pressure on the rentals and wage levels by the Indian competition, the fight for employment during and after the slump, and finally the privileged position which the Indians enjoyed in the administration and police [79] added racial unrest to social tension. It is common desire to simplify complicated developments and look for a visible scapegoat. The Burmese peasant, deprived of the privilege of permanent occupation of the land he tills and of belonging to a village society, can be easily won for rebellion and disorder by a vehement, very often exaggerated propaganda. He is more likely to attack the immediate enemy who stands in his way than the colonial system, which for him used to be far more abstract and difficult to grasp. The fight against the Indians was fought by criminal individual attacks, by riots and strikes, by a propaganda of hate, political pressure, and, in recent years, by administrative discrimination.

The first organized rebellion against the British rule took place in 1930, under the leadership of a religious charlatan, Saya San. It started in the Tharawaddy district and spread quickly. However, it degenerated into a looting campaign principally directed against the Indians and was soon suppressed. The official Report relates this rebellion to the serious economic conditions, especially to the heavy recent drop of the rice price, though it had a political, rather than economic, origin. "All classes of agriculturists have been hit terribly hard by the disastrous fall in the price of paddy, and economic distress no doubt helped to make them lend a ready ear to inflammatory preaching against the government." [80] Certainly a drop in the price of paddy from 150 Rs. per 100 baskets (the average price since 1918) to less than 70 Rs. explains satisfactorily the back-

79. Census of India, 1931, Chapter VIII, p. 155. Subsidiary Table VII-B reports that out of 1,000 army and policemen, 400 were Indian immigrants and only 296 were Burmese. However, according to Virginia Thompson, op. cit., p. 3, the share of the Burmese in the defense services has increased since 1941, in connection with the war.

80. Report on the Rebellion in Burma up to May 3, 1931 (CMD. Papers 3900, Vol. XII, London, 1931), pp. 10, 12.

ground for the rebellion of a rootless peasant group, without calling for the additional remark in the mentioned Report (p. 10) that "in spite of a high standard of literacy, the Burmese peasantry are incredibly ignorant and superstitious."

This rebellion, like other riots in Rangoon in the same year, was characterized by the always latent racial antagonism against the Indians, which became acute in this period of economic tension. The Report continues (p. 13),

Until recently, the average Burman found no difficulty in supporting himself comfortably, and he then tolerated the existence of the Indian laborer in Burma. Conditions have now changed. In the first place, a number of Indians have settled down as peasant cultivators in Lower Burma districts, and the Burman now finds himself living side by side with a considerable Indian population, who by reason of their lower standard of living are able to offer higher rent than he can. In the second place, economic pressure has compelled the Burman to take the coolie work more than he needed to in previous times, and he is beginning to feel the competition of the Indian laborer, with which he finds it hard to compete, as the standard of living of the Indian laborer is much lower than his own.

Furthermore, the rising tide of a national feeling in Burma is mentioned, and it is concluded that it is very difficult to get evidence, as the sympathy of the villagers is entirely with their own people. There is a risk of this disturbance spreading to other districts.

An official press communiqué [81] issued by the government of Burma on May 19, 1931, discusses the anti-Indian movement, asserting that it is mainly, if not entirely, of an economic nature. The communiqué points out (p. 19) that the Burman resents the competition of Indians, especially "as the Indian is ordinarily willing to accept lower wages than the Burman and also to pay higher rent for agricultural land." The communiqué admits that action is necessary to alleviate the economic situation and states that orders were given not to collect the principal of outstanding government loans and to remit land revenues in cases of genuine inability to pay. The uprising was followed by a month of anti-Chinese riots. However, the agitation against the Chinese in Burma is rather

81. *Ibid.*, pp. 16 ff.

negligible, their social stratification and general attitude not being
as contrary to the Burmese as is the Indian.

Burmese-Indian antagonism has constantly increased and has
resulted time and again in clashes and riots. The most serious anti-
Indian riots occurred between July and December, 1938. They
had their origin in a literary, religious conflict. Beginning in Mandalay and Rangoon, they spread throughout the rural districts of
Lower Burma. During this period, the fight against Indian influence, property, and labor was carried on in a wave of direct
attacks, demonstrations, obstructions, strikes, burning, and looting.[82] An investigation [83] stated that one of the causes of these riots
was "the spreading of an anti-social creed amongst the youth of
Burma by the political Thakin Association," [84] a nationalist movement which attacked foreign economic and political domination
and which today is strongly represented in the government of
Burma. This movement cooperated with organizations like the All
Burma Cultivators' League which fought for a radical solution of
the land problem.

In the years shortly before the war the tension increased and resulted in extreme political developments. War and the Japanese
occupation gave the growing national movement the essential experience in practical policy and in organizing armed forces. After
a short period of well-organized and partly armed resistance against
the reestablishment of colonial rule after the war, the final agreement between Great Britain and the Burmese national movement
(London, January 27, 1947) became the basis for a peaceful and dignified retreat of British rule.

CONCLUSIONS   Analysis of the economic and social development
in Lower Burma during the past fifty years must first of all state
as a fact the contrast between the highly successful development
of the economic resources and the social disintegration of the native
farming population. It is very easy to overemphasize one side of the
picture. It is equally easy to put both features in a fixed relationship,
to assert that they are dependent on each other and that the misery

82. Christian, *op. cit.,* pp. 244, 245.
83. *Report of the Riot Inquiry Committee* (Burma, Home Department, Rangoon,
1939).
84. See Chapter VIII, below.

of the population was the price paid for the development of the country. But the question remains whether this price was not too high. Such considerations may surely be interesting from a historical, political, and ethical point of view, but they hardly contribute to a serious analysis of the economic problems involved.

In this connection another contrast in the Burma picture seems to be more important—the contrast in the economic and social level of the people of the fertile, highly commercialized plains of Lower Burma and those of the less privileged but more stable Upper Burma, with its diversified agriculture. Commercial agriculture has, of course, also entered Upper Burma, and the farmers there tend more and more to cultivate the land for the purpose of selling their produce. The process of commercialization in Upper Burma, however, was not pushed by speculative interests, but developed in a natural, organic way. Therefore, it did not lead to disintegration, but rather to higher economic and social levels of living. The variety of cultivation not only guaranteed an average level of living throughout the year, but at the same time kept the people comparatively "free from the reproach of undue conservatism" which is so often leveled at farmers.[85] In contrast with the farmers in the Delta land, they proved ready to introduce new methods and crops [86] and by a harmonious, organic, development, produced surpluses capable of export without creating an unbalanced credit economy. Furnivall asserts that the cultivators in Upper Burma have benefited by the introduction of the groundnut crop and that many parts of the dry zone, miserably poor a generation ago, are now rich in gilded pagodas, well-founded monasteries, brick houses, gay clothing, a varied diet, and other signs of wealth.

Even the more stabilized conditions in Upper Burma, however, prove the severity of the credit problem in any agricultural area which has crossed the border line dividing domestic from commercial agriculture. Even Upper Burma will soon have to face problems similar to those of the Delta land if no adequate solution of the urgent credit problem is found.

The contrast between Upper Burma and the Delta land demonstrates clearly the different ways in which two areas with different productive potentialities developed from domestic to commercial

85. Furnivall, *op. cit.*, pp. 98–100.   86. *Ibid.*

agriculture. The one more privileged by climate, soil, and investments became the center of destructive landlordism with a distressed and unstable population, while the less favored area was
able to develop a more balanced economy. This contrast may not
only be of value as a basis for judging colonial development, but
also a hint for practical economic policy in future.

Certainly, the difference in productivity has to be taken into consideration, especially the unparalleled development of the rice production in the Delta lands. However, the economic structure of
Lower Burma's rice economy has to carry the weight of a distorted
tenure system and of dangerous social and racial tensions, liabil-
ities which may equal, if not exceed, the value of the assests. As Furnivall said, "Society [in Lower Burma] is organized for production
rather than for decent living, and for acquisition rather than for
production." [87]

War and the Japanese invasion did not ease the problem of Burmese indebtedness. The hope failed that the records of the Chettyars were destroyed during the invasion and that the Burmese
farmers would be restored automatically to their land.[88] The public
relations leader of the Chettyars, A.M.M. Vellayan, was farsighted
and able enough to gather up the originals of practically all Chettyar
deeds and mortgages. He presented them for safe-keeping to the
government of India in 1944. When he went to New Delhi to de-
posit the documents,[89] it required 36 bearers to carry them.

Therefore, the Burman's great problem is still to get his land
from the Chettyar, as the Chettyar's problem is to get his money
from the Burman.[90] This unsettled situation is likely to result,
again and again, in unrest and turbulent expressions of dissatisfaction. The present government of Burma, a democratic socialist
government, has, however, formulated a social and economic program resembling that of the government of the Indonesian Republic. But, in contrast to the Indonesian Republic, Burma seems more
stabilized and, therefore, in a position to concentrate on her eco-

---

87. *Ibid.*, p. 81.
88. "Blue Print" for Burma, issued by the Conservative Imperial Affairs Committee,
London, 1944, stated incorrectly that these documents were destroyed during the
occupation.
89. J. Russell Andrus, "Burma; an Experiment in Self-Government," p. 262.
90. Christian, *op. cit.*, p. 120.

nomic future. Burma's parliament has been given power to liqui-
date all large landholdings as soon as possible. On the whole it
seems safe to say that the reform work in Burma will start in the
agricultural sector of the economy, where the needs of the people
are the most urgent and the possibilities for international complications the least.

A most detailed five-year plan for the rehabilitation of rice production has already been drawn up, and the farmers' economic
position will be strengthened through well-organized consumers'
cooperatives in every town and village. Industrialization is another
important part of the program, with, in the first place, the development of hydroelectric power and the establishment of a chemical
industry to supply the farmers with cheap artificial fertilizer.

The solution of the land problem remains the most urgent
task. The government is planning legislation to provide the legal
and economic means for the redistribution of land and for an efficient agricultural credit system. While the Chettyars seem inclined to accept a fair liquidation of their investments, the Burmese
landlords are already in vehement political and economic opposition against the government.[91] No doubt, a large-scale effort by the
new Republic of Burma, will be needed if the task of restoring the
rights of a people to its native soil are to be solved in a legal way.
Indeed, the basic problem of redistributing the land must have
priority over all other political and economic problems of postwar
reconstruction. A resettlement policy will have to be initiated in
gigantic dimensions on the scale of the expropriation of the native
farming class. Anything less would not be an effective solution for
the economic and social problems of the country.

91. Virginia Thompson, "The New Nation of Burma," *Far Eastern Survey*, XVII,
No. 7 (April 7, 1948). Virginia Thompson emphasizes in this connection that there
is a strong trend to normalize the relationship to India, since that country is Burma's
natural market.

4

Malaya

INTRODUCTION: MALAYA AND THE IMMIGRANTS   "British Malaya"
was the traditional collective name for the Straits Settlements
(Penang, Malacca, and Singapore), the Federated Malay States
(Perak, Selangor, Negri Sembilan, and Pahang), and the Unfederated Malay States (Perlis, Kedah, Kelantan, Trengganu and
Johore). On February 1, 1948 however, the "Malayan Federation"
was inaugurated which established an intimate political association
between the 9 Malay States and the British settlements Penang
and Malacca. Singapore has not yet joined the Federation. With
the establishment of this Federation which is under British protection and supervision, the old distinction between Federated and
Unfederated Malay States has been abolished. This distinction,
however, reflects an historic and economic development which, by
no means, has been concluded by the new form of political organization and which will have to be applied if we want to analyze the
typical features in Malaya's economic structure. In this chapter
(also on the map) we will, therefore, still use the terms Federated
and Unfederated Malay States.

The degree of Great Britain's political control over Malaya was
always commensurate with the degree of foreign (Western, Chinese, or Indian) economic penetration. The lowest degree of economic penetration combined with the least political control is
found in the former Unfederated Malay States; the maximum of
political control is in the Straits Settlements, the economic center
of Malaya. The establishment of the Malayan Federation recognizes
the fact that the former Unfederated States are approaching the
stage of intensive foreign economic penetration.

Malaya does not share the problems of population pressure and maldistribution that are common in most areas in Southeast Asia. Rather there is a complicated immigration problem. The Malay population continued subsistence farming and refused to supply labor for the rubber and tin industries. As a result, the volume of foreign immigration during recent decades has been directly proportional to the development of production for exports.

THE POPULATION OF MALAYA ACCORDING
TO MAIN RACIAL DIVISIONS
(*In thousands*)

	1911	*1921*	*1931*	Estimated *1938*
Europeans (all white)	11	15	18	28
Eurasians	11	13	16	18
Malays (all Malayans)	1,438	1,651	1,962	2,211
Chinese	917	1,175	1,709	2,220
Indians	267	472	624	744
Others	29	33	56	58
Total	2,673	3,359	4,385	5,279

Source: Malayan Year Book, 1939.

In 1921, the Malays still exceeded the Chinese population by about 500,000 and comprised around 50 percent of the population.[1] Today they are a minority of about 42 percent in their own country, outnumbered by the Chinese population. The regional distribution of the population by nationality is intimately related to the degree of foreign economic penetration, and to the gradual advance of rubber plantations from the west coast to the east coast. While the Malays represent only 25.6 percent of the population in the Straits Settlements and 34.7 percent in the former Federated States, (key regions of foreign penetration), they still number 69.6 percent of the total population in the former Unfederated Malay States. The Chinese comprise 59.6 percent of the population in the Straits Settlements,[2] 41.5 percent in the Federated States, but only 21.4 percent in the Unfederated States. The corresponding figures for the Indians are 11.9 percent, 22.2 percent, and 7.2 percent.[3] As

1. All statistics in this chapter are quoted from the *Malayan Year Book, 1939* (Singapore, 1939), or other official sources. See also Rupert Emerson, *Malaysia, a Study in Direct and Indirect Rule* (New York, 1937), p. 20.
2. In Singapore the Chinese constituted 74 percent of the population, in Penang 0 percent; of all these Chinese, 50 percent were born in Malaya.
3. Karl J. Pelzer, *Population and Land Utilization*, (New York, 1941), p. 48. The figure for Malays includes Malays and Immigrated Malayans.

the fluctuation of immigration is determined by the export poten-
tiality of Malay rubber and tin (primarily for the American and
secondarily for the European market), the statistics reflect clearly
the critical years beginning 1930, the period of recovery in 1934–35,
and the new decline in 1938.

MALAYA: MIGRATION 1929–1938

EXCESS OR DEFICIT ARRIVALS FROM FOREIGN OVERSEAS PORTS

	Chinese	Malays	Southern Indians (Tamils)
1929	109,801	6,633	1,624
1930	28,586	1,758	−51,247
1931	−112,965	−3,110	−71,811
1932	−97,580	−3,996	−61,320
1933	−31,178	304	−11,175
1934	61,639	3,425	66,666
1935	90,986	−3,060	33,045
1936	75,801	−4,326	7,909
1937	180,502	−3,850	84,365
1938	53,180	−5,748	−23,251

Source: Malayan Year Book, 1939, p. 42.

The predominantly immigrant character of the population is illustrated most clearly by the fact that in 1931 less than 57 percent of
the total population in Malaya was born in the country (in 1921 the
proportion was 54.3 percent).[4]

Most of the people are engaged in agriculture. The Chinese work
mainly as laborers in the mining industry, and to some extent on
rubber plantations, but are also engaged as farmers and merchants.
The Indians are generally plantation workers and provide the main
supply of labor for the rubber industry.

In recent decades Malaya's economy has been marked by large-
scale rubber and tin production. The former was developed during
the last generation and depends almost wholly upon the demand
of the American automobile industry. Even more than tin, rubber
has determined the economic pattern of the area and also the racial
structure of the population. Malaya's economy has become tied to
the economic cycles of the Western world, and calls for a fluctuating
population proportional to the demand of labor. In the years just

4. Virginia Thompson, Postmortem on Malaya (New York, 1943), p. 21, mentions
that the census statistics are slightly inaccurate on account of the tendency of Chinese
and Malays to overstate their age.

MALAYA

before the war, rubber exports reached record heights—538,-000 tons (S.S. $450 million) [5] in 1940 as compared with 375,000 tons in 1938, and 370,000 tons in 1939.[6] As the world's largest producer of rubber and tin, Malaya maintained a key position in the balance of international payments, thereby compensating in great part for Great Britain's negative trade balance with the United States.[7]

FOREIGN INVESTMENTS The volume of foreign investments in Malaya places her in an outstanding position in the world economy.[8] In 1937, aside from a public debt [9] of about $U.S. 60 million, entrepreneur (including Chinese) investments totaled approximately $U.S. 575 million. These large amounts of capital have developed rubber production, the tin dredging industry, and numerous other export products, such as copra, palm oil, pineapples, phosphates, coal, and gold.

TOTAL WESTERN INVESTMENTS IN MALAYA, 1914–37

(In Millions of U.S. Dollars)

Year	Rentier [a]	Entrepreneur	Total
1914	43.7	150.0	193.7
1930	112.7	447.0	559.7
1937	82.5	372.0	454.5

Source: Helmut G. Callis, Foreign Capital in Southeast Asia, p. 56.

[a] Rentier investments including outstanding public debt and industrial debentures (in 1940, U.S. $22.5 million).

Rubber companies account for two-thirds of the entrepreneurial investment, and tin dredging companies for one-sixth. Up to the end of 1941 the greater part of the rubber industry was controlled by the British with an investment of about $U.S. 200 million. Companies domiciled in the British Empire owned 1.1 million acres of rubber plantations.[10]

5. The Straits Settlements Dollar (SS. $) had a sterling exchange rate of 2s 4d, equal to 46 U.S. cents.
6. Generally speaking, 50 percent of Malaya's exports went to the U.S.; in 1940, 75 percent of the rubber, 78 percent of the tin; see Michael Greenberg, "Malaya, Britain's Dollar Arsenal," *Amerasia* (June, 1941), p. 147.
7. *The Network of World Trade* (Geneva, 1942), pp. 59 ff.
8. Helmut G. Callis, *Foreign Capital in Southeast Asia* (New York, 1942), p. 48.
9. The public debts were largely incurred for purposes calculated to assist the exploitation of the colonial resources by private finance. See Ernest O. Houser, "Britain's Economic Stake in Southeast Asia," *Far Eastern Survey*, Vol. VI, No. 25 (Dec. 22, 1937).
10. Callis, "Capital Investment in Southeast Asia and the Philippines," *Annals,*

About 70 percent of entrepreneurial investments are British, thus securing for Great Britain a predominant economic control in agriculture and mining, in trade, banking, and industry. British enterprises, such as the Straits Trading Company, and the Eastern Smelting Company, maintain an actual monopoly for tin smelting in Southeast Asia, sustained by a prohibitive duty on tin ore exported from British Malaya, except when destined to be smelted in the United Kingdom or Australia. The remainder of the Western investments are held by American, Dutch, and before the war by Japanese interests. In 1936 the U. S. Department of Commerce [11] estimated the total American capital in Malaya at $U.S. 23.7 million, mainly invested in rubber plantations, trading and shipping, tin mining, and the distribution of petroleum products.

A relatively small staff of only 28,000 Europeans and Americans, aided by about 20,000 Eurasians controlled these large investments and supervised the industry. The number of resident Europeans as owners of independent plantations, mines, and so on was rapidly declining because of advancing capital concentrations, the bulk of European interests tending to become concentrated in big joint-stock companies with main offices in London. This development has further emphasized the colonial features of the Malayan economy.[12]

Chinese business investments are estimated at $U.S. 200 million, and are second only to the British.[13] Technically they should not be termed foreign, since the Chinese influence in Malaya is centuries old, and more than 50 percent of the Chinese in Malaya, mainly the investors, were born in the country. However, the Chinese remittances from Malaya, especially to Hong Kong, amounted to considerable sums, in 1930 alone to $H.K. 42 million,[14] thus indicating close ties with the Chinese mother country.

March, 1943, p. 24. Lennox A. Mills, *British Rule in Eastern Asia; a Study of Contemporary Government and Economic Development in British Malaya and Hong Kong* (London, 1942), p. 213, quotes the nominal value of the external capital outstanding in Malaya rubber corporations on Dec. 31, 1936, at £53.6 million. This figure does not include money invested and subsequently lost, and the considerable investments not denominated in pounds sterling.

11. *American Direct Investments in Foreign Countries, 1936* (Dept. of Commerce, Washington, 1938), pp. 7, 21.

12. Emerson, *Malaysia*, p. 30.   13. Callis, *Foreign Capital in Southeast Asia*, p. 57.

14. Carl F. Remer, *Foreign Investments in China* (New York, 1933), p. 185. The Hong Kong dollar was equal to 33 American cents.

Chinese capital is mainly invested in tin mining, which was started by the Chinese in primitively equipped mines long before the British came. Before the war, 36 percent of the total output came from Chinese owned and managed mines, and an additional 11 percent of mines were sublet to Chinese. Chinese capital is also invested in rubber plantations, and the Chinese rubber acreage has constantly increased during the last generation. In addition, Chinese investments can be found in trade, pineapple canning, saw milling, vegetable growing, and in the fishing industry.

As in other dependent countries of this area, the export production of raw materials has been overemphasized in Malaya. No large-scale manufacturing enterprises have been developed. There are only minor industries, mostly engaged in the processing of agricultural products, or in the production of various types of consumer goods not competing in the small local market with the imports from Great Britain.[15] Shortly before the war, the Malayan tariff system was adjusted to the principle of imperial preference, which would seem to indicate that there are but small prospects for the future development of a local manufacturing industry.[16]

LAND UTILIZATION; DISTRIBUTION OF POPULATION   The total area of Malaya is about 32,700,000 acres, of which 6 million acres, or 18.4 percent, are alienated for agricultural purposes. About 5.4 million acres, or 15.5 percent, were under crop in 1940, 3.5 million of which were planted with rubber. The areas planted with rice and coconut were about 800,000 and 600,000 acres, respectively.[17]

Only the western part of the peninsula, especially the former Federated Malay States, comprising two-fifths of Malaya, is commercially developed. Half of the cultivated land is planted with rubber trees. In this center for rubber production, mainly in the states of Perak, Selangor, and Negri Sambilan, as well as in the Straits Settlements, a land problem is beginning to develop. At the

15. Kate L. Mitchell, *Industrialization of the Western Pacific* (New York, 1942), pp. 185, 187, 189.
16. Virginia Thompson, *Postmortem on Malaya*, pp. 210 ff. The degree of imperial preference varied widely, however, throughout Malaya. Johore and Kedah, the most advanced Unfederated States, agreed to tariff identification with the rest of the peninsula, but they avoided the Customs Union. However, Malaya as a whole decided on a buy-British policy.
17. *Malayan Agricultural Statistics, 1940* (Kuala Lumpur, 1941).

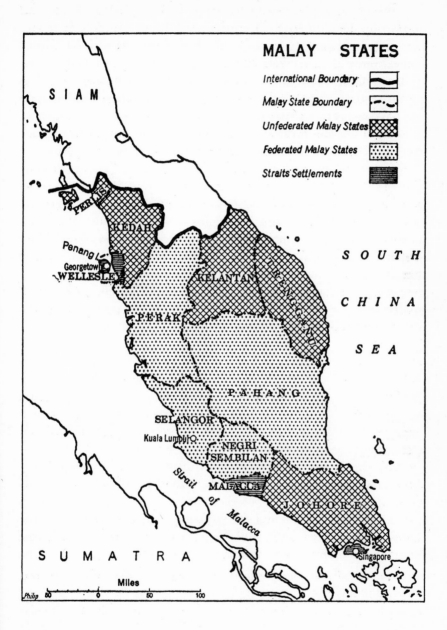

MALAY STATES

International Boundary
Malay State Boundary
Unfederated Malay States
Federated Malay States
Straits Settlements

SIAM

SOUTH

CHINA

SEA

PERLIS
KEDAH
Penang I.
Georgetown
WELLESLEY
KELANTAN
TRENGGANU
PERAK
PAHANG
SELANGOR
Kuala Lumpur
NEGRI
SEMBILAN
MALACCA
JOHORE
Singapore

Strait of Malacca

SUMATRA

Miles

Philip   50   0   50   100

same time vast undeveloped agricultural areas are still available in the former Unfederated States, with the exception of Johore. In 1938, the total population was estimated at about 5,300,000, one million more than in the census of 1931. The population density in the agricultural area seldom reached 100 persons per sq. mile, though greater densities were encountered in Kedah and Perlis (118,159, respectively, per sq. mile), and in Selangor (169).

In 1940, rubber production used 3.5 million acres, i.e., 63 percent of the total crop area, of which rubber estates (100 acres and more) covered 2,120,000 acres, and small holdings (under 100 acres), 1,360,000 acres. This latter group harvested about 39 percent of the rubber production. In Johore and Kedah—the most advanced of the former Unfederated States from a colonial point of view—a considerable number of small holdings were engaged in rubber farming (1.2 million acres), while subsistence farming was predominant in the other Unfederated States. About 41 percent of the rubber acreage of Johore and 30 percent of Kedah consisted of small holdings.[18] However, there was a marked trend towards land concentration over most of Malaya.

LAND CONCENTRATION IN MALAYA, 1931–38

	Federated States	Straits Settlements	Unfederated States	Total
(In Thousands of Acres)				
Acreage 1931–34				
over 100 acres	970	215	713	1,898
under 100 acres	566	130	568	1,264
Acreage 1935				
over 100 acres	1,040	208	774	2,022
under 100 acres	540	126	507	1,173
Acreage 1938				
over 100 acres	1,032	207	793	2,032
under 100 acres	581	128	555	1,264

Source: *Malayan Agricultural Statistics, 1940.*

The table above shows that the acreage of holdings under 100 acres remained numerically stable while the expanded area accrued to the large estates. This trend can be recognized all over Malaya, especially in the former Unfederated States, where a considerable

18. *Malayan Agricultural Statistics, 1940,* Table VI; Kate L. Mitchell, *op. cit.,* pp. 180–81; Emerson, *Malaysia,* p. 37.

number of small holdings changed to rice farming after the slump of the early thirties, automatically increasing the share of the large estates in rubber farming.

This development was further emphasized by the International Rubber Regulation Scheme, which was introduced to save some £100 million of British and foreign investments in Malaya from complete collapse. In fact, great British plantations, together with other Western rubber interests, pushed native rubber farms into the background by buying up the export rights of small holders. By the end of 1936, 37 percent of the rubber trees on small holdings in the Federated Malay States were not being tapped.[19]

The rubber estates (over 100 acres) are almost completely in foreign hands. The accompanying tabulation shows the ownership by nationality in 1940.

ESTATE OWNERSHIP IN MALAYA, 1940

(In Thousands of Acres)

Nationality	Federated Malay States	Percent	Straits Settlements	Percent	Unfederated States	Percent	Total	Percent of Total
European	879	81.5	133	64.	566	68.	1,578	74.5
Chinese	138	12.8	62	30.	153	18.2	353	16.6
Indians	50	4.6	11	5.3	33	4.	94	4.4
Others	12	1.1	1.5	0.7	82	9.8	95.5	4.5
	1,079	100.	207.5	100.	834	100.	2,120.5	100.

Source: *Malayan Agricultural Statistics, 1940,* Table VII. The term "European" includes all white races. In the corresponding statistics for 1931 the Japanese share amounted to 3.6 percent; the Malay to 0.9. Both groups are now included in the column "Others."

For the last decade prior to the war no essential changes in ownership have taken place. The only exception is that of the Unfederated Malay States where the European holdings have increased from 64 percent to 68 percent, indicating the advancing penetration even into the still Malay-dominated States. In addition, the Chinese share is slowly but certainly advancing; Western and Chinese capital together dominate more than 90 percent of the rubber industry.

In actual distribution, according to size of farms, plantations

19. Callis, *Foreign Capital in Southeast Asia,* p. 52; *Annual Report,* Straits Settlements and Federated Malay States, Dept. of Agriculture, 1936 (Kuala Lumpur, 1937), p. 7. E. O. Houser, *op. cit.,* emphasizes the value of political control and of having friendly cooperating governments in the surrounding territory for the preservation of foreign investments in Southeast Asia, clearly manifested in the time during and immediately after the slump.

from 1,000 to 5,000 acres comprise 51.8 percent of the total acreage, and those over 5,000 acres, 19.5 percent.[20] The largest estates are owned by Europeans, the middle group by Chinese, and the smallest by Chinese, Malays, and Indians.

The Malays constitute the majority of small rubber growers. The sector of the small holdings varies in different parts of Malaya; it is smallest (36 percent) in the former Federated Malay States, and highest (41.2 percent) in the underdeveloped former Unfederated States. The Malays generally have the smallest holdings with an average size of only 4 acres, while the Chinese holdings average 18 acres, their total acreage being around 700,000 acres, or 55 percent of the total area of the small holdings. One of the characteristics of land distribution in Malaya is the fact that more than three-fourths of the rubber-crop area is in the hands of Western and Asiatic foreigners, while the Malays control only 22 percent.[21]

The other main crop in Malaya is rice, ranking next to rubber.[22] In 1940, 800,000 acres were planted with rice, of which 730,000 acres were planted with wet rice. Until shortly before the war, rice production was actually a Malay monopoly. About 540,000 acres of rice land are located in the former Unfederated Malay States, while there are only 70,000 acres in the Straits Settlements where the Malay population is very small. In 1940 the bulk of the rice crop, about 70 percent, came from the Unfederated States, while the Federated States contributed only 23 percent to the total rice output. Three-fourths of the rice acreage is located in areas dependent on weather conditions, sufficient irrigation being almost unknown beyond the borders of Perak.

After the slump, rice acreage expanded by 100,000 acres, but Malaya is far from being self-sufficient in this dietically essential crop. An output of only 330 thousand tons in 1940 necessitated the importation of about 600 to 650 thousand tons, or two-thirds of the annual consumption. In spite of the expansion of acreage, the dependence on imports from Siam and Burma has by no means decreased in the last decade. While the output after 1919 increased by almost 50 percent, and after 1933 by more than 10 percent, the im-

20. W. I. Ladejinsky, "Agriculture in British Malaya," in Foreign Agriculture, V (Washington, 1941), 103 ff.
21. Emerson, Malaysia, pp. 37–38.   22. Malayan Agricultural Statistics.

ports were nevertheless 50 percent higher in 1940 than in 1933.[23] The ratio of local production to total consumption has remained more or less unchanged at 35 percent.

This disproportion in rice production constitutes one of the most serious effects of Malaya's rubber economy. The area planted with rice is only about 23 percent of the rubber area, although rice is the staple food for 99 percent of the population. Rice imports are a heavy financial burden, especially in periods of depression, which hit severely the very sensitive rubber and tin economy.[24] The slump in 1929 revealed the risk of an overemphasized cultivation of rubber with its accompanying inadequate food production.

After the slump the authorities tried to encourage the expansion of rice farming, and to support it by establishing government mills.[25] These were intended to serve as protection against the Chinese rice mills, whose price-fixing practices were detrimental to native security, but progress was frustrated by the dependence of the native farmer upon credit and advance payments from Indian or Chinese shopkeepers.[26]

It is but natural that the mere rhetorical encouragement from the government could not change the rate of food production to any considerable extent, especially after a renewed rubber prosperity had come to Malaya. Rice production was barely increased. The Malays continued to produce only for subsistence, and not for the market, mainly because of the lack of any real support from the government. However, it must be stressed that the cultivation of about 750,000 acres of rice land by a population of only two million Malays was a significant achievement, a fact which is frequently

23. Malaya's rice imports in 1940 amounted to 635,000 tons for S.S. $51 million; in 1933, 433,000 tons for S.S. $24 million.

24. From 1928 to 1933 the average London rubber price (per lb.) dropped from 10¾d. to 2 11/32 d. and raised slowly to 6 7/32 d. in 1934.

25. In 1940 the government operated 5 State mills and planned to establish 2 additional mills.

26. Mills, *op. cit.*, p. 261, reports that in certain districts from 40 to 90 percent of the rice cultivators were not free to sell to the mills because they were in debt. Their creditors were Indians who had mortgages on their holdings, or Chinese shopkeepers who had given advance payments in cash or kind, while the crop was still on the field. See D. H. Grist, *An Outline of Malayan Agriculture, Malayan Planting Manual No. 2* (Straits Settlements and Federated Malay States Dept. of Agriculture, Kuala Lumpur, 1936), pp. 33, 38, 39.

underestimated. This is evident when one considers the extent of cultivation of the newly irrigated lands in the Sungei, Manik, and Krian areas, without any financial assistance by the administration in the difficult first three or four years.[27] Even the organization of cooperative credit institutions failed, because the government provided the cooperatives with by-laws rather than with funds, in the erroneous belief that the native farmers would be able to finance their own credit institutions with their "savings"—native farmers, however, seldom have anything left for savings.[28]

Shortly before the war, the colonial administration broke the virtual native monopoly of rice production.[29] Fearing the severance of connections with rice-supplying countries, it wanted to expand the rice production of Malaya. Up until that time only the Malay sector of the population had been self-sufficient, but it seemed essential now to encourage the Chinese and Indians to cultivate their own rice, against possible emergencies. This broke with the traditional British policy (agreed upon with the native Sultans) of reserving all potential rice land for the Malays. The administration gave assurances, however, that it would not give the same concession to new immigrants, and that the extended rice production should serve only for local consumption and not for export. The Malays protested vehemently this intrusion upon their last privilege. They claimed that the lack of sufficient rice acreage was the result of government failures, of inadequate financial assistance, and of lack of agricultural instruction. They further maintained that the deficiency in food production was entirely the effect of governmentally encouraged immigration, and of the wrongful use of agricultural land for mining. They asked the government to subsidize and improve the traditionally Malayan rice industry and not to "outrage the Malay's heritage." [30] This fight for rice lands created a strong racial tension, up until then unknown in Malaya.

27. Virginia Thompson, *Postmortem on Malaya*, p. 40.
28. W. I. Ladejinsky, *op. cit.*, pp. 159 ff. Mills, *op. cit.*, p. 287, is more optimistic for the cooperatives.
29. Based on the Stockdale Report of 1938 (Sir F. Stockdale, *Report on a Visit to Malaya, Java, Sumatra and Ceylon, 1938*, London, 1939), a new agrarian policy was introduced which should maintain a proper balance between the areas of commercialized agriculture and the areas essential for native farming. Greater crop diversification and scientific instructions were main issues of the report. See also Virginia Thompson, *op. cit.*, pp. 32 ff.
30. Virginia Thompson, *op. cit.*, p. 36.

However, the war boom in the rubber and tin industries, which absorbed almost the entire Indian and Chinese manpower, and the somewhat restrained policy of the colonial administration combined with a more active assistance to Malay agriculture,[31] relieved the tension to a certain extent. As a result, when the reserved areas in Johore, Selangor, Perak, and Penang were opened up for Chinese rice farming, the allotted acreage remained small in relation to the total of newly opened agricultural lands. This whole development, however, revealed the latent racial tension involved in Malaya's rice problem, and intimately related to the dependent economy of the country.

The process of Western colonization has not only determined the pattern of land utilization, but also the racial distribution of the population. The development of the rubber and mining industries has pushed the native Malay population more and more towards the east, into the areas of the former Unfederated Malay States, while a dense immigrant population is concentrated in the western part of Malaya in settlements near rubber plantations.[32] The Malays considered the east as safe from Western penetration, and therefore preferred this undeveloped area to the irrigated lands on the western coast, mainly because there they could only get temporary land licenses, since a complete survey of all potential tin-bearing regions had not yet been made.[33]

The essential difference between Malaya and other countries in this area, such as Java, is the abundance of arable land, and an almost unlimited reserve of virgin soil waiting for cultivation. Where a land problem was about to develop, as in some rubber production centers, the British administration answered the claims of the Malays by establishing Malay reservations. These were the areas which on the eve of World War II were partly opened up for rice cultivation by the Chinese. The abundance of arable land, even during a

31. In January, 1940, the government guaranteed a minimum price of S.S. $2.50 a picul for standardized paddy, sold to the State Rice Mills, and agreed to pay a bonus on the purest strains. Additional measures—distributing of fertilizer to farmers, waiving the water rate on rice land, government marketing—were planned when the war in the Pacific broke out. For a discussion of the entire problem, see Virginia Thompson, *op. cit.*, pp. 32 ff.

32. E. H. G. Dobby, "Settlement Patterns in Malaya," *Geographical Review*, XXXII (1942), 211 ff.

33. Virginia Thompson, *op. cit.*, p. 38.

period of most intensive colonization, gave the Malays the possibility of retaining their characteristics as "a people with a highly developed culture of their own, and with a distinct and well formulated attitude toward life.[34] They refused to become laborers in the colonial enterprises, and generally preferred to continue their small independent farming in less accessible areas.

The colonizing power in Malaya was not confronted with the difficult problem of acquiring the needed areas for large-scale plantations as in Java; its only problem was to obtain adequate farm labor, the native farming population not being an available source.

RUBBER FARMING Rubber production, in spite of its dimensions, is not yet adequately developed and needs continued scientific improvement. Conditions improved essentially after 1928, when Ormsby-Gore, Under-Secretary of State for the Colonies visited Malaya, Ceylon, and Java, and reported his findings to Parliament.[35] He first of all criticized the organization and operation of the British plantations as being too costly, with their "complicated and expensive mechanism of directors, agent firms, visiting agents, managers, and share holders." According to his investigations, the costs of production here were about 75 percent higher than on Dutch estates. This was mainly the result of the restriction schemes of the Stevenson plan,[36] which had induced the plantation companies to neglect research and to look to the administration for assistance in price fixing on the basis of the costs of production of the least efficient company. Ormsby-Gore asked for the immediate abolition of the restriction schemes and the general recognition of the necessity to reorganize Malaya's rubber industry. He was successful, and the restriction schemes were eliminated by Parliament immediately upon the adoption of his report. However, rubber cultivation in

34. Emerson, Malaysia, p. 18.
35. Parliamentary Papers, CMD, 3235 (1928), pp. 134–54, especially pp. 141–48.
36. In the early twenties the Stevenson plan for the control of rubber exports had been introduced in Malaya and Siam, but not in the Netherlands East Indies. The Dutch government refused to cooperate, which brought about the ultimate failure of the entire restriction scheme, though it controlled 70 to 75 percent of the world's production. But the native small holder in the Dutch colony, with his very low costs of production, increased his output considerably and thus frustrated the regulation scheme.

Malaya is still less efficient than the much smaller production of the Netherlands East Indies.

Ormsby-Gore considered the lack of native participation in rubber cultivation as the most serious threat to the European estates "with their high overhead expenses and costly management." The native small holder can adjust his production according to the price situation, and the quantity he brings to the market is to a great extent determined by the current price. The amount, however, of production on the big European estates depends on the area planted with trees mature enough to tap. Overhead expenses virtually force the plantations to continue tapping regardless of the current price, because their fixed charges remain, irrespective of the state of the market.[37]

Malaya is still behind the Netherlands Indies in adopting strains of higher yield. While the average annual yield in all Malaya is 350–450 pounds of rubber per acre, the yield from bud-grafted trees, as introduced in the Netherlands Indies, is capable of reaching a thousand pounds and more.[38] The variation in yield is largely determined by heredity, and it is, therefore, important that all the trees on an estate be grown from buds obtained from highly qualified parent trees. This process, called "bud-grafting," needs many years of experiment and selection. The establishment of a proven progeny (called clone), of a highly qualified parent tree requires about ten years. The high standard of rubber production in the Netherlands Indies is the result of a successful application of bud-grafting in most intimate cooperation with the Research Institute established in Buitenzorg, Java, in 1913. Rubber research in Malaya, however, lagged far behind, partly because of the effects of the first World War on the colonial administration, and partly because of red tape. When bud-grafting finally was introduced, the demand for grafts became so great that they at times were taken from not fully proven clones, thereby creating new problems.[39] Not until 1928 did Malaya start a systematic improvement of the rubber strains, which included the importation of bud wood from the Netherlands East Indies on a large scale. The Malaya Rubber Research Institute, established in 1925, was then enlarged considerably. A staff of thirty

37. Mills, *op. cit.,* pp. 193 ff.   38. Ibid., pp. 200 ff.
39. D. H. Grist, *op. cit.,* pp. 78–81.

scientists was attached to the Institute in the years just prior to World War II.[40] Methods of grafting and fertilizing, and of treatment of pests and root diseases were improved. Advanced forestry methods were instituted for improving and conserving the soil on estates with mature trees, thereby raising standards of cultivation. Finally, new methods of preparing the rubber for shipment, using ammonia as a preservative, were developed. Reorganized estate operations succeeded in reducing the costs of production by lowering the administration expenses and absorbing the management of the smaller estates. But in spite of these favorable changes, the total area planted with bud-grafted rubber was only around 350,000 acres in 1940, or 10 percent of the total rubber acreage. Progress was greatest in the last year before the war—70,000 acres of bud-grafted trees were added, twice as many as in 1939, and three times the amount in 1937.

Much has still to be accomplished before Malayan estate farming can reach the standards of pre-war Dutch production. It is still marked by overorganization, by the existence of individual units of uneconomic size, and by plantations of obsolete trees, which could be replaced with higher-yielding stocks. Though the introduction of bud-grafting made possible a certain standardization of estate rubber and thus diminished the competitive threat of the native rubber, the quality has yet to be improved. The Rubber Research Institute has endeavored to train the small-scale native landholders by means of persuasion and by sending out field officers from the agricultural department (Asiatic rubber instructors). It had modest success in introducing new methods of tapping, rubber preparation, and disease control, but was actually unable to improve the methods of cultivation, especially as far as bud-grafting on a larger scale was concerned.[41] The small native holders continued to plant as many trees as possible, and remained rather indifferent to fertilizing, selection of seedlings, bud-grafting, and so on.

Though the standard of Malayan rubber is largely decided by the estate production, the economic and social status of the native rubber producer is of the greatest importance for the agricultural

40. Mills, *op. cit.,* p. 210.
41. See Annual Reports on Agriculture in Malaya, Straits Settlements and Federated Malay States, Dept. of Agriculture *1934,* pp. 31–32; *1935,* pp. 30–31; *1936,* pp. 30–33; *1937,* p. 8.

economy as a whole. It is, therefore, essential to analyze his actual position within the agriculture of Malaya. Native rubber holdings are mainly in the former Federated States, while most of the Malays in the former Unfederated States remain rice cultivators. The exception is Johore, where in 1940 the total area of small holdings planted with rubber was as large as 400,000 acres. Though the income of the native rubber cultivator in foreign-dominated areas follows the general profit trend, he nevertheless remains a conservative peasant and refuses to adopt modern methods. He pays no attention to the marketing of his produce, and relies, to his serious disadvantage, upon the Chinese dealer as middle man between himself and the world market. He is satisfied with cash returns which cover his immediate needs, and is not interested in putting forth the extra exertion needed for treating and marketing his produce. The Chinese has to accomplish this additional work for him.[42]

His basic problem is his dangerous dependence on such a highly fluctuating commodity as rubber. Unlike his countrymen who remain rice farmers, he is pushed into the risks of the world market, and his social existence fluctuates as much as the market for his crop. Though living in a country with no land problem and where he enjoys a certain amount of government protection, he is nevertheless without any stable economic basis.

Unlike the European rubber estates, where scientific methods of tapping and bud-grafting are mostly applied, the Malay small holdings are still run very primitively. The yield per tree is therefore relatively low.[43] Though rubber is usually supplementary to the Malayan's other crops, it is his only cash crop; he depends on it to pay taxes and to buy what he cannot produce for himself. He will, therefore, adjust his tapping to the current price situation. This means that he will increase tapping when prices drop in order to secure his minimum subsistence; this is contrary to the policy of the large plantations and inconsistent with a realistic rubber economy.[44] His costs of production are very low, as he has no highly developed organization and no labor costs. He is, therefore, ready to sell at any price, and can still make a profit when the plantation is losing money. Naturally he is opposed to regulation schemes that

42. Emerson, *Malaysia*, p. 38.   43. *Ibid.*
44. W. I. Ladejinsky, "Agriculture in British Malaya," pp. 103 ff.

protect the plantations against losses but prevent him from making his badly needed cash income. In this way the economically weak native producer, only interested in his immediate income, antagonizes the big rubber interests which determine the policy and are the deciding factor in any regulation. This conflict, latent in periods of prosperity, has a tendency to grow into serious tension in critical times.

The history of rubber regulation in Malaya shows that even the best-calculated program is no remedy against the effects of complete economic dependence on the world market. When a new regulation scheme was introduced in 1934, the rubber market had collapsed. Between 1928 and 1932, prices had fallen to about 20 percent of the 1928 level, and had recovered slowly to about 60 percent in 1934. Within the same period, world production had increased from about 660,000 tons to over a million tons, with a world consumption of about 900,000 tons. However, in 1934, accumulated surplus stocks amounted to almost 70 percent of that year's world production. This was the economic background which in May, 1934, induced Great Britain (representing Malaya, Ceylon, India, Burma, Sarawak, and North Borneo), the Netherlands East Indies, and later Siam, to agree to restrictions of rubber exports from June 1, 1934, to December 31, 1938. The conditions in the rubber regions had already then reached a very critical stage. Large-scale cultivation had been considerably reduced; hundreds of thousands of plantation workers had been discharged, and wages were drastically cut. The restriction schemes set up a basic quota of 504,000 tons for Malaya. An International Rubber Regulation Committee, representing producers and consumers, fixed the permissible additional exports for each quarter. Any expansion of the already existing rubber acreage was generally prohibited. In 1939, the restriction agreements were renewed for an additional five years.

Though the plan succeeded in establishing greater security both for the plantations and for their approximately 600,000 (mostly Indian) laborers, it failed to create an efficient control of the market. The International Rubber Committee could diminish the fluctuation of prices but could not control the relation between production and consumption. Within a few months in 1937 the export quotas had to be cut by an additional 30 percent and prices were considerably reduced. These fluctuations made the problem of regular employment extremely difficult and showed clearly that production regulation can neither stabilize the dependent economy of Malaya, nor improve the social levels of its population. This can only be done through increased production.[45] Certainly the restriction schemes could claim some success in protecting the larger investments and smoothing out the effects of the business cycles, but they failed completely in stabilizing the economy of the country as a whole. As a matter of fact, this control added to the economic differences between foreign and native rubber producers. Since the Malays had been encouraged by the administration to plant rubber as their only cash crop, they considered the restrictions on their production unjustified, and consequently contested the right of the administration to collect money taxes which they could only pay from their rubber receipts. Unlike the European and Chinese planters, native farmers have neither planting associations nor any influential legal counsel to represent their interests. But there is no doubt that they strongly opposed the restriction schemes. It is rightly asserted that they have little possibility of balancing their losses; they cannot apportion them among numerous shareholders and they cannot soften the burden of depression by drawing on reserves, as the plantation companies do. If the native farmer is out of business he is out of cash and cannot buy his daily rice. Because of his economic helplessness, the large estates have been able to buy up his export rights when rubber prices were low, and have thereby strengthened their own position. These conditions within Malayan rubber production prove that native participation in the cultivation of export crops constitutes a great problem and, under present conditions, is no step toward a solution of the problem of colonial production.[46]

The pre-war boom in raw materials returned large profits to Malaya's rubber industry, but competition was also stimulated in other countries (as in South America and Africa), as was the production of substitutes. The permissible export quota went up from 75 percent in the last quarter of 1939 to 80 percent in the first half of

45. Harold B. Butler, *Problems of Industry in the East* (Geneva, 1938), p. 45.
46. Sir Allan Pim, *Colonial Agricultural Production* (London, 1946), p. 9, does not give full credit to this problem, nor is it discussed in his chapter on Malaya (pp. 45 ff.); see also the Preface by G. E. Hubbard.

1940, and soared to 125 percent in August, 1941. It was difficult, however, to export the full amount permitted, mainly because it was found that certain plantations had been overassessed,[47] and secondarily because of difficulties in finding an adequate labor supply.

Taking the years immediately before the war as a basis for analysis, the future aspects of Malaya rubber do not look very bright. An Anglo-American agreement has removed the ban on the export of seeds and bud woods in order to increase the planting in unrestricted areas, such as Africa and South America, thus lessening America's dependence on Far Eastern rubber. Furthermore, the expanded production of native producers in Sumatra and Borneo constitutes a low-cost competition which endangers the position of the Malayan plantation rubber. In addition, the competition of synthetic rubber became noticeable for the first time when higher freight rates and expensive war-risk insurances inflated the production costs of natural rubber. The synthetic production seems even able to reduce its own extremely high costs of production.

Malaya's rubber producers have much to accomplish if they want to face successfully the difficulties of the postwar period with its intensified competition. The extension of research, the scientific selection and grafting of trees, have actually made possible a quadrupled yield per acre, and a highly standardized production. Sooner or later, a market situation may develop which will overthrow all international restrictions, and the definite battle with the synthetic producers will begin. Quality and costs of production will then be the factors deciding the future status of the Malayan economy.

LABOR   The great rubber and tin industries in Malaya, built up as they are by foreign capital, depend upon the import of an adequate labor force from abroad. In this way, Malaya became the country in Southeast Asia where foreign capital and immigrant labor could establish an efficient export economy, while the indigenous population remained on the periphery of the economic system. The alien enterprises, in cooperation with the colonial administration, solved the labor problem by importing immigrants from India and China. At first, this recruiting was combined with heavy penal sanctions which led to very bad labor conditions. However, after the first World War, changes in the system were effected and conditions

47. Virginia Thompson, *Postmortem on Malaya*, p. 107.

of work were made more attractive through effective inspection and social services.[48]

Malaya has drawn heavily on the inexhaustible population reservoirs of overcrowded South India and South China, receiving since the beginning of the century an uninterrupted stream of Tamils and Chinese coolies. The Indians constitute the main labor force on the rubber estates, (75 percent), while most of the Chinese work in the mines. Some Javanese immigrants work in Johore and on the east coast. Malay workers are found only in the former Unfederated Malay States, which have a rather dense, homogeneous, and well-balanced Malay population. There they provide the labor required by the government departments.[49]

In recent decades, the labor policy of the large estates has been guided by the dependence upon an adequate regular labor supply, which could only be provided by a well-organized import of reliable labor. The process of capital concentration and consolidation and the prevalence of large enterprises also called for a more stable, more reliable, and better nourished labor force. These considerations ruled out indentured labor, which was expensive and inadequate in quantity, and also barred the continued use of ignorant, half-starved and terrorized coolies.[50] After contract labor was abolished by law,[51] workers were raised above the starvation level of India and China, and Malaya became an attractive market for Asiatic laborers. The Indian government played a very active part in this improvement. In contrast to the Chinese government, which was rather indifferent to the fate of nationals abroad, India was concerned with the conditions offered its emigrants and developed, in the course of time, a strong control mechanism. The Indian Immigration Committee, originally created (1907) to control the recruiting of Indian labor, developed into a powerful administration concerned with all the problems involved.[52] By the Immigration Act of 1922, the emigration of Indians to Malaya

48. Emerson, *Malaysia*, p. 46.
49. *Malayan Year Book, 1939*, Chapter XV; A. S. Haynes, "Industrialization as an Indispensable Means of Maintaining the Level of Prosperity in Tropical Regions; the Position of Malaya," *Comptes rendus, du Congrès International de Géographie* (Amsterdam, 1938), II, Sec. III, 543.
50. Emerson, *Malaysia*, p. 46.
51. Recruiting of indentured or contract labor was abolished in 1910.
52. During the depression, immigration was suspended and extensive repatriation was carried through.

finally came under the control of the government of India and the Malayan administration. Plantation companies were forced to accept their terms for standard rates of wages, and so on. The improvement of labor conditions in Malaya and the growing social reputation of the country rendered unnecessary any further recruiting; [53] instead, the flow of free labor was increased, especially after an agent of the Indian government had been established (at Kuala Lumpur in 1923) with the right to inspect all places where Indians were employed. An Indian Immigration Fund was set up, through assessments on all employers of Indian labor, including the government. This fund paid all expenses connected with the immigration of Indian labor, including medical attention and the repatriation of destitute laborers. Finally, in 1931, the Indian government, pressed by the nationalist movement, prohibited all "assisted" immigration to Malaya which was suspected of not being voluntary.[54]

Labor regulations have been set up in Malaya, under the influence of Western ideas, especially from New Zealand and England. These provide, for example, for maternity allowances and a two months' holiday after childbirth, and for the protection of children and adolescents.[55] The administration of the Federated Malay States issued a labor code in 1912, which later was amended and supplemented twelve times. Its main provisions were likewise enacted in the Unfederated States and regulate even today the conditions for the entire immigrant labor force. The administration introduced a consistent labor policy for all of Malaya in respect to wages, housing, sanitation, water supply, and labor agreements. However, this

53. The recruiting system differed from the earlier indentured or contract labor inasmuch as the coolie was not bound by contract to serve for a stipulated period on a particular estate.

54. An order effective from June 15, 1938, prohibited all persons from emigrating from the provincial government of Madras to the Straits Settlements, the Federated States, etc., for the purpose of unskilled work. The term "emigrate" and "emigration" means, under the Emigration Act of India, the departure by sea "of any person who departs under an agreement to work for hire" and of any person who is assisted to depart otherwise than by a relative "for the purpose or with the intention of working for hire or engaging in agriculture." This ban is universal and includes all departures which are assisted, and which in effect can be considered as assisted, even if the worker leaves India at his own expense. See Federated Malay States Dept. of Labor, *Annual Report 1938* (Kuala Lumpur, 1939), pp. 16 ff.

55. Virginia Thompson, *Postmortem on Malaya*, p. 127, mentions, however, that many of the health measures existed only on paper, and that the problem of providing medical care on smaller estates was never solved.

social system completely collapsed in the depression, since it was based almost exclusively on the plantations. Plantation work was reduced to a minimum, workers were dismissed and finally deprived of all social benefits. In the years 1930–33, about 200,000 South Indians were repatriated at the expense of the Immigration Fund. Nevertheless, in the years before the second World War, agricultural laborers fared better in Malaya than in many other areas of the Far East. Their social level was comparatively high, even higher than in the Philippines.[56] For the poor and frequently jobless Tamils from South India, Malaya was a promised land where conditions for labor were good and where effective regulations gave protection and assured cash incomes.

It is a characteristic of the rubber estates that, in spite of their outstanding position in one of the world's key industries, they preferred to depend on a flexible labor force. Therefore, they did not establish such conditions that would have induced the immigrant workers to settle down. As the estates were completely dependent on industries abroad which were extremely sensitive to the business cycle, and hence highly speculative, they preferred a status which made possible quick adjustment to the fluctuating market situation, including reduction of the labor force to a minimum in periods of depression.

For years, Malaya's labor population has been a function of the rise and fall of the prices for two commodities, rubber and tin. As foreigners in the country, immigrants have little chance to earn a livelihood outside the industry in which they were originally employed. Many serious students of Malaya's economy consider this dependence of hundreds of thousands of workers on the prosperity of a single industry as a potential danger to social peace in the country. Some of them propose the organization of "some form of settlement, particularly for the younger generation, who have spent all their life in Malaya and would be completely dépaisés if they had to return to India or to China." [57] But this proposal has not met with a sympathetic response from the big plantation owners.

Under the protection of their home country, Indian plantation

56. Mills, *op. cit.*, pp. 2, 225–26.

57. Harold Butler, *op. cit.*, p. 48. Actually, only three agricultural settlements were established, covering not more than a thousand acres.

laborers received a daily wage, whereas Chinese workers were paid by the weight of latex they collected. In May, 1938, the actual wages for male workers on the large estates throughout Malaya were not less than 50 cents a day, while female workers got 40 cents for nine hours work.[58] The fall in price and production during the latter part of the year forced wages down to 45 cents and 35 cents, respectively. The Labor Report for 1940 (p. 2) gives standard wages of 40 cents and 32 cents for Indian labor. In the course of that year, however, earnings showed a steady increase on account of war-stimulated production and full employment.

In 1937, the Central Indian Association of Malaya (CIAM) assumed leadership of the Indian community and tried to raise its political and social standard in accordance with the demands of the Indian National Congress, whose viewpoint was that Indian workers in Malaya might not be badly treated but that they could be treated better.[59] The CIAM demanded equal political status for them and recognition of the labor question as part of the greater and more important political problem as a whole. It further demanded land settlements for Indian workers, but only in connection with fixity of tenure, freehold rights, and a clear political status. The negotiations ended in a deadlock in 1938, and the general condition of Indian estate-labor remained unchanged. Its level was determined by the abundant supply maintained through voluntary immigration. This migratory flow did not slow down until the end of 1939 when war employment began to affect the labor market in India, where rising wages, together with the fear of a rice shortage and a Japanese invasion of Malaya, counteracted the readiness to migrate.

In recent years, labor conditions have not been as well balanced as Harold Butler noted on his journey during the winter of 1937–38. The fact that the bulk of the labor population in Malaya stayed only temporarily without ever feeling at home may doubtless have delayed the advance of trade unionism and prevented open conflict for some years. However, the political activity and radicalism which marked the thirties in India and China spread its influence to the alien labor forces in Malaya, especially the Chinese.[60]

58. Straits Settlement Currency. Federated Malay States Dept. of Labor, *Annual Report 1938* (Kuala Lumpur, 1939), p. 39.
59. Virginia Thompson, *op. cit.*, p. 137.   60. *Ibid.*, pp. 146 ff.

Immigrant labor became the bearer of revolutionary ideas; political issues, rather than economic, were decisive in the development of an organized labor movement. Strike movements changed character, and were no longer directed against specific abuses, but were undertaken on general issues. In the beginning, the chief battlefield was the mining industry and the municipal enterprises in Singapore. As early as 1937, however, Chinese estate laborers had joined the strike wave, primarily because their wages were not being increased with the returning prosperity in the rubber industry. The strike was mildly successful; it resulted in the establishment of an advisory committee on Chinese labor, with control over wage regulation.

The slogans of the Indian National Congress and of the Kuomingtang more and more dominated the spirit of the non-Malay Asiatic population, and resulted in very effective strikes. It was a still unorganized labor class which fought this fight, trade unions usually not being formed till after the dispute; even the old Chinese societies and guilds, which were originally mutual aid societies and traditionally conservative, joined the struggle.

Unbalanced economic conditions in 1938 added to the unrest. Large unorganized strikes in the mining industry of the Straits Settlements led the government to set up the necessary machinery for arbitration. Some very progressive laws [61] were drafted, and these should promote the development of the trade union movement and of collective bargaining in Malaya. But the administration failed to implement these bills for three years after they were drafted.[62]

In this period of increasing unrest, Chinese associations for the first time showed an active solidarity with Indian strikers, and a united labor front in Malaya seemed imminent. Throughout the years 1938–39 agitation continued among nearly all labor groups, threatening to endanger the fulfillment of the increased export quotas and hence hamper economic recovery. Political emotions at the outbreak of the war, together with depressed social condi-

61. The Industrial Courts Bill, the Trade Unions Bill, and the Trade Disputes Bill (against illegitimate strikes) were drafted in 1938.
62. Virginia Thompson, *op. cit.*, p. 153, quotes the Central Indian Association of Malaya (CIAM) as suspecting employers and government as actually opposed to trade unionism and collective bargaining. The reluctance of the government (the largest employer) to implement the bills, has, according to this author, given substance to this charge.

tions growing out of higher costs of living, increased the intensity of the strikes. A considerable labor shortage in the booming rubber and tin industries supported the strikers and resulted in a 20–30 percent wage increase, the eight-hour day, a weekly holiday, and full pay for sick leave.

Political propaganda ran far ahead of actual trade unionism, thereby frustrating the hopes and calculations of both administration and employers to control and neutralize the labor movement.[63] The China War Relief Fund, originally only a collecting agency of the Chinese government in the war against Japan, but later in intimate connection with the communist section in the Chinese resistance movement, developed into a political center with radiations throughout Malaya. Communist influence was particularly strong among the Chinese, who classified their opponents as pro-Japanese traitors. The Indian workers were influenced by the Chinese attitude, and strikes and unrest grew in strength in spite of increasing wages.

The government decided to consider the strike movement as politically unwarranted. The strike of the Singapore harbor workers [64] in March, 1940, was chosen as the staging ground for a serious effort at repression, but the wave could not be halted. Finally, the administration and the employers resorted to an improvement in working conditions as the most effective means of quelling the unrest. During the first six months of the war, wages were raised by more than 33 percent, housing conditions were improved, new schools were built, and a survey was started of the nutritional standard of the workers.[65] Progressive social legislation was introduced, dealing with night work for women and minors, and workmen's compensation (for any injury resulting in total or partial disability) was extended to agricultural workers. Though the position of labor in Malaya was thus considerably improved during the first two years of the war, the new positive social policy could not change the social and economic pattern overnight.

In general, the social level of the Indians remained lower than

63. *Ibid.*, p. 165.
64. The Singapore harbor workers were organized in the General All Trade Union, a branch of the Anti-Enemy Backing Up Society connected with the China War Relief Fund. Virginia Thompson, *op. cit.*, p. 158.
65. *Ibid.*, p. 159.

that of the Chinese. Even when the Indian rubber tappers struck for higher wages in 1940, they did not ask for the income level of the Chinese, thus indirectly admitting their own lower efficiency.[66] However, the growing excitement of the Chinese workers did not fail to affect the Indians, who, in 1941, participated in great numbers in the estate strikes in Selangor, and in the colliery strikes throughout Malaya. Though the wages in 1941 had gone up to 60 cents a day in most parts of the country, and though the Indian remittances to Madras had increased by 40 percent, tens of thousands of Indian estate coolies joined the strike movement, many of them using the political slogans of the Indian Congress Party.[67] In the middle of strikes and demonstrations, the Trade Unions and Industrial Courts bills were finally enforced, "when both capitalists and officials came to regard the new legislation more as a means of controlling labor than of fostering its evolution." [68]

Hereafter, the registration of trade unions made progress, but was somewhat delayed by lack of leadership and organizing capacity.[69] The Chinese led here, too, while the Indians remained rather indifferent, probably because the CIAM satisfactorily supervised the working conditions of the Tamils. Later, however, several trade unions were registered with mixed membership, as, for example, the Batu-Arong Labor Association, which represented the workers in the Malayan collieries and included Chinese, Indians, and Malays.

The new labor legislation was used to secure the production conditions necessary to Malaya's increasing export quotas. In August, 1941, five months before the war in the Pacific, the government, which was responsible for filling the quotas, yielded to the pressure of the rubber and tin industries and declared strikes illegal during wartime. Strikes in basic industries and transportation were outlawed. Troops were called out to reinforce the "peace maintenance

66. *Ibid.*, p. 160.
67. *Ibid.*, pp. 161 ff. The striking estate workers in Selangor demanded that a framed picture of Ghandi be placed in the coolie lines, and that the Congress flag be flown at the estate entrance.
68. *Ibid.*, p. 162.
69. Federated Malay States, Dept. of Labor, *Annual Report, 1940* (Kuala Lumpur, 1941), p. 9. *Labor Conditions in Ceylon, Mauritius, and Malaya*, a Report by Major G. St. J. Orde Browne (Labor Advisor to the Secretary of State for the Colonies), Parliamentary Papers, CMD, 6423 (London, 1943), pp. 109 ff.

units," and the British authorities had to declare a state of emergency in some regions. In the middle of 1941, armored-car units and troops were used on the peninsula to quell disorders that were termed by the British Governor, "a direct challenge to the government." [70]

From a general point of view the import of a mobile labor force turned out to be very expensive for the employers in Malaya. It transplanted the social ideas of the two great Asiatic revolutions to the narrow stage of Malaya, where there were already most serious economic problems. Malaya, once the model country in Southeast Asia for good interracial relationships and social progress, became a center of social and racial tension.

LEVELS OF LIVING—HEALTH CONDITIONS   Various levels of living, differentiated by nationality, mark the social situation in Malaya. At the bottom of the scale are the Indians, with the Chinese and Malays somewhat above them. Generally speaking, however, the level of living is considerably higher than in other countries in Southeast Asia. For years the per capita rice consumption, a fairly sure index to living conditions, has been relatively high: in 1936–40, the four-year average was 184 kg.[71] Considering that the population of Malaya obtains most of its calories from rice, the per capita consumption can still be regarded as comparatively high. For decades it increased steadily with the single exception of the depression period, 1931–35, when it went down to 170 kg. According to official statistics,[72] the full daily ration of uncooked rice in 1938 for an adult plantation worker without family was 1 *kati*, or 1⅓ lbs. For this he had to pay, according to the average retail price, 1 d. out of his daily wages of 40 Strait Settlement cents (equal to 11½ d.). This relation between rice price and earnings must be considered as favorable. The attraction which Malaya exerted on the Tamils and Chinese coolies coming from crowded and starving countries can well be understood.

The complete dependence of Malaya's economy on the business

70. Michael Greenberg, "Malaya, Britain's Dollar Arsenal" *Amerasia* (June, 1941), pp. 144 ff., especially p. 150.
71. V. D. Wickizer and M. K. Bennett, *The Rice Economy of Monsoon Asia* (Palo Alto, Calif., 1941), p. 328, Table VII.
72. *Malayan Year Book, 1939*, Chapter XV, p. 124.

cycle nevertheless marked the life of the individual laborer with uncertainty and instability. Depression and slump not only resulted
in unemployment, but fostered conditions in which repatriation
was the only alternative to starvation. Furthermore, most of the
famous welfare institutions, especially those giving medical care,
were kept up by the estates and, therefore, depended on the general
economic situation. The wages of those who continued to work
during the depression were heavily cut and fell at a much faster
rate than they had risen in times of prosperity.[73] Finally, the unemployed plantation workers who were not repatriated faced distress and hopelessness. The amount of social services rendered,
including the unemployment service, never went beyond the first
stages of development in Malaya as a whole, though it differed in
the various sections of the country and, although the Straits Settlements in 1938 carried out a fairly adequate relief program, a most
reluctant attitude toward social problems was prevalent in the Federated States. There was considerable unemployment among white
collar workers even in times of prosperity. Thus, the Bangkok
Times reported in March, 1941, during the peak of the boom, that
hundreds of unemployed persons in Kuala Lumpur were sleeping
on the pavements, exposed to all kinds of weather.[74]

Because of a very efficient malaria control and sanitation measures enforced on the estates,[75] the health standard was comparatively high, particularly among the plantation workers. However,
as the policy of the government was only preventive and hygienic, it was unable to bring about any essential improvement
in nutrition. Pandit Nehru traced the inferior efficiency of Indian
laborers in comparison to the Malays and Chinese to their inferior
diet. In recent years the need for creating a more permanent labor
force has led some employers to consider improving the diet of
laborer's children. Where this has been carried out, the frequency
of hospitalization has notably decreased.[76] Typical deficiency
diseases, such as beri-beri (vitamin B_1 deficiency) and xero-
phthalmia (vitamin A deficiency) can, however, still be found in

73. Virginia Thompson, *Postmortem on Malaya*, p. 136.   74. *Ibid.*, pp. 141, 163.
75. League of Nations Health Organization, Intergovernmental Conference on Far
Eastern Countries on Rural Hygiene, 1937 Preparatory Paper: *Report of the Malayan
Delegation* (Geneva, 1937), p. 27.
76. Virginia Thompson, *op. cit.*, pp. 127 ff.

the country. But most serious is the protein deficiency caused by the high prices of most forms of protein, such as meat, milk, and eggs. Dried fish, the only source of protein within the reach of the Tamil, is far from sufficient, so that he and his family must be considered as undernourished.[77]

CONCLUSIONS Malaya's economy can be considered either as favorable or unfortunate, depending on the viewpoint taken. Its place in world economy and the large returns on invested capital certainly justify an appreciation of the economic achievements in this British colony. Furthermore, the general level of living is comparatively high as compared with other countries in the area. However, other considerations lead to a more pessimistic point of view. Malaya as a whole certainly has achieved a maximum of wealth, but has paid for it with a maximum of dependence, the effects of which are evident in all sectors of her economic and social life. Thus, the volume of production is decided by the developments on the world market to a far greater extent than is the case in other areas, since agriculture is almost completely based on the production of the most sensitive export crops. Consequently, subsistence production is very limited, which further increases dependence by necessitating large-scale imports of rice, that can be paid for only with returns from the exports.

The administration and the colonial enterprises were fully aware of the weak foundation of Malaya's economy and of the heavy economic risks involved. This is why they preferred a flexible labor force to a permanent one, and wanted to reduce the risk of economic dependence by an imigration machinery which would provide needed recruits in times of prosperity without imposing any responsibility for them in periods of depression. This policy diminished economic risks, but created a serious political labor problem, which, however, was not fully understood until a few years before the war in the Pacific.

While in periods of prosperity the unfavorable effects of economic dependence are generally concealed, dependence on labor from abroad becomes most evident. This dependence is a typical

77. League of Nations Health Organization, *Report of the Malayan Delegation*, pp. 26 ff. *Labor Conditions in Ceylon, Mauritius, and Malaya* (The Orde Browne Report), p. 101.

economic feature in a country where a disproportionate development has taken place, and its high degree in Malaya is proof of the artificiality of the economic structure.

It seems to be a basic principle in colonial economy that the effects of dependence can neither be avoided nor reduced without transferring tensions and frictions to other sectors of the economic and social life. In Malaya this feature was aggravated by the fact that dependence on labor from India and China created a simultaneous dependence on the political ideology of these countries. Thus the political development in Malaya became a function of her labor situation.

It is beyond the limits of this study to analyze the alternative solutions of the economic and social problems in Southeast Asia, but in this special case their nature and proportions may be indicated. Economically, Malaya may have to face the possibility of a heavy reduction, perhaps a partial liquidation, of the basic rubber industry. This will threaten the very existence of the bulk of the immigrant population. The only alternative will be agricultural reorganization (including construction of irrigation works) and large-scale diversification of the economy.[78] Politically, Malaya will have to coordinate the interests of the Malays with those of the Chinese and Indians in the country, the majority of whom will finally settle there. The entire social and racial problem, so dangerous today, can be solved only by a broad policy that presumes a reorganization of the entire economy.

Fortunately, the Malays participate only to a limited extent in export agriculture. They have been left in possession of the greater part of their land, where they produce their sustenance, and a surplus in periods favorable for trade. Thus, they may become the agricultural backbone of an economic reconstruction in which the immigrants will be placed in other sectors of a diversified economy.

The case of Malaya is particularly striking. Though, from a colonial point of view it was the most successful country in Southeast

78. Rupert Emerson, *Malaysia,* p. 193: "If the economic base of the Federation can be broadened by an effective encouragement of food crops and of other export crops and industries, if the Malayan and the Chinese and Indian coolie can be given a real and significant place, it will begin to take on some of the characteristics of an economically sound and socially healthy community; but even this minimum program is more than can be expected within the framework of imperialism."

Asia, it nevertheless displayed, on the eve of World War II, a most serious economic and social crisis. Malaya proves that even outstanding economic success cannot balance the contradictions of an economy dependent on a fluctuating world market, but that these contradictions grow proportionately to the economic expansion.

In the postwar period the economic and political reorganization of war-battered Malaya was delayed by great and complex political and racial problems. The powerful triumph of the national movements in other areas weakened, ironically enough, the capacity of Malaya to amalgamate its differentiated population into *one* movement for political emancipation. While the development to statehood in India has strongly impressed the Indian population in Malaya and has forced them to choose between loyalty to India and loyalty to Malaya, the Malay national movement shows a strong Indonesian orientation which stands in the way of a large Chinese following.

Concentration on the great political and economic tasks is still lacking because the racial question is absorbing the attention of Malaya's population. In the past, Great Britain was in a position to maintain the balance of power by conducting a pro-Malay policy. Immediately after the war, however, the British seemed decided to centralize the administration and make important concessions to the non-Malay population, a policy which automatically would weaken the position of the Malays. Special emissary of the British Colonial Office Sir Harold MacMichael concluded in 1945 a series of treaties with the Malay Sultans to the effect that the Malay States ceased to be protected states and became colonial protectorates, a change which was more important from a legal than from a political matter-of-fact point of view. These treaties represented the first step to unite Malaya and were followed by an official British White Paper of 1946 ("Malayan Union and Singapore," CMD 6724) recommending the creation of two separate colonies—a crown colony (Singapore) and a colonial protectorate (called the Malayan Union) comprising the Federated and Unfederated Malay States, and the Straits Settlements with the exception of Singapore. Most essential was, however, the proposal for a Malayan Union Citizenship, the requirements for which were very favorable to the Chinese and Indian population.

The Malays, with influential, though unofficial, British support, reacted vehemently against this policy and demanded a revision of the treaties and the White Paper. Their opposition was directed not so much against the planned British control of the Malayan Union and its defense and external affairs as against all arrangements which would give political rights to the Chinese and Indians.

At a constitutional conference held in Kuala Lumpur in August, 1946, the Malays met with the utmost success. The various proposals made at the conference showed that the idea of centralized administration was on the retreat, while the federation of the Malay states and the nominal sovereignty of the Sultans were to be restored. This, however, would automatically mean that the requirements for citizenship would be most unfavorable for the Chinese and Indians, the majority of whom would remain foreigners in the country.[79]

In fact, the new Malayan Federation which replaced the Malayan Union of 1946 is based on separate treaties between Great Britain and the sovereign rulers of the nine Malay States, who were confirmed in all their power and privileges.[80] The Malayan Federation is a British protectorate in which the British High Commissioner decides foreign policy and controls defense. The individual states within the Federation are to enjoy administrative autonomy, while the High Commissioner and British advisers will have great influence in the Federal government and in economic matters.

Seen as a whole, the Malayan Federation is a most conservative approach towards the solution of the basic problems in Malaya. Once more British colonial interests have cooperated with the native rulers, a step which is bound to lead to serious conflicts with the other racial groups, representing today the majority of the population in Malaya. The economic reorganization of the country, however, demands above all an atmosphere of racial cooperation, that is, the *mutual* effort of Malays, Chinese, and Indians in the reconstruction of their country.

79. P. R. Bauer, "Nationalism and Politics in Malaya," *Foreign Affairs*, XXV, No. 3 (April 1947), 509 ff. See also Max Seitelman, "Malaya in Transition," *Far Eastern Survey*, XVI, No. 10 (May 21, 1947), 109 ff., and "Political Thoughts in Malaya," *ibid.*, No. 11 (June 4, 1947), pp. 128 ff.

80. The treaties were signed in Kuala Lumpur, January 21, 1948. The rulers also undertook to promulgate constitutions for their states and to make provisions for elections in due course, both to the central legislature of the Federation and to the State Councils.

5

Indo-China

INTRODUCTION: FRENCH COLONIAL POLICY   Indo-China, which consists of Tonkin, Annam, Laos, Cambodia, and Cochin-China, has been compared to a pole balanced by two baskets of rice. The pole is the Annamite range; the baskets are the delta valleys of the Red River (to the north in Tonkin) and of the Mekong River (to the south in Cochin-China), both of them ancient centers of rice cultivation.

The French conquest of the large areas between the Mekong and Red Rivers had been prepared by the activities of traders and missionaries towards the end of the eighteenth century. The treaties of 1884 and 1885 definitely established a French Protectorate over Annam and Tonkin, thus eliminating the old Annamite Empire. French penetration started in the south with the conquest of the three provinces of Cochin-China (1862), was advanced by the accession of Cambodia (1864), and ended with the military control of the Tonkin delta (1874).[1] The only section which was governed directly as a colony was Cochin-China while native rulers remained in nominal control of most of the country. However, French colonial power was always the basic reality, the method of indirect rule being used for administrative expediency.

In Indo-China which was declared an "assimilated" colony,[2] France has established the most protectionist system in Southeast Asia. Both theoretically and practically, it came to depend almost completely on the interests of the mother country. Free trade was

1. Charles Robequain, *The Economic Development of French Indochina* tr. Isabel A. Ward (London and New York, 1944), pp. 3 ff.
2. This principle is embodied in the French Law of January 11, 1892, to define the relations between France and the Union. See Duvergier, *Collection complète des lois, décrets,* etc. (Paris, 1892), pp. 5 ff.

established with France, and products from other countries were subject to the same tariffs as in France. The establishment of the Indo-Chinese Union in 1887 coincided with a complete change in French economic thinking. The rapidly growing heavy industries in France demanded protected markets, and the man in the street resented the prophets of liberal thinking who were ready to share the colonial market with other countries. The French industries demanded further (and were supported by public opinion) "that colonial production must be limited to supplying the mother country with raw materials and with non-competitive products." [3] The law of 1892 provided for some flexibility but the French government, rather than the colonial administration, had the final word, and Indo-China's particular position was seldom considered. French metropolitan interests and the demands of the customs treasurer generally took priority over the interests of the colony.

The first World War and the period of prosperity which followed strengthened the position of French industries in Indo-China. In 1928, a new law was enacted which practically did away with the old customs system and granted to the colonial administration the authority to adjust its tariffs to its needs. The basic principle of assimilation was maintained in the new law, although it was now used to serve the French interests invested in the colony. The protectionism of the colonial investors surpassed by far the claims of the industries in France and resulted in new tariff rates on foreign commodities, most of which exceeded those of the home tariff. These tariffs further aimed at exclusive protection for French export industries against Chinese and Japanese goods. This tended to isolate Indo-China from the rest of Asia.

The Imperial Economic Conference of 1934–35 emphasized the trends towards absolute protectionism and strengthened the ties between France and Indo-China. Some limited exceptions were made, however, which gave Indo-China the privelege of adjusting its commercial situation to the geographic position by a certain degree of autonomy in governing its relations with neighboring states.[4] Within the treaties and agreements, however, French eco-

3. Meline (Director of the Association of French Industry and Agriculture), quoted by Robequain, *op. cit.*, p. 129.
4. Robequain, *op. cit.*, pp. 128 ff., 132–33.

nomic interests remained the dominating factor. Though the policy of assimilation had been formally abandoned, it did not alter the state of dependence, but, rather, emphasized the importance of French vested interests. Economic development in Indo-China has been generally hampered by complete subordination to these interests.[5]

FOREIGN INVESTMENTS, EXPORTS, AND BALANCE OF PAYMENTS   In 1938, a total of U.S. $464 million were invested in Indo-China, of which $382 million were in business enterprises. Western capital (95 percent French) amounted to $302 million; Chinese, to $80 million. All outstanding rentier investments in 1938 ($82 million) were French. Average profits from business were estimated at 7 percent. More than one-third of the French capital was invested in agriculture, the remainder in processing industries, mining, trade, and banking. The relatively large share in agriculture was owing to the rapid development of rubber production in recent decades. Before the war, the value of French rubber holdings was estimated at U.S. $45 million. In addition, French capital was invested in rice, tea, coffee, sugar, and cotton plantations.[6]

Chinese capital monopolizes the rice trade and dominates the retail business in Cochin-China and Cambodia; 80 percent of the rice mills and roughly half of the wholesale trade in other commodities were in Chinese hands. The Chinese are also well represented in a number of light industries, and they own saw mills, match factories, and mechanical workshops. In 1930, their remittances to Hong Kong were estimated at 5 million Hong Kong dollars.[7]

Aside from Chinese capital, foreign capital other than French is almost absent; a virtual monopoly has been secured by French protectionism and paternalism, combined with direct discriminating restrictions against foreign economic activity.[8] Indo-China has

5. Ibid., p. 388.
6. Helmut G. Callis, Foreign Capital in Southeast Asia, pp. 80, 85 ff., and "Capital Investment in Southeast Asia and the Philippines," p. 28.
7. Carl F. Remer, Foreign Investments in China, pp. 179 ff., and table on p. 185.
8. For instance, mining companies were obliged to have three-fourths majorities of French nationality on their Boards of Directors. Foreigners were excluded from land concessions. According to the U.S. Department of Commerce, American Direct Investments in Foreign Countries (1936), p. 16, American companies operating in Indo-China and Thailand had a capital of only 3.3 million dollars.

become primarily a producer of argicultural and industrial raw materials.[9] As a result of French policy, which considers a colony exclusively as a source of raw materials and a market for manufactured goods, no essential manufacturing industries have been allowed to develop in Indo-China. Like other countries in the area. it has become primarily a producer of raw materials for export.[10]

Rice production is the backbone of the economy. It is not only the staple food for the population, but represents from 40 to 45 percent of the total exports. In 1939, Indo-China exported about 1.6 million tons of rice, out of a production of 4 million tons. In recent years, rubber has ranked second; exports in 1939 amounted to around 70,000 tons, representing a value of almost 1 billion francs.

Indo-China is the world's third largest exporter of rice and rubber. Coal, tin ore, iron ore, and other minerals are the other major exports. In 1939 and 1940, an export excess of 1.1 and 1.9 billion francs, respectively, was achieved, while the average in normal years was only 600 to 700 million francs. Even this considerable export excess, however, was normally insufficient to cover the annual transfers of commercial profits (600 to 800 million francs). For several years this resulted in a deficit in the balance of payments, and not until an excess export of around 1 billion francs was reached in 1937 did a surplus in the balance of payments of around 280 million francs appear for the first time. Payments were balanced by new capital imports, since the heavy transfers of profit prohibited the accumulation of capital in the colony. Increasing indebtedness, with little organic growth of capital equipment, has characterized the development of this assimilated colony.[11]

SURVIVAL OF NATIVE HANDICRAFTS Unlike other countries in this area, native handicrafts have survived. The purchasing power of a large part of the native population has remained so low that the imported French goods have been inaccessible.[12] Although some of

9. Kate L. Mitchell, *Industrialization of the Western Pacific* pp. 151 ff.

10. Some manufacturing industries, however, were established in 1939 against administrative opposition, but they carefully avoided competition with French imports.

11. *Balance of Payments, 1938* (Geneva, 1939), pp. 55 ff. Callis, *Foreign Capital in Southeast Asia*, p. 84.

12. Mitchell, *op. cit.*, p. 153; concerning the handicrafts in Indo-China, the author asserts that they still exist "because of the exceptional intensive character of French

the handicrafts are gradually disappearing, in 1938, 1,350,000 people were still dependent on them for their livelihood, while a large part of the farming population found additional income in the village handicraft industries. Of about 6.5 million Annamites in lower Tonkin, 200,000 devoted the greater part of their time to this work, and 800,000, at least some weeks of the year. Native handicrafts are still very common in the northern part of the country, where land holdings are very small. They represent chiefly the preparation of foodstuffs, cotton and silk spinning, embroidery, manufacturing of fishing nets, wood work, some metal work, pottery and tile making. They are carried out almost entirely without modern equipment and generally lack organization. They are closely connected with agriculture, in the main based on vegetable raw materials, and supplement the income of the peasant who uses his off-season time for artisan work. The returns are small, even in relation to the low agricultural income, and are therefore unable to improve to any extent the position of the rural population.[13]

As late as 1938, the French government emphasized the importance of these handicrafts for the economic development of the country, declaring officially that promotion of them is "one of the best methods of combating the rural pauperism resulting from over-population." [14] But the government refused to establish an essential industrial production, which would have lessened dependence on imports of textiles, machinery, and chemicals and, to a still higher degree, would have combated the rural pauperism.

POPULATION AND LAND UTILIZATION   Indo-China comprises an area of about 285,000 square miles. In 1936, the population amounted to about 23 million,[15] of which 90 percent were peasants. The general population density was 81 per square mile. The greater part of the people, about 19 million, live in the delta valley, comprising an area of less than 40,000 square miles. In other words, 80 percent of the population occupies less than 14 percent of the

colonial exploitation, which precluded any form of economic development that might have raised the purchasing power of the native population."

13. *Labour Condiitons in Indo-China* (International Labour Office, Studies and Reports, Series B., No. 26, Geneva, 1938), pp. 170 ff. Robequain, *op. cit.*, pp. 243 ff.

14. Quoted from Mitchell, *op. cit.*, p. 162.

15. *Annuaire Statistique de l'Indochine, 1936–37 services de la Statistique Général* (Hanoi, 1938), pp. 17 f. Most of the figures are taken from this handbook.

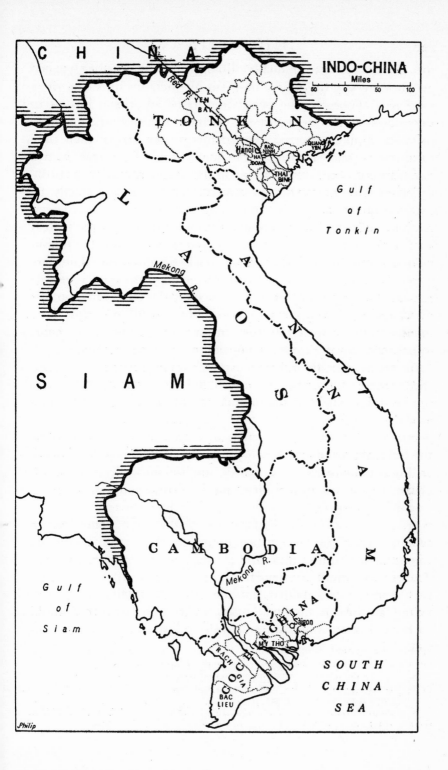

INDO-CHINA

Miles

50   0   50   100

CHINA

Red R.

YEN BAY

T O N K I N

Hanoi
BAC NINH
HA DONG
QUANG YEN
THAI BINH

Gulf
of
Tonkin

L A O S

Mekong

S I A M

C A M B O D I A

Mekong R.

Gulf
of
Siam

COCHIN CHINA

Saigon

MY THO

RACH GIA

BAC LIEU

A N N A M

SOUTH
CHINA
SEA

Philip

total area.[16] Between 4 and 5 million people live on the remaining 245,000 square miles (about 20 per square mile). Out of the 2.8 million families representing the 19 million people, 1.9 million own their land and 900,000 make their living by wage earning and share cropping; 70 percent of the landed families, however, live in the overpopulated Tonkin area, and their plots are seldom large enough for their subsistence. In 1936, the population density in Tonkin was 195 people per square mile; in Cochin-China, 185; in Annam, 99; and in Cambodia, 44.

The cultivated area of about 6 million hectares comprises only 8 percent of the total land area of the colony. According to official French statistics for 1937, 5 million ha. were planted in rice,[17] 500,000 in corn, 300,000 in rubber, and the remainder in sugar, coffee, tea, and other crops. Of the total rice acreage, 1.2 million ha. are in Tonkin, 800,000 in Cambodia and 2.3 million ha. in Cochin-China. Cochin-China supplies 55 percent and Tonkin 35 percent of the rice production of the country, but only the newer, still underpopulated, provinces of Cochin-China can produce an export crop.[18] The other parts of Indo-China consume the rice they grow and depend on the newer rice areas in times of emergency or famine.

Rice cultivation and population density are intimately related in Indo-China, where the population has mainly settled on rich alluvial plains of recent origin. In the Red River delta, 7.5 million people are concentrated on about 6,000 square miles, 4.5 million people on 6,000 square miles of plains along the coast of Annam, and 3.2 million on 6,200 square miles of plains in central Cochin-China. Further, a million people live on about 7,800 square miles in western Cochin-China, and 2.4 million on about 12,500 square miles in southern Cambodia.

Almost 75 percent—16.7 million—are Annamites, who live on the plains of Tonkin and Annam and on the east side of Cochin-China. These people have retained the impress of Chinese culture ever since they were conquered by the Chinese a thousand years

16. Jean de la Roche, "A Program of Social and Cultural Activity in Indochina" Institute of Pacific Relations, French Paper No. 3 (New York, 1945), p. 42.
17. V. D. Wickizer and M. K. Bennett, *The Rice Economy of Monsoon Asia*, Appendix, Table I, quotes for 1937–38 a rice area between 5.6 and 6 million ha.
18. Virginia Thompson, *French Indo-China* (London, 1937), pp. 123 ff.

ago. They are industrious farmers, good fishermen, and skillful workers. The Cambodians, with a population of 2.9 million, tend to be indifferent, inactive, and less energetic farmers than their neighbors. Their district seems to be predestined for penetration by the Annamites, who, in the course of time, have established extensive colonies in Cambodia. The Tai, representing 1.3 million, inhabit Laos and are likewise indifferent to agriculture. They prefer hunting and fishing.[19] The mountain regions of Tonkin, upper Laos, and the Annam range are populated by tribes (numbering about a million) which have only a few arable valleys and plains at their disposal. They are primarily of the type "who till with fire and sow with the sword."

More than 300,000 Chinese live in Indo-China, the majority in Cochin-China, the rest mostly in Cambodia. They are traditionally merchants and traders, ranging from small shopkeepers to wealthy rice exporters. Chinese land-owning farmers are found in Cambodia, Chinese coolies on plantations in the south, and Chinese artisans in the towns.[20]

The population problem in the Tonkin delta is very serious. Here, an area of about 6,000 square miles must support about 7.5 million people, that is, a demographic density of more than 1,250 inhabitants per square mile. Nutrition densities of more than 1,950 per square mile are not uncommon, and even higher than that can be encountered in various provinces, as in Hadong, with 2,927, in Yenbay, with 2,971, and in Quang-Yen, even with 5,980 inhabitants per square mile.[21] In 1931, the average nutrition density in Tonkin was 1,916. Such densities are outstanding, in view of the fact that 95 percent of the population is engaged in farming. The density is greatest where the land renders the best possibilities for drainage and irrigation, that is, along the estuary of the Red River, where consequently the social and economic problems are most delicate.

The term "excess population" refers to the actual level of living, and in an agricultural area, therefore, to the scarcity of land. Pierre

19. Henri Gourdon, *L'Indochine* (Paris), p. 60.
20. Virginia Thompson, *op. cit.*, pp. 165 ff.; *Labour Conditions in Indo-China,* pp. 243 ff.
21. *Labour Conditions in Indo-China,* pp. 217 ff. In order to bring the densities of the population level of the census year 1936, the figures must be increased by about 10%.

Gourou hesitates, however, to apply this term to the actual conditions in the delta and argues that the agricultural technique used there requires a relatively large labor force.[22] The fact, however, that the normal rice ration per year in Tonkin is only 136 kilograms per inhabitant, compared with an average of 250 kilograms in the rest of Indochina, should be reason enough for the statement that there is excess population. In addition, the high rate of population increase in the delta lands has further increased the disproportion between production and consumption since the last census.

Problems arising from an excess of population exist also in other parts of Indo-China, especially in those districts of Annam bordering Tonkin, where land holdings are small and the nutrition density is between 1,560 and 1,690. The situation improves gradually towards the south, where one finds average nutrition densities of 1,003 in Cambodia and 600 in Cochin-China. Indo-China is, therefore, a typical example of maldistribution of population.

SIZE OF FARMS AND LAND TENURE   The size of farms and the form of land tenure differ in the various parts of Indo-China, which is but natural in a country with such an unequally distributed population. While the peasants in the densely populated areas of Tonkin, Annam, and Cambodia till their own plots, Cochin-China is a country of large estates where the land is tilled by tenants and farm labor. Almost 99 percent of the peasants in Tonkin, 90 percent in Annam, and 95 percent in Cambodia are owner-cultivators, while the figure for Cochin-China is only 64.5 percent.

The Tonkin delta is the most minutely subdivided area in the colony. About 62 percent of the farming families own less than 0.36 ha. (1 mau), and 20 percent even less than 0.18 ha.; 91.5 percent of the farming families hold less than 1.8 ha. (5 mau). This overwhelming majority of the entire farming population of Tonkin cultivates only 40 percent of the total rice area.[23] The minute parceling, partly due to inheritance policy, has serious disadvantages. The situation is similar in Annam, where 69 percent of the peasants own less than half a hectare of rice land.

22. Pierre Gourou, *Land Utilization in French Indo-China* (translation of *L'utilization du sol en Indochine française,* (New York, 1945), Part II, pp. 92 ff. *Labour Conditions in Indo-China,* pp. 218-19.
23. Pierre Gourou, *Land Utilization,* Part II, pp. 276 ff.

Although land utilization in Tonkin is characterized by a system of small-scale ownership, it remains a fact that the legal proprietor is frequently not the economic one. He is often practically a tenant, being obligated to make annual payments to the moneylender who has allowed him to remain on the holding. In addition (and this is the case in the whole country, not only in Tonkin), large landowners are frequently anxious to conceal actual property relations. Inaccuracy in registration and concealed transfer of ownership by special agreements often make it impossible to figure the actual dimensions of the large estates. An official inquiry in the very densely populated province of Thai Binh [24] disclosed that 122,000 small owners with less than 1 *mau* shared 61,000 *mau*, while 253 large owners held 28,000 *mau* directly, and, in addition, controlled 43,000 *mau*, the owners of which, in fact, were share croppers of the big estate owners, though still registered as owners. Another inquiry reported by Gourou verified the desperate situation in certain villages of the Bac Ninh province, where there is a high percentage of small proprietors. Out of 1,672 proprietors examined, 1,528 owned less than 3 *mau* (1.08 ha.) and of those, more than 1,000 owned less than one-half *mau* (0.18 ha.).

In Cochin-China, the pattern is very different. Almost 72 percent (180,000) of the total number of farmers have up to 5 ha. under cultivation, and only 86,000 of them own less than 1 ha. In spite of this relatively favorable proportion, the share of the small owner in the total rice area is only 12.5 percent. The large holdings—those with more than 50 ha.—comprise 45 percent of the area (in Tonkin, 20 percent, in Annam, 10 percent). Only 6,200 farms belong to this group, and many of them are under the same owner. In general, all holdings above 10 ha. are divided into parcels from 5 to 10 ha. each and are worked by tenants.

Cambodia keeps a middle position between Tonkin and Annam on one side and Cochin-China on the other. The holdings average about 1 ha. in the river valleys and from 1 to 5 ha. in the interior. Tenancy is not frequent.[25]

As in Java, the ancient institution of community land is still known in Indo-China, especially among the Annamites. The vil-

24. Pierre Gourou, *op. cit.,* pp. 280–81.
25. *Labour Conditions in Indo-China,* pp. 192 ff.

lage community, the basic administrative unit of the Annamite Empire, owns part of the land. Every three years, the communal land is distributed in equal shares to each member of the community. This old Malayan institution corrects, to some extent, the practice of extensive subdivision of land in Tonkin and Annam and is preserved on 20-25 percent of the total rice area.

One of the most characteristic features in the pattern of land tenure is the uncertainty of ownership. This is partly due to inaccuracies in the old village land registers of the Annamite Empire and, to some extent, to the fact that the boundary between the land and water area is changing frequently. The French colonial administration tried to establish a stable basis for individual land ownership by gradually introducing a normal system of land registration. In 1931, 15 million holdings had been surveyed in Tonkin; 3.6 million ha. out of an arable surface of 5.1 million in Cochin-China; 120,000 ha. in Cambodia, and 140,000 ha. in Annam. So far, the initiative of the French administration has created clear-cut tenures, a prerequisite for regular transactions and for obtaining cheaper credit.[26] However, the traditional feeling of the Annamite peasants has counteracted the useful effects of these reforms. They refuse to sell their inadequate holdings and migrate to fertile new lands because the tomb of their ancestors is generally on the land and they are afraid to disturb their spirits. They have therefore preferred excessive indebtedness, and have accepted the hardest conditions if only they could remain on the land, even as tenants.[27]

Under French control, the land situation has changed considerably. Before the French colonization, inequalities in landed wealth had been counterbalanced by the joint communal responsibilities of the villages. People deprived of rice fields turned for support to the communal lands, the cultivation of which was shared periodically.[28] But under French administration these communal lands were partly neglected, and land concentration increased rapidly. While the average size of the holding decreased with the increase of population, the French administration favored the establishment of large estates by a generous concession policy and by patronizing

26. *Ibid.*, pp. 195 ff.
27. Paul Bernard, *Le Problème économique indochinois* (1934), pp. 233 ff.
28. Robequain, *The Economic Development of French Indo-China*, p. 82.

and subsidizing plantation owners. Ample credits were at their disposal, while the peasants were obliged to turn to the usurous moneylenders for financial support. During the last 50 years, European
plantations have developed on a large scale. Between 1890 and
1937, the area of European estates increased from 11,000 hectares
to more than 800,000, mainly in Cochin-China and Cambodia, but
partly also in Tonkin and Annam.[29] The cultivation of the land has
remained, nevertheless, in the hands of small cultivators, tenant farmers or sharecroppers "whose wretchedness is increased by their
debts." Robequain mentions that land speculation also involved
communal lands because of the complicity of the village mandarins
and head men.[30]

Large estates are found all over Indo-China, though their number and size vary in different parts of the country. The statistics below show legal, rather than economic, ownership. Actual conditions in Tonkin would reflect a much more pessimistic picture.

HOLDINGS BY SIZE IN PERCENTAGE OF RICE ACREAGE

Districts	Total Rice Acreage (in Thousands of ha.)	Large Estates over 50 ha. Percent	Medium Estates 5 to 50 ha. Percent	Small Holdings under 5 ha. Percent	Community Lands Percent
Tongking	1,200	20	20	40	20
Annam	800	10	15	50	25
Cochin-China	2,300	45	37	15	3

Source: Bulletin économique de l'Indochine (Hanoi, 1938), II, 746 ff. (Report of the
Inspector General of Agriculture).

Cochin-China is today a country marked by large estates. Here,
especially, the French colonial administration has favored the establishment of a landed class who now control more than 80 percent of the rice fields. About 60 percent of the land of Cochin-China
is leased out, and 200,000 landless families are engaged in share-
cropping. Under French rule, rice cultivation extended rapidly to
what had been waste lands, now irrigated by canals. These
new lands were developed almost exclusively by large-scale cultivators—rich natives, European corporations, or individual French

29. Jean de la Roche, "French Indochina's Prospective Economic Regime," Institute of Pacific Relations. French Paper, No. 2 (New York, 1945), p. 2.
30. Robequain, op. cit., p. 83.

colonists, mostly on a credit basis. While, in the old central province of My Tho, 80 percent of the farms have an area of 1 to 5 ha., only 38.3 percent of the farms in the "new" province of Bac Lieu are of this size.[31] European-owned rice plantations, almost all in French hands, cover about 250,000 ha.[32]

In Cochin-China only one adult male peasant out of four is an owner-cultivator and far too little communal land is available in the newly established villages. Consequently, the most serious land problem has developed, though there is an abundance of land in relation to the population.[33] French policy has prevented the best and most extensive territories from being used for the settlement of the excess population of Tonkin and Annam.[34] Nor did it grasp the opportunity to redistribute the lands of the large estates when so many great landowners became insolvent during the slump. At the end of 1932, the total indebtedness of Cochin-China's rice farmers amounted to about 22 million U.S. dollars, of which more than 50 percent was owed by 655 landowners controlling 200,000 ha. The colonial administration, however, felt obliged to maintain the big estates and in 1932 issued a Special Decree establishing a general service for long-term agricultural loans in Indo-China, guaranteed by the Governor-General. This Decree also provided for a land settlement office for redistribution of land in those cases where the indebtedness was oppressive. The records prove, however, that the effect of the Decree was to stabilize and consolidate the large estates, rather than to redistribute the land.[35]

LANDLORD-TENANT RELATIONSHIP—INDEBTEDNESS   The general features of the landlord-tenant relationship do not differ much from those in other countries of Southeast Asia. The plot of leased land averages 5 ha. As a rule, the tenant has to pay the landlord about 40 percent of the crop (the percentage, however, varies some-

31. Robequain, op. cit., pp. 83–84.
32. Ibid., pp. 193 ff., and Gourou, op. cit., Part III, p. 344.
33. Jean de la Roche, "A Program of Social and Cultural Activity in Indochina," p. 8: "These conditions create a permanent political unrest and make for the existence of an agricultural proletariat which has no hope of bettering its conditions, but is rather due to ever growing indebtedness and abject misery."
34. Yves Henry (General Inspector of Agriculture for the Colonies) "La Question Agraire en Indochine," La Dépêche Coloniale, December 16, 1936, quoted in Labour Conditions in Indo-China, p. 193.
35. Labour Conditions in Indo-China, pp. 197 ff.

what with the fertility of the soil), but considering the expenses for cultivation, he seldom gets more than 50 percent for himself. Hardly ever is the tenant allowed to dispose freely of his own share of the crop, as the landlord claims the control of the entire produce. This additional claim weakens the marketing position of the tenant.[36] Furthermore, the landlord-tenant relationship is generally combined with traditional feudal customs, precisely stipulating onerous gifts and services in favor of the landlord. If lucky, the tenant can supply the rice for his family, but he is at the mercy of the landowner for additional needs, especially in cases of emergency.[37]

The landlord is the main source of credit for the tenant. He furnishes the needed capital and rice to the tenant cultivator—who is quite frequently devoid of cash—at a rate which is officially estimated at about 50 percent for 8 months or one year, but which frequently goes up to 70 percent or more.[38] Gourou quotes, as rate for rice loan in Cochin-China an interest of 50 percent to 100 percent for a six-month loan. Aside from the landlord, professional Annamite and Chettyar moneylenders are available sources of credit; their rate of interest on personal property varies between 20 percent and 80 percent for three-month loans. Rates up to 120 percent are not unheard of. The Annamite creditor usually considers a loan secured by land as the most favorable way of acquiring the property and, therefore, calculates the payments so that they cannot be paid out of the produce of the land.[39] French legislation has tried to restrict the legal Annamite rate to from 3 percent per month to 8 percent per annum, but in vain, because it is impossible to regulate a social disequilibrium by legal norms without an adequate economic policy.

In Indo-China, as elsewhere, the landlord-moneylender is the

---

36. *Bulletin économique de l'Indochine*, 1938, Vol. II, 747–48.
37. Gourou, *op. cit.*, Part III, pp. 347 ff.
38. *Bulletin économique de l'Indochine*, p. 750.
39. Gourou, *op. cit.*, Part III, p. 347. The usurers were able also to interfere in the activities of the licensed pawn shops by intervening in the traffic of pawn shop tickets. *Labour Conditions in Indo-China*, pp. 208 *et seq.* The Chettyars in Indo-China seem to be at least as greedy as in Burma. Their rates seem to be moderate, nominally 12% per annum, but by adding the interest to the capital—the total sum is shown on the receipt—and dividing this total into 12 equal fractions to be repaid one at a time, the actual rate of interest may easily be double the figure indicated to the farmer.

worst influence on the general agricultural development. The land-lords depend far more on the interest from the loans they make than on the production of their rice fields. That explains why own-ers of large estates prefer to divide their lands into small farms and lease them to tenants for primitive, traditional cultivation.[40] Gourou emphasizes that usury is the surest and most economical means of rounding out a domain, that the debtors with a status similar to servitude often seek escape in flight, and that indebted-ness on this scale destroys stability and reduces the intensity of land use.[41] Certainly a system of land utilization based on money interest and not on agricultural production must finally reduce the pro-ductivity of the entire economy.

Cochin-China, the center of landlordism, is also the focal point of usury and general indebtedness. Gourou quotes a report from 1937 by M. Roger Sylvestre, the colonial administrator of the prov-ince of Bac Lieu, as stating:

There is no one who is neither borrower nor lender. The *tâ dien* (ten-ant) borrows from his landlord, the latter, if need arises, from a large capitalist; the coolie will establish credit with his foreman; the latter with his employer; the fisherman with the fisheries contractors; the small trader with the large merchant. Those with an independent calling, ar-tisans and officials, contract with the Chinese merchants or with the usurer.[42]

The situation in Tonkin is not very different. Gourou describes the lot of the Tonkin peasant as follows:

The Tonkin peasant is led to borrow by poverty; when he has exhausted his resources following a bad harvest, he has to borrow. . . . The inter-est on cash loans is extremely variable, generally ranging between 3 and 10% per month. The lender covers himself by a mortgage on the harvest, or goods of the borrower; for loans in kind, the interest paid, also in kind, varies from 30 to 50% for one rice-growing season; that is to say, from 60 to 100% per annum.[43]

Even in Cambodia, where conditions are more favorable, the absence of equitable credit institutions has rendered a tempting

40. Robequain, *op. cit.*, p. 193, indicates that French colonists shared in the money-lending practices of native landlords.
41. Gourou, *op. cit.*, Part III, 345–47. *Labour Conditions in Indo-China*, pp. 208 ff.
42. Gourou, pp. 344 ff.		43. *Ibid.*, p. 281.

opportunity for exploitation of the native farmers. The Chinese
trader generally takes a rate of 100 percent for a six to eight-month
loan. If the peasant does not repay on time, the Chinese creditor
takes the whole (surplus) of the harvest himself, pays the taxes, and
reduces the peasant to a form of peonage.[44]

Though the French authorities recognized very well the oppressed position of the heavily indebted Annamite peasant, they
still fought usury mainly by legal measures and, therefore, without
success.[45] Where they tried to combat it indirectly by providing
credit at moderate rates,[46] they also failed because they did not
reach the level of the most urgent need for money.

There have been different credit institutions in various parts of
Indo-China, but they have all been based more on government
guarantees rather than on their own resources. The losses were
generally met by the bank of issue. In Cochin-China, where property rights were better cleared by the more efficient surveying system, a regular agricultural credit system was maintained, in the
form of mutual credit societies. However, according to their regulations, loans could be granted only with land as security, and, the
credit activities, therefore, did not reach the level of the tenants.
Certainly, these institutions financed the extension of rice cultivation, but, at the same time, they fostered the process of land concentration. In addition, they gave the landlord the opportunity to
lend to distressed tenants and farmers, at exorbitant rates of inter-

44. *Ibid.*, pp. 386–87.
45. A decree of July 17, 1926, restricted the recourse to imprisonment for debt in
the case of commercial matters. The Decree of May, 1934, fixed the legal rate of interest at 5%, and the maximum rate by agreement at 8%. In order to circumvent eva-
sions of this law, the Decree of October 9 and December 2, 1936, required official wit-
nesses to private loan contracts and severe punishment for moneylenders violating
the Decree.
46. In Cochin-China, a mutual agricultural credit system has existed since 1910.
In 1936, the loans granted amounted to 8.5 million piastres, on a capital of around 1
million piastres; the rate of interest was restricted to 12% and later reduced to 10%.
A People's Agricultural Credit Scheme, as in the Netherlands Indies, was introduced
in Tonkin and Annam in 1926. Later, it was supplemented by a system of advances
on the security of agricultural land, as in Cochin-China, to administer the credits
granted to mutual aid societies set up under Annamite and Cambodian legislation.
A central supervising body, the Mutual Agricultural Credit Office, was established
in 1933. The system comprised a communal bank, provincial banks and a central
fund. The place of the communal banks was provisionally taken by communal committees of mandarins, whose activities in examining the loan applications were not
always advantageous for the bank. See *Labour Conditions in Indo-China*, pp. 211,
213 ff., Robequain, *op. cit.*, pp. 168 ff.

est, the money he had borrowed at cheap rates. On the whole, the credit system in Indo-China, though called a mutual credit system, did not ease the situation, but actually aggravated it by increasing the tenant farmer's need for credit.

In this connection it must be mentioned that the popular agricultural credit system in Annam and Tonkin also provided loans at a rate of 12 percent per annum on personal security or movable property, but the scale of these loans was limited, as they were granted only for periods up to 18 months and in amounts not exceeding 500 piastres. In 1939, loans were granted by 13 provincial banks up to a total of 2 million piastres. During the depression, however, the loans based on personal security and movable property decreased considerably, as the steady fall in the quotations for rice and other products reduced the borrower's capacity to give security.

The report on labor conditions in Indo-China[47] gives various reasons for the deficiencies in the French credit system: the excessive independence of the various organizations, the alarming discrepancy between the capital available and the loans granted, and especially the inability to reach the small producer. The system, though often called a mutual agricultural system, was actually based not on mutual aid but exclusively on government funds and guarantees. It cannot be considered a cooperative enterprise, as no joint risk was involved. Consequently, no cooperative spirit could develop.[48] As the small farmer is not in a position to save enough money to refund a loan, the government has to come to the rescue, and government control, instead of mutual supervision, therefore has dominated the credit system.

Pierre Pasquier, Governor-General of Indo-China, illustrated the defeat of the credit system in the following statement:

If only most of the loans had been granted directly to the needy *nhaqué* or the poverty-stricken *tâ dien!* The depressing fact is that the credit facilities so far granted have had no psychological or economic effects.

47. *Labour Conditions in Indo-China,* pp. 214 ff.
48. *Ibid.,* pp. 280 ff., is optimistic for the prospects of a future cooperative movement in Indo-China, as social traditions have created customs and institutions which might be considered as some sort of spontaneous cooperation (for instance, communal lands, mutual aid in connection with funerals, assistance in the case of floods, and so on). The Report emphasizes in this connection the old Annamite tax system; taxes are fixed as a lump sum for the whole village, which remains responsible for dividing it and collecting the individual taxes.

It has indeed proved almost impossible to bring these advances within the reach of the small farmer, the *tá dien* or *nhaqué,* except through the large or medium-scale landowners. . . . All the efforts made by my administrative officers to improve the situation of these poor people are therefore brought to naught; any attempt to lower the cost of production of rice by reducing the interest on loans is doomed to failure in advance. The large and medium-scale landowners charge a tremendous commission, equal to the difference between the interest charged on loans by the rural funds and the rates at which they lend money directly or which they charge for standing security. Their maleficent influence prevents any direct contact between the authorities and the rural masses.[49]

At the outbreak of the recent war, the peasants of Indo-China were in a helpless state of dependency. For years, they had been forced to approach the landlord or moneylender for advances, and always they had had to be at the disposal of their masters for laboring services of any kind; always indebted, they had no chance ever to repay the loans, and the accumulated rates of interest soon multiplied the capital debt.

Agriculture in Indo-China has gradually evolved . . . to a position in which there are two very distinct elements: on the one hand the large and medium-sized landowners—Annamite or French—who exercise their influence through the authority of the mandarins, the local councils and chambers of agriculture, etc., their associations, the press and the credit system; on the other hand the working masses: smallholders, tenant-farmers, share-farmers, wage earners, all more or less subject to the other group.[50]

LEVEL OF AGRICULTURAL CULTIVATION   More than in any other country in Southeast Asia, the most intensive application of human labor is still the essential way of land cultivation in Indo-China. Agricultural machinery is still unknown, and work animals are much less used than in Burma or Siam. Gourou reports the struggle for existence between man and his animal in the Tonkin delta,

49. *Ibid.,* p. 215. Address to the Grand Council of the Economic and Financial Interests of Indo-China, on November 25, 1931.

50. *Ibid.,* p. 193. The report asserts that, according to certain writers, the policy of the French administration that resulted in such unfavorable social conditions was partly carried through in order to win the upper class of the inhabitants for French rule.

where a laborer is paid 2 francs a day and a buffalo 4 francs.[51] This misproportion in the evaluation of human and animal labor is responsible for the typical Tonkin idyll, which shows the man working in the rice field while the buffalo is resting in a water hole. Cultivation in Indo-China is typically small-scale. The large estate owners are not in favor of large-scale farming, but prefer to use the most primitive methods of cultivation, with the tremendous amounts of labor involved, for the exploitation of the soil. Hereby the fact of excess population is partly concealed. Even the application of the most elementary technical methods would reveal the true extent of the existing excess of population. The surplus of labor in Tonkin is estimated at more than twice the amount of labor needed for cultivation of all arable land.[52]

The Annamite is skillful as a cultivator, but he is by experience deeply convinced of the worthlessness of his labor, and therefore does not even try to obtain high yields at low costs. This fatalistic attitude of the farming population blocks the way for agricultural progress and proves that agricultural improvements presume a certain capacity for economic calculation which is not reached on a level of ill-paid labor.[53]

The inferiority of the Annamite cultivation is largely due to lack of selection of seeds, inefficient agricultural equipment, and lack of fertilizer. This results in a low average yield and mediocre produce without any standardization.[54] The response of the world market is the low quotation for rice from Indo-China.

The French administration tried to raise agricultural standards by practical education, school gardens, and technical services for seed selection, cattle rearing, and other procedures. In 1929, a rice office was established to study and organize the rice cultivation of the country. Finally, an Institute of Agricultural Research was founded, dealing mainly with the crops of higher altitudes, such as tea, coffee, rubber, and cinchona. The endeavors of the administration, however, met with little success, since, under the given circum-

51. Gourou, op. cit., Part III, p. 241.
52. Labour Conditions in Indo-China, p. 219.
53. Gourou, op. cit., Part III, pp. 294–95.
54. In 1928, the yield per ha. was 12 quintal in Indo-China; in Java, 15; in Siam, 18; in Japan, 34. There is no justification for such a low output in Indo-China. See Labour Conditions in Indo-China, p. 204.

stances, the agricultural educational work was not coordinated with positive measures for the solution of the credit problem. For example, it is useless to explain proper methods of fertilizing so long as the price of fertilizer is beyond the economic capacity of the peasant and so long as credit at reasonable rates is unobtainable.[55]

Not even the public works initiated by the administration to increase the rice acreage and provide the fields with adequate water supply have been able to raise the general agricultural level of the colony. Nevertheless, these works were of great importance for Indo-China, especially for Cochin-China, where the rain is sufficient but not dependable and where even heavy rainfalls do not supply the uninterrupted flow of water which can be provided by irrigation.

The French were especially active in construction works in Cochin-China, where the problem was to reclaim new land. Here, French engineers greatly improved and extended the few canals dug by the Chinese and Annamites. In 1930 alone, about 165 million cubic meters of soil were excavated, and it can rightly be said that these dredging operations are among the great works in technical history.[56] They increased the rice acreage from 376,000 ha. in 1868 to 2.3 million ha. in 1940. In addition, the canals became essential communication lines between the different settlements in the region. The increase in the capital value of the soil was more than thrice the expenditures. Between 1880 and 1937, the value of the cultivated area in Cochin-China increased by 421 percent, the population by 267 percent, but the rice export from Saigon by as much as 545 percent.[57] However, the work is far from being completed. There are still no transverse canals between the principal arteries and the secondary and tertiary ones, small irrigation installations which the peasants themselves could easily construct if they had initiative. By means of transverse canals, the whole area could be drained and the tides regulated and used for irrigation or drainage of surplus water, according to requirements. Robequain asserts

55. Robequain, op. cit., p. 228. No official statistics are available regarding secondary crops, as for instance, corn, sweet potatoes, and beans. However, they do not seem to have considerable importance, with the exception of corn. See ibid., p. 230.

56. Labour Conditions in Indo-China, pp. 199 ff.

57. The rice exported from Saigon is virtually the crop of the new areas in Cochin-China. See also Robequain, op. cit., p. 220, and Labour Conditions in Indo-China, pp. 199 ff.

that only a small number of rice plantations along the main canals are actually benefited by the tidal changes in the water level.

In contrast with Cochin-China, the problem of the overpopulated Red River delta (Tonkin) has been to increase output.[58] The Red River has always had to be tamed by a system of dikes. However, the old Annamite dike system had many defects and time and again, the floods of the river broke through and caused starvation and famine. After one such disastrous flood in 1927, the French administration reconstructed the dikes and thus eliminated one of the main reasons for the recurrent periods of starvation in the Tonkin delta.

Another great problem for rice cultivation in Tonkin and Annam is drought. The rainfall in this region is very irregular and undependable, and droughts are not uncommon. In the thirties, the French administration began the construction of several giant irrigation works. The level of certain rivers was elevated by dams and water was led to the fields by a system of canals adjusted to the topography. An area of about 250,000 ha. is now fully irrigated, and schemes for irrigating an additional 500,000 ha. have been prepared. In Annam, dam and canal networks providing gravity irrigation for around 90,000 ha. have been constructed, and even in Cambodia similar projects have been completed. Since 1933, the average yield per hectare for a single yearly crop in Tonkin has been between 500 and 600 kilograms of paddy, but where irrigation has made possible the harvesting of two crops, the yield in the future may be increased to between 1,800 and 2,000 kilograms per hectare. Though the attainable increase of the rice output in the Tonkin delta is estimated at 300,000 tons annually, it is still doubtful whether the new irrigation system will pay because of disproportionately high expenses per hectare.[59]

The French administration considers the drainage and irrigation works as the main weapon in the war against poverty and misery in Indo-China. However, this is merely a technical weapon, while the real problem has broad economic and social implications. The indebted Tonkin and Cochin-China peasant can hardly be influenced by impressive engineering as long as his own economic problem is not solved. Robequain mentions the expected economic

58. *Labour Conditions in Indo-China*, pp. 201 ff.
59. *Labour Conditions in Indo-China*, pp. 202 ff.; Robequain, pp. 222 ff.

results of large-scale irrigation, but appeals at the same time to the Annamite farmer for cooperation. He maintains that the promised results are impossible if the peasants remain unwilling "to take the trouble to cultivate their rice fields properly." [60] But it may be doubtful if they will ever take this "trouble" under the existing system of land tenure. It is a fact that, in the last thirty years, the volume of rice production in Indo-China as a whole did not increase sufficiently to match the population increase (more than 40 percent). The average rice production in 1935–1940 was only 300,000 tons more (not even 10 percent) than the average of 1910–1915. This comparatively small increase can be explained by the low agricultural level of the distressed peasant, which counteracted the technical progress embodied in the construction works. For example, while the rubber plantations based on French capital and scientific research expanded and flourished, the cultivation of rice and other native crops, based mainly on native cultivation methods, remained stagnant.

LABOR   In countries like Indo-China, the position of labor is mainly decided by the general low level of living of the agricultural population. Consequently, progress through labor legislation can only be obtained when social conditions in general are improved at the same time. The importance of the laboring population in the social pattern of Indo-China can hardly be overestimated.

The special problem of labor in Indo-China is not alone the uneven distribution of population, but, equally, the demand for labor by the large rubber estates in the new provinces in the south. The rapid development of the large rubber investments has necessitated an early solution to the labor problem of the plantations. Still today, contract labor is the usual type of plantation labor in Cochin-China and Cambodia; it is not encountered in either Tonkin or Annam.

Until the slump, there was a phenomenal increase in the number of coolies imported to the south: 3,684 in 1925, 17,777 in 1926, and 18,000 in 1927. The planters were strong enough to keep the administration out of the recruiting business, which was in the hands of unscrupulous labor agents. Virginia Thompson [61] reports that

60. Robequain, op. cit., p. 227.
61. Virginia Thompson, French Indo-China, pp. 153 ff.

sorcery, the use of drugs, and gross misrepresentation of the labor contract by the agent have characterized labor hiring. The miserable coolie has often been forced to consent to what is really three years of slavery. Agents have earned up to 12 piastres for each coolie hired, many of whom later died on the malaria-infested plains of Cochin-China.[62] The coolie was completely at the mercy of the native foreman, or *cai*, who collected a commission on his wages and induced the coolie to borrow from him at excessive rates. He profiteered on food, medical supplies, and treatment. Brutalities resulting in wholesale desertion or suicides were frequently reported.[63] Often, the planters administered their own justice and police control, thus increasing the social tension on the plantations. The assassination of the head of the labor recruiting office on the eve of the Annamite New Year in 1929 revealed the feelings of the peasant against the labor situation in Indo-China. A letter was pinned to his body listing the crimes which had led to his execution.

This ruthless recruiting system soon aroused general resistance especially in Tonkin. Annamite nationalists successfully used the return of exhausted coolies in their fight against plantation capitalists. The northern provincial authorities supported their viewpoint on the ground that a large-scale exodus of labor would inevitably bring about a rise in labor costs.

The government, however, did not abolish direct recruiting, as requested by the Chamber of Agriculture in Tonkin and by Annamite nationalists, but introduced a system of authorized recruiting which forced plantation owners to state the real labor conditions under which the migrating workers would work.[64] Recruiting was permitted only in specified areas and by recognized agencies. Government medical examination and minute control in the ports of embarkation gave additional security against abuses. The workers remained continuously under medical supervision, and the employers were obligated to render substantial medical care.

The contracts had to be in accordance with standard contracts, guaranteeing a minimum of well-being to the immigrants: three

62. In 1927, the mortality on southern plantations was from 4 to 5 times as great as the average death rate.
63. Between Jan. 1, 1928, and June 30, 1928, more than 1,700 workers deserted, out of a total of 30,000 (*Labour Conditions in Indo-China*, p. 84).
64. Legislation dated Oct. 25, 1927, supplemented in 1928 and 1930.

years' employment, ten hours daily work, rest periods, wage regulation, provisions for women and children, and food rationing (700 grams dry rice per person). Furthermore, a compulsory deferred pay system (5 percent wage deduction) was introduced.

Supervision was in the hands of civil administrative authorities. However, no special labor inspectorate was established. The report of the International Labor Office [65] criticizes this omission and states that the administrative officer is generally uninterested and lacks the time to study labor conditions. His inspection is frequently unsatisfactory, and his relationship with the planters is "too intimate and too friendly" to permit him the independence of mind and decision which is often necessary. Moreover, his visits are announced in advance, thereby destroying some of their effectiveness.[66]

There can be no doubt, however, that government supervision of the recruiting system has had some results. Laborers have become interested in the plantation where part of their wages are deposited, and fewer, therefore, desert. But of greatest importance is the efficient malaria control in all public works projects supervised by the officials and doctors of the Pasteur Institute of Indo-China. The general assistance given by the Institute has largely eliminated the demoralizing influence of this disease. As a result of malaria control, plantations have reported that cases of unfitness for work have decreased by 20 to 30 percent and that the efficiency of labor has increased by 40 percent.[67] The mortality rate decreased from 5.4 percent in 1927 to 2.32 percent in 1930. This is still a very high death rate, in view of the fact that it involves persons in the prime of life who have passed three medical examinations.[68]

It is difficult to estimate fully the success of this labor legislation, since the recruiting of workers was stopped during the depression. Aside from this, however, it is a recognized fact that industrial prosperity generally worsens the health conditions among plantation workers. Mortality increases because the expansion of rubber plantations involves the most exhausting and dangerous work, namely the clearing of the brush. The depression eliminated this factor.

65. *Labour Conditions in Indo-China,* p. 268.   66. *Ibid.,* p. 264.
67. *Ibid.,* pp. 90–91; but the report stresses that the situation still necessitates increasing efforts. The number of cases of malaria treated increased from 43% of the average number of workers during the second half of 1933 to 57.9% in the first half of 1934.
68. *Ibid.,* p. 92.

Legislation concerning non-contract labor, of great importance for Tonkin and Annam, was first introduced in 1936. It was equally important for the plantations in central and south Annam and Laos, where there was a rather limited demand for labor, which easily could be supplied by the near-by overcrowded districts. In Indo-China, as in the Netherlands East Indies, contract labor has been the first target of labor legislation, as the system can be maintained only when a minimum of social security is guaranteed. The extension of effective labor legislation to the field of free labor is generally the second step.

The victory of the Popular Front in France (1936) brought about this broader social legislation. A wave of strikes rolled over Indo-China. Labor unions were established, and the country experienced, for the first time, an extensive social movement. The Decree of December 30, 1936, gave Indo-China a series of labor laws that granted fixed rates for non-contract agricultural or industrial labor. The Decree stipulated compulsory minimum wages, limited working hours, prohibition of fines, prohibition of night work for women and children, regulations for company stores, for health and safety, for labor inspection, and other similar items. Employers were, naturally, opposed to the introduction of these reforms, and, at times, the opposition was so strong that the enforcement of the laws had to be suspended, which however, automatically resulted in the rise of new radical reform movements. The report of the International Labor Office refers to this resistance of the employers with the words that "they do not seem prepared to admit that social protection should be considered, not as an optional charge depending on the margin of profit, but as a strict obligation for which allowance must be made in the initial calculations of any business." [69]

The social legislation, however, did not change the general situation of the day laborer, who still is subject to usury by the *cai*, the shopkeeper, or the professional moneylender. His position is particularly weak, as he is usually employed only one day out of every two.[70] Generally, he can pay off his debts by work, but for every dollar he borrows, he owes ten days of work, which would otherwise

69. *Labour Conditions in Indo-China*, pp. 134, 262, and especially p. 266. Robequain, *op. cit.*, p. 78.
70. Paul Bernard, *Le Problème Économique Indochinois*, pp. 23–24.

have brought him two dollars and fifty cents. He can also pay off his debt by putting to work one or more of his children, who are required to live with the creditor—a rudiment of slavery. It would take us too far afield to mention all the different methods of usury which are reported, some of which stipulate interest rates for petty loans varying from 240 percent to 3,650 percent per year.[71]

Wage reductions during the slump and the fight for reforms have frequently resulted in strikes and turbulent dissatisfaction. Plantations reported many incidents which in some cases led to bloodshed.[72]

Under the existing circumstances, the labor pattern in Indo-China can probably be changed only by a broad resettlement policy. Furthermore, the contract system, though it guarantees a higher level of social protection, should be abolished, as it considerably restricts the personal freedom of the laborers. Already before the war the colonial administration considered the contract system as merely a temporary arrangement and endeavored to develop a spontaneous migration that would gradually provide an adequate voluntary labor supply to the plantations in Cochin-China.[73] Some steps have been taken to settle workers in the vicinity of the plantations, but no statistics are available on the success of this plan. The Report of the International Labor Office recommends a closer approach to non-contract labor, without abandoning the benefits of contract labor.

LEVEL OF LIVING AND HEALTH CONDITIONS; INDIRECT TAXES   Annamite society today displays the typical features of a disintegrating native community—very similar to Java and other countries in Southeast Asia. The Annamite bourgeoisie is economically based on rice cultivation and moneylending—a typical basis for wealth in an area open to commercial agriculture but without adequate credit facilities. The growth of this upper class was paralleled by a corresponding increase in the agricultural proletariat, because its moneylending activities excluded the introduction of agricultural machinery even if this had been expedient from an economic point of view.[74] The proletariat in Indo-China increased considerably

71. Gourou, *op. cit.*, Part III, pp. 348–49.
72. *Labour Conditions in Indo-China*, pp. 148–49.   73. *Ibid.*, p. 264.
74. Robequain, *op. cit.*, p. 86.

under the French rule, though this development occurred "unwittingly and contrary to its own interests." [75]

The living conditions of this proletariat differ largely, depending on the place of the laborer in the economic pattern of the country. But the border lines are fluctuating, and the individual laborer has no stable existence. In spite of the general features of poverty and misery, there are considerable differences in the level of living of a peasant on his small plot in Cochin-China and of a Tonkin laborer contracted for three years' work on a rubber plantation, or of an occasional laborer in a coal mine near his village. It is hardly possible to evaluate them correctly by means of statistics. But the whole proletariat faces starvation if the harvest is bad or if an accident involves unforeseen expenses. [76]

In addition, the regional differences are important. The normal annual rice ration per person in Tonkin is only 136 kilograms, in comparison with an average of 250 kilograms for Indo-China as a whole. The Tonkin peasants are generally undernourished. Substitute products such as Indian corn and tubers allow them to subsist, but their conditions are miserable. [77] "Far too many children still die in infancy, not only on account of inadequate hygiene arrangements, but also because they are nursed by exhausted mothers . . . their bodies are often puny and stunted. The result of more abundant and more rational food may be seen in the healthy look of servants and soldiers, who are fed by the European." [78]

With regard to the relationship between wages and costs of living, the Report of the International Labor Office states that the fall recorded in the cost of living for the indigenous working class amounted to 20 percent from 1931 to 1933, while the fall in wages fluctuated only between 7 percent and 17 percent. However, the report eliminates the possibility that the purchasing power of wages actually was increased, by pointing to the basic fact that at no time, either in 1930 or in 1936, has the budget of an Annamite worker shown any surplus, and that it has always been impossible

75. *Ibid.*, pp. 85 ff.   76. Paul Bernard, *op. cit.*, p. 25.
77. *Labour Conditions in Indo-China*, pp. 218 ff.
78. Charles Robequain, *L'Indochine française* (Paris, 1935), p. 167. Virginia Thompson, *French Indo-China;* p. 149: They enjoy release from hunger only at harvest time.

for him to save anything. The cost of food alone accounts for three-fourths of his expenditures.[79]

The tenant farmer is hardly better off. Paul Bernard reports on the budget of a tenant cultivator family in western Cochin-China, with an area of 5 ha. and an annual consumption of 250 kilograms of rice per member. The budget is as of 1931, when the slump had not yet reached its lowest point. The expenditures, which are considered a strict minimum, amounted to 164 piastres, while the total income of the family, including extra money earned, amounted to only 154 piastres.[80]

Certainly, the times of death-dealing famines are long past, but the Annamite population is undernourished in many districts, especially in the north, and at more or less regular periods of the year. This causes reduced resistance against epidemics and a seasonal increase in the incidence of endemic diseases, especially malaria, which first of all affect the poorly nourished part of the population.[81] The Pasteur Institute of Indo-China and the government have doubtless made a remarkable effort in combating diseases by general and individual prophylaxis, and by improving the water supply. But here, as everywhere else, nutrition remains the basic problem for the generally poor health conditions. In Indo-China, it is primarily a question of quantity of food, and only secondarily is it a problem of quality. However, the quality problem also can be traced back to the state of poverty, because protein-rich items (meat, fish, and so on) are inaccessible without increased purchasing power.[82] This situation is clearly illustrated by the statistics on infant mortality. In 1936, the death rate for children under one year was 240 per thousand in Saigon, and 230 (1937, 210) in Hanoi. Though it has decreased considerably in the last decade, it is still very high.[83]

Public health in Indo-China was also affected by the French internal revenue system which was most undemocratic and contributed to the misery of the population. It was based on indirect taxes,

79. *Labour Conditions in Indo-China*, pp. 145 ff.
80. Paul Bernard, *op. cit.*, pp. 22–23.
81. League of Nations Health Organization, Intergovernmental Conferences of Far Eastern Countries on Rural Hygiene, 1937 Preparatory Papers, *Report of French Indo-China* (Geneva, 1937), pp. 92 ff.
82. *Ibid.*, pp. 95 ff.
83. *Annuaire Statistique de l'Indochine, 1936–37* (Hanoi, 1938), pp. 29–30.

which were intended to make the colony financially independent of France, which goal has been practically obtained.[84] In 1936, around 40 percent of the colonial revenues were still derived from indirect taxes and monopolies.[85] Administration of the monopolies was sabotaged by fraud, corruption, and inadequate profits, which caused terrific price increases. The Annamite village notables represented the most effective contrabandists, protected by their elevated position. Seen from the point of view of public health and nutrition, the monopolies had different effects. The opium monopoly kept the price of legal and illegal opium so high that it was unobtainable for the bulk of the rural population. Actually, only Chinese merchants and traders and well-to-do Annamites smoke opium, which consequently plays a very small part in the mental pathology of Indo-China.[86] The alcohol monopoly, though maintained only as a kind of sales monopoly, raised the price exorbitantly and burdened the narrow budget of the Annamite, who needs alcohol for religious rites. In the budget of 1936, an amount of about 5 million piastres appeared as consumption tax from alcohol.[87]

The salt monopoly was very poorly organized. Consumers had to pay both the French holding company for the concession, as well as the Chinese lessor, instead of only the Chinese producer, as had been customary in the past. With the introduction of the salt monopoly, prices were tripled. In addition, the provisioning of the interior of the country was very inadequate. In 1936, the salt monopoly added around 5 million piastres to the budget. Though the distribution of salt was improved later on, it was still inadequate in many parts of the interior before the war, and the inadequate

84. Paul Doumer, Governor-General from 1897 to 1902, put the colony on a paying basis by the introduction of a taxation system based largely on monopolies. He created a federal budget with indirect taxes and 5 local budgets from direct taxes. See Doumer, *Situation de l'Indochine* (Hanoi, 1902), p. 9. He practically established the Indochinese Union by the strong federal framework of reforms. However, the entire system of monopolies roused much opposition in France and Indo-China, especially in the case of the opium monopoly, which involved a great moral problem. It was subject to several reforms. On account of general political considerations, the distilling monopoly for Tonkin and Annam, which had contributed to large-scale corruption, finally was lifted, and free distilling by licensed companies and individuals was granted.

85. *Annuaire Statistique*, p. 262.

86. League of Nations Health Organization, *Report of French Indo-China*, pp. 127 ff.

87. *Annuaire Statistique*, p. 221.

consumption of salt affected the health of the natives, especially the children. Certainly, the monopoly system was not one of the main reasons for the poverty and misery of the native population, but it narrowed additionally the margin of their small budgets. It contributed much to discontent and was one of the major grievances of the Nationalist Party before the war.[88]

CONCLUSIONS   The economic and social status of Indo-China on the eve of World War II was delicate in more than one respect. Certainly, the outstanding technical contribution of the French colonial administration had eliminated periodical famine and conquered entire provinces for rice cultivation. But even this performance was unable to relieve the poverty and misery of the population, which itself increases proportionately to the advancing sanitary and medical control.

The still prevailing principle of "assimilated" economy—a clear formulation of economic dependence—must be considered responsible for the failure of the French administrative policy in the colony. It has kept the native population at a low level of agricultural development and tied to a system of production where human labor competes successfully with animal labor. By neglecting the economic and social progress of the population, the economic effects of the technical advance were crippled. The conditions in the country were determined by land scarcity in the north, landlordism in the south, and the unsolved credit problem generally.

It is to the credit of French students that their statements strongly reflect the state of social distress and human misery in the French colony. The manifold contradictions in economic and social developments have indeed revealed "that there is something radically wrong with a system which to an ever greater extent imposes Western economic methods and increased requirements on the Indo-Chinese worker, but which at the same time tends to result in a constant reduction of his purchasing power." [89] In the last years before the war, the numerous landless proletariat which had grown up as a result of the overpopulation in the Tonkin area and of the land concentration in Cochin-China constituted a social danger.[90] It

88. Virginia Thompson, *French Indo-China*, pp. 182 ff., 188–91.
89. *Labour Conditions in Indo-China*, p. 148.   90. *Ibid.*, p. 193.

was possible to control the floods of the Red and Mekong rivers, but it proved to be impossible to make productive use of the abundance of human labor, which would have improved the general level of living.

Indo-China, with its uneven distribution of population, has some similarities with the Netherlands East Indies. Indeed, if we compare Tonkin with Java, and Cochin-China with the Outer Provinces, we find similar problems of excess population, minute subdivisions of land, native village economy on one side, and the problem of migrating labor on the other. We also meet the social and psychological problem of transferring the excess population from the overcrowded provinces to newer, less populated land, and even the same restraints and difficulties. However, while the problem in the Netherlands East Indies seems too large to control, the far smaller proportions in Indo-China suggest a practical solution. Its population problem could be solved by an extensive land settlement scheme, well-financed and efficiently organized. As the report on *Labour Conditions in Indo-China* says:

Money is necessary to set up a central settlement organization and maintain a staff of specialized local officials; money is necessary for the transport of the emigrants; money is necessary for the preliminary surveys, for the construction of villages and the making of roads, for clearing and drainage, and for the advances of rice and cash which must be granted to the settlers. The aggregate of all these sums may well be some hundreds of millions of piastres. . . . Land settlement in Indo-China would therefore seem to be essentially a matter of credits.[91]

Cooperative organizations, properly adjusted to Annamite customs and way of thinking will ease the process of large-scale settlements.[92]

91. *Ibid.*, p. 279.
92. The French administration realized very well the necessity of organized migration for the population of the Tonkin area, but was never able to dispose of amounts sufficient for even limited action.

Resettlement experiments during the first 30 years of French administration were frustrated, as the Annamite peasant did not respond to the call for individual migration. He was restrained by attachment to his native village and the ancestral rice fields, and by religious and superstitious prejudices. Therefore, the French changed to a policy of collective migration, which could more easily overcome a part of the psychological handicaps. Finally, in 1937, they started the transfer of 500 families to the province of Rach-Gia, where two villages were to be established. There were also some large-scale programs, for instance, the settlement of 50,000 Tonkin families

A reconstruction of Indo-China's economic and social life is as much a psychological as an economic problem. Resettlement policy will have to be coordinated with a serious endeavor to develop the productive forces of the population without any consideration for an "assimilated" policy. It will have to introduce a higher valuation of human labor, based on adequate education and training. However, colonial history in Indo-China indicates that this can hardly be achieved without basic political and economic changes.

Developments in the postwar period have not yet disclosed a solution to the political and economic problems. Immediately upon the end of hostilities in the Pacific, the Annamite Republic, *Viet Nam,* was declared (September 2, 1945), and was at once attacked by France. But, on March 6, 1946, France was forced to recognize Viet Nam and drew up a plan according to which an Indo-Chinese Federation was to be established within a French Commonwealth. This Federation was to consist of the free and independent Viet Nam, composed of Tonkin, Annam, and Cochin-China, and the constitutional monarchies Cambodia and Laos, which are more or less controlled by France. But the great French interests in Cochin-China resented such a solution. Consequently, Franch recognized only Tonkin and Annam as belonging to Viet Nam, while Cochin-China was established as a separate republic which by a popular referendum should decide for or against joining Viet Nam.

Viet Nam, however, is not willing to accept the possible exclusion of Cochin-China, the natural outlet for overpopulated Tonkin and Annam. Therefore, it reacted vehemently against the French ad-

---

in the Transbassac. However, these plans never went beyond the initial stage, mainly because of lack of funds.

In addition, migration to the southern plains is a very complicated problem. The Cochin-Chinese dislike the Annamite mass migration. Though the land is lying waste today, they are afraid of land scarcity 50 years ahead at the present rate of population increase and land concentration. The Annamite, on the other hand, is afraid of a rice cultivation different from the one he was accustomed to in Tonkin.

Meeting these objections, the government recommended "select" or "model" colonies and asked the big landowners of Indochina to establish colonies of Tonkin laborers on their property. However, this kind of settlement will hardly solve the population problem, and will not contribute to the establishment of an independent labor and farmer class.

See *Labour Conditions in Indo-China,* pp. 222 ff.; Robequain, *op. cit.,* p. 64. The former, p. 238, asserts that a real, large-scale immigration from Tonkin can succeed only if the adequate psychological conditions are established (for instance, retaining of the Annamite's share in the communal property in their native village for a transitional time).

ministration for postponing the planned popular referendum in Cochin-China until "order is restored," and is skeptical that Cochin-China will ever be given the opportunity of an honest plebiscite.

But, this is not the only reason for disagreement between France and Viet Nam. Viet Nam does not want French leadership in matters of defense and foreign affairs and is not satisfied with the status, offered by France, of merely administrative autonomy. Consequently, it rejected the French proposals in September, 1947. France then refused to negotiate with the legal government of Viet Nam and tried to reach an agreement with Bao Dai,[93] the former Emperor of Annam, thus once more attempting to maintain French influence and securing French economic interests by indirect rule.

Since December, 1946, an actual state of war has existed between France and Viet Nam. However, while the French armies secured the highways and occupied the cities, many thousands of villagers have deserted their rice fields and are fighting as guerrillas. This has brought about a paralysis of the entire economic life and has postponed the urgently needed political and economic reorganization of the country and the rehabilitation of its distressed population.

93. Bao Dai abdicated in August, 1945. He has a good nationalist record. He was first Councillor to the President of Viet Nam and later a member of the legislative assembly. During the new conflict with France, however, he detached himself more and more from the government of Viet Nam and might now be ready for greater concessions both politically and economically.

6

The Philippines

INTRODUCTION The economic, social and political development of the Philippine Islands is unusual when compared with that in other countries of Southeast Asia. Under Western control for almost four hundred years, the population has become Christian by faith with the exception of the Mohammedan Moros and some isolated mountain tribes. For the people of the Islands, Western culture and economic influence have become identical with national history and but little has remained of oriental traditions and customs. The Philippines, therefore, are highly susceptible to the influx of Western education and culture and to the transplantation of Occidental economic and political ideas.

Spain brought the Christian faith and the Church to the people of the Islands. It also brought suppression and exploitation, but created at the same time the basis for national consciousness. A gradually growing movement of resistance spread from island to island and brought the various tribes and groups into contact with each other. They learned to act together, and to think in national terms. Then America added the technical and spiritual means for a national development by an extensive cultural, economic, and political education.

While American business in the Philippines more or less followed the road of typical colonial penetration, American administrators and educators wholeheartedly devoted themselves to establishing the foundations of a modern Philippine Commonwealth by training Filipinos in adminstrative methods and teaching them the principles of democracy. This experiment in political engineering had to be based on the existing semifeudal economic and social structure of the Islands, which was maintained and not changed by American policy. Thus the political problem remained intimately connected with the basic agrarian factors.

During recent decades the Filipinos have enjoyed a privileged position among the Western-penetrated areas of Southeast Asia. To an ever-increasing extent they have participated in the development and administration of their own country. They were the only dependent nation in the Far East, certain of achieving political independence; it was granted to them on July 4, 1946. Therefore, they lost some of the mental characteristics of a dependent nation and learned, at least politically, to speak the language of the West.

The basic structure of the Islands, however, was not essentially influenced by this process. The Philippines, for centuries a Spanish colony, retained under American control the typical features of economic dependence. Reciprocal free trade, subject only to minor restrictions, was instituted between the United States and the Philippines by the provisions of the United States Tariff Act and the Philippine Tariff Act, both dated August 5, 1909.[1] These regulations became the basis for almost complete economic dependence on the American market and for the highly protected position of American imports into the Islands.

At the beginning of the twentieth century, shortly after the American occupation, more than 80 percent of the Philippine exports went to Europe and Asia, and only 13 percent to the United States, while in 1940 more than 80 percent of the total exports was directed to America. In the same year American products constituted 80 percent of the total imports. America's economic position in the Islands remained unchanged after the establishment of the Commonwealth in 1935. The Independence Law (H.R. 8573) did not grant Filipinos the right to conduct independent trade negotiations or to contract loans in foreign countries without the approval of the President of the United States.

In 1940, the total exports of the Islands amounted to 305 million pesos (1.00 peso = U.S. $0.50) of which 258 million pesos' worth of

1. The so-called Payne-Aldrich Tariff Act. It provided for free trade between the United States and the Philippine Islands with certain limitations. In the first year after the passage of the Act the total Philippine trade with the United States rose by 40%. The Law was opposed vehemently by the Philippine National Assembly which feared the political consequences of a too intimate economic cooperation which might lead to economic dependence on the United States.

products went to the United States. The biggest export item was sugar, with about 900,000 tons valued at almost 95 million pesos. Next followed coconut products, 50 million pesos; Manila hemp, 30 million; and tobacco, 10 million. More than any other industry in the Islands, the sugar industry was based on a preferential position in the American market, secured by the free trade relationship. Philippine sugar has no other market.

In 1940 American exports to the Philippines amounted to 210 million pesos. They consisted mainly of technical equipment for Philippine export industries such as iron and steel products, machinery and trucks, but provided also the majority of the general consumption goods, especially cotton material and cigarettes, thus practically preventing the growth of an extensive Philippine consumption industry. The Philippines have almost exclusively small-scale and household manufacturing, in addition to important processing and mining industries. After the establishment of the Commonwealth the National Development Company, owned by the Philippine government, endeavored to develop a cotton-textile industry. Modern spinning and weaving mills were established, but their output remained low compared to the needs of the home market.

After the war, Philippine exports began to recover much faster than was anticipated, thanks to the high postwar world prices for copra. Already in 1946 the export of copra amounted to 78 million pesos, while the figures for the export of abaca and tobacco were only 9.6 and 2.5 million pesos, respectively. Sugar was not yet listed among the items exported in 1946; substantial production reaching prewar levels cannot be expected until 1949–50. The greater part of the exports went to the United States (valued at 75.3 million pesos out of a total export of 106 million pesos). The total imports in 1946 amounted to 590 million pesos, of which goods to the value of 515 million pesos came from the United States.[2]

The economic setup always showed the features of a dependent economy; the Islands have to pay for their imported foodstuffs and ready-made goods by a large-scale export of commercial crops and are, consequently, hindered in establishing a diversified economy.

During the period of American control, an almost uninterrupted

2. Philippine Bureau of Census and Statistics, Manila, 1947.

chain of investigations and hearings, missions and commissions [3] were set up to study trade relations, and the impact which the approaching political independence, involving the elimination of the free-trade relationship, might have on the economic status of the Islands and upon American investments there. Political relations between the United States and the Philippines long ago lost the glamor of political imperialism and have been reduced to a problem of economic adjustment. The general economic unpreparedness for independence, the future position of the Philippine export industries on the American market, the diverging interests of competitive American groups and the necessity for a period of gradual adjustment are the substance of hearings on the different bills for independence. Until the outbreak of the war in the Pacific, Filipino political leaders placed chief emphasis on full and complete political independence, while after the war they frequently stressed the priority of the economic aspects of the problem. The frank and open discussions in Congress on the future of the Islands added much to an understanding of the basic problems of economic dependence in general, and of the implications of political and eco-

3. Hearings before the Committee on Territories and Insular Possessions (now the Committee on Insular Affairs), Senate: Philippine Independence, Hearing on S. 912, Providing for Withdrawal of the U.S. from the Philippine Islands, Feb. 11–March 2, 1924, Washington, 1924. Independence for Philippine Islands, Hearings on S. 204, S. 3108, S.I. Res. 113, S. Res. 199, S. 3379, S. 3822, June 15–March 10, 1930, Washington, 1930. Independence for Philippine Islands, Hearings on S. 3377, Feb. 11 and 13, 1932, Washington, 1932 (including Hearings before House Committee on H.R. 7233, Jan. 22–Feb. 12, 1932). Complete Independence of Philippine Islands, Hearings on S. 1028, Feb. 16–March 15, 1939, Washington, 1939.
Hearings before the Committee on Insular Affairs, House, Philippine Independence Hearings on H.I. Res. 131, H.R. 3924, H.I. Res. 127, H.R. 2817, Feb. 17 and 25, 1924, Washington, 1924. Philippine Local Autonomy Hearings on H.R. 8856, Apr. 30–May 5, 1924, Washington, 1924. Independence for the Philippine Islands, Hearings on H.R. 5182, May 5 and 6, 1930, Washington, 1930. Hearings on S. 204, S. Res. 199 to Investigate Feasibility of Tariff Autonomy of Philippine Islands, Washington, 1930. Further report to S. 3822 (submitted by Mr. Hawes), Washington, 1930. Philippine Independence, H.R. 8573 and Report to Accompany H.R. 8573 to Provide for Complete Independence of Philippine Islands, Submitted by Mr. McDuffie, March 13, 1934, Washington, 1934.
Hearings before the Committee on Ways and Means, House: Philippine Trade Act of 1945, Hearings on H.R. 4185, H.R. 4676, H.R. 5185, October 15–19, November 14, 15, 1945; February 15 and March 15, 1946, Washington, 1945.
Hearings before the Committee on Finance, Senate: Philippine Trade Act of 1946 on H.R. 5856, April 2, 3, 4, and 5, 1946, Washington, 1946.
See also Joint Preparatory Committee on Philippine Affairs, Report of May 20, 1938, Parts I, II, III, Washington, 1938. The present study is based partly on the mentioned protocols and reports.

nomic independence. The hearings revealed the intimate connection between foreign trade, land utilization, and levels of living on the one hand, and the importance of a diversified economy for the status of political independence on the other.

FOREIGN INVESTMENTS   Foreign capital maintains a strong position in the Islands. Its share is even greater than the statistics suggest, since a considerable part of the Spanish capital in recent years became listed as Filipino capital when some leading Spanish families acquired Filipino citizenship.

American investments are very important in the Philippine economy, although they are not large in relation to other American investments abroad. An estimate in 1943 of an American economic stake of 200 million dollars (1 percent of total United States investments in the world and only 25 percent of those in Southeast Asia) is fairly correct.[4] For the year ending December 31, 1939, United States holdings of Philippine government and government guaranteed bonds were $37.5 million. Direct American investments [5] of approximately $165 million were placed in key economic positions. They were greatest (25 percent) in the mining industries; [6] 20 percent was invested in public utilities, almost 15 percent in sugar centrals, 12 percent in plantations, and the remainder in lumber and coconut industries, in general manufacturing and engineering companies and embroidery.

The type of investments rather than the actual amount is the strength of American capital in the Islands. To a considerable extent it controls the sugar mills and other processing industries based on agricultural products. The investments in the sugar industry, by some estimated at $22.5 million, by others at $30.6 million, con-

4. Helmut G. Callis, *Foreign Capital in Southeast Asia* (New York, 1942), pp. 16 ff.; see also his, "Capital Investment in Southeast Asia and in the Philippines," *The Annals* (March, 1943), pp. 22 ff. Both studies are based on estimates of the U.S. Tariff Commission of 1937 (Philippine Trade Report, No. 118, 1937, pp. 189 ff.). Ona K. D. Ringwood, "Some Statistics on the Philippines," *Foreign Policy Reports*, Oct. 1, 1945, however, gives a higher estimate, $258 million, probably based on the figures of the Bureau of Insular Affairs.

5. Including the investments of American citizens permanently residing in the Islands.

6. Callis estimated American investments in mining (June, 1935) at around $38 million. More recent statistics estimate American mining investments as high as $70 million.

trolled about one-third of the sugar centrals. United States capital also had a strong hold in the processing of coconuts.

The Spanish share in Philippine economy is still considerable and has outlived Spain's political rule. Direct Spanish investments are estimated at $90 million [7] but might be even larger. Spanish capital is invested mainly in sugar and coconut plantations, but also in industries related to the processing of sugar (about $20 million) and tobacco. Based on this economic position, the Spaniards retained a disproportionately strong political influence, even during the American period. Their social concepts, derived from Spanish feudalistic traditions, became the general pattern of the Filipino upper class.

Aside from American and Spanish capital, the only other Western investments worth mentioning are those of the British (with $45 million in 1935) who have a strong position in the Manila Railroad Company.

Chinese capital is a very influential factor. It was estimated conservatively at $100 million of which some 25 percent is invested in retail trade. More than 75 percent of the 2,500 rice mills in the Islands are owned by Chinese, who dominate the rice trade and also control 10 percent of the capital invested in the lumber industry. They are prominent in warehousing, shoemaking, cordage, soap manufacturing, and the processing of coconuts, and have a strong hold over the trade in gold. Unlike other foreign capital in the Philippines, Chinese capital is not imported but is acquired in the Islands. Japanese capital was eliminated by the war. It was estimated at $25 to $30 million, invested mainly in abaca (hemp) cultivation in the Davao province in Mindanao and in retail business all over the Islands.

POPULATION AND LAND UTILIZATION   According to the latest census of 1939, the total population of the Philippine Islands was about 16 million; today it is estimated at more than 18 million. In 1939, the number of births totaled about 600,000 and the number of deaths not quite half this figure. Between the census years of 1918 and 1939, the average annual population increase was 2.2 percent.[8]

7. Callis, *Foreign Capital in Southeast Asia*, p. 22.
8. The statistical data in this and the following chapters are taken mainly from the *Census of the Philippines, 1939,* Commonwealth of the Philippines, Commission of

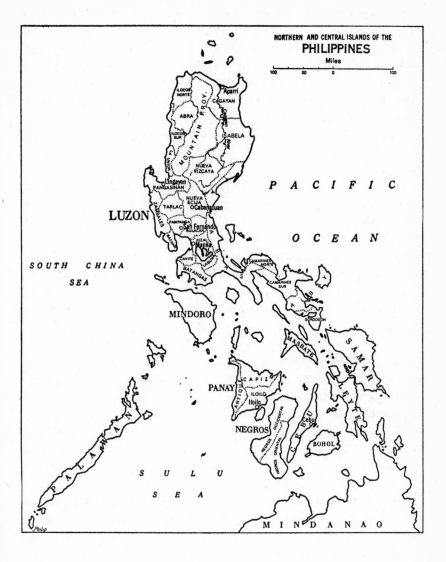

NORTHERN AND CENTRAL ISLANDS OF THE
PHILIPPINES
Miles
100   50   0   100

ILOCOS
NORTE
Aparri
CAGAYAN
ABRA
ILOCOS
SUR
ISABELA
M O U N T A I N   P R O V.
NUEVA
VIZCAYA
Lingayen
PANGASINAN
NUEVA
ECIJA
TARLAC
Cabanatuan
PAMPANGA
San Fernando
RIZAL
Manila
CAVITE
BATANGAS
CAMARINES
NORTE
CAMARINES
SUR
SORSOGON

LUZON

P A C I F I C

O C E A N

SOUTH   CHINA
SEA

MINDORO

MASBATE

SAMAR

LEYTE

PANAY
CAPIZ
ANTIQUE
ILOILO
Iloilo

NEGROS
Cebu
C E B U
NEGROS OCCIDENTAL
NEGROS ORIENTAL
BOHOL

P A L A W A N

S U L U
S E A

M I N D A N A O

According to recent statistics (July 1, 1941) the population density is estimated at 147 persons per square mile. The population, however, is unevenly distributed.[9] The coastal plains of Luzon and Cebu are generally overcrowded, while Mindanao and other of the larger islands in the south are sparsely populated. The maldistribution can best be illustrated by comparing the density figures for some of the main provinces on Luzon with the central and southern islands: in the province of Laguna there are 601 inhabitants per square mile; in Cavite, 480; in Pampanga, 454; in Bulacan, 326; in Nueva Ecija, 197; and in Nueva Vizcaya, bordering Nueva Ecija, only 30. On the island of Cebu there are 568 people per square mile; on Panay, 363; on Bohol, 312; whereas in the province of Davao on Mindanao, the figure is 39, in Cotabato 34, and on the forest covered island of Palawan, only 16. In 1939, the nutrition density was 1,052 persons per square mile on an average, but was much higher in some provinces, as in Ilocos Sur where it was 2,091; in Ilocos Norte, 1,733; and in Cebu, 1,995 persons. More than 70 percent of the Filipinos live in rural areas and are engaged in farming. But only the smaller part of the agricultural population till their own soil. By far, the largest number work as tenants or hired farm labor.

The influence of foreigners is exceedingly strong, though they number only 1 percent of the total population. More than two-thirds of them (about 120,000) are Chinese. Among the white communities the most important are the American and the Spanish (before the war with 9,000 and 5,000 members, respectively). The economic and political influence of these groups, however, is far greater than the modest figures suggest. Since the establishment of the Commonwealth an increasing number of Spaniards have taken out Philippine citizenship without giving up their prerogatives. Spanish and Chinese mestizos constitute an influential extension of the foreign community into the political and economic life of the Islands.

The 7,000 islands of the Philippine Archipelago comprise a land

the Census (Manila, 1940–41); the Yearbook of Philippine Statistics, Commonwealth of the Philippines (Manila, 1941), and other official sources.

9. Reginald G. Hainsworth and Raymond T. Moyer, Agricultural Geography of the Philippine Islands, a Graphic Summary (U.S. Dept. of Agriculture, Office of Foreign Agricultural Relations, Washington, December, 1945).

area of 114,800 square miles. About 55 percent is still covered by forest, about 18 percent is grass and open land, while only 23 percent (about 6.5 million ha.) is farm land, of which 59 percent was under cultivation in 1939. The cultivated land, as defined by the Philippine Census, includes not only the field-crop area but also the area planted with coconut, fruit and nut trees, amounting to 16 percent of the total land area of the Islands. According to an estimate of the Bureau of Forestry [10] a permanent forest of only about 11 million ha. is needed to maintain a balanced soil cover, which leaves more than 18.5 million ha. as an alienable and disposable area, of which more than 16 million ha. is considered arable. This figure reveals the vastness of potential agricultural land, located mainly on the undeveloped islands of Mindanao, Leyte, Samar, Mindoro, Palawan and South Luzon.

Rice is the main crop; in 1938, 1.82 million hectares or 38.4 percent of the total crop area was planted with it. The area has almost doubled since 1910, and has thus kept pace with the increase of population. However, the Philippines are not self-sufficient in rice, even though it is the staple food of the population. In an average year, during the period from 1936 to 1939, about 64,000 metric tons of cleaned rice were imported from China and Saigon, representing about 10 percent of the amount consumed. In the last five years before the war, rice cultivation was declining. It decreased from a maximum of 2.05 million hectares in 1935–36 to 1.9 million in 1937–38.[11]

While the rice area decreased, the corn area was expanded considerably, indicating that corn—an essential part of the diet in several parts of the Islands—has become an acceptable substitute. Between 1934 and 1938 the corn area increased by 40 percent and by 1938 comprised about 810,000 hectares, about half the area cultivated in rice.

Before the war only 55 percent of the cultivated land was used for the growing of subsistence crops, while more than 1.6 million hectares (34.7 percent) of the remaining acreage was planted mainly with export crops and showed a clear tendency toward expansion.

10. Karl J. Pelzer, *Population and Land Utilization* (New York, 1941), p. 127.
11. V. D. Wickizer and M. K. Bennett, *The Rice Economy of Monsoon Asia* (Palo Alto, Calif., 1941), Appendix, Tables I and IV B.

Coconuts had the largest share in the export crop area with 1.3 million hectares, then followed abaca with 291,000, sugar cane with 230,800, and tobacco with 58,700 hectares. There is little doubt that the cultivation of subsistence crops is inadequate to meet the needs of a growing Filipino population. In the Philippines, as elsewhere in Southeast Asia (although not to the same extent as in Malaya), export crops have been developed at the expense of subsistence farming. Free trade relations with the United States have determined the pattern of land utilization which favored the cultivation of export crops.

SIZE OF FARMS AND LEVEL OF AGRICULTURAL CULTIVATION   The great majority of Filipino farms are small. More than half are of less than 2 ha. and of these almost half are less than one hectare. Only 31 percent of the holdings are larger than 3 ha.[12] However, the figures vary considerably from province to province; in the densely populated Ilocos provinces and on Cebu about 50 percent of the holdings are smaller than one hectare. The small farm is most frequently found in the sugar provinces. In Pampanga, 20 percent are less than 1.5 ha., in Negros Occidentale more than 40 percent, and in Negros Orientale, almost 70 percent. In the province of Nueva Ecija, the rice granary of the Islands, the holdings are somewhat larger; about half are between 1 and 2.9 ha.

The tenant operated farm is generally somewhat larger. In 1939 the average was 2.88 ha., of which the tenant, however, was able to cultivate only 2.22 ha, on the average.[13] More than half of the share tenants, about 54 percent, had farms of less than 2 ha. Tenant cultivation is still at a very low stage of development in spite of the efforts of American controlled institutions and in spite of similar efforts carried on by the Commonwealth. But, as in other countries of this area, the rigid tenure system, combined with the effects of indebtedness and usury, blocks the way of agricultural progress among the majority of the peasants.[14] The level of Philippine agriculture is almost precapitalistic and lacks modern organi-

12. *Census of the Philippines, 1939*, Vol. II.
13. Karl J. Pelzer, *Pioneer Settlement in the Asiatic Tropics* (New York, 1945), p. 96.
14. Owen L. Dawson, "Philippine Agriculture, a Problem of Adjustment," *Foreign Agriculture*, Vol. 4 (Washington, 1940), pp. 383 ff., especially p. 395. Dawson asserts that progressive effort is poorer than in Java, and somewhat better than in Japan.

zation of production with the exception of some sugar-producing districts located near modern sugar centrals, as on Negros. Here modern machinery and efficient organization of production have been introduced, and wage labor (not tenant labor) is utilized almost exclusively. With the exception of sugar, the exports of the Islands have been produced by methods handed down through the years and adaptable only to a modest subsistence economy.[15]

Most of the rice lands yield only one crop per year and lie idle during the dry season. Double cropping is practiced only on 6 to 8 percent of the total crop area. Where effective irrigation has been introduced, however, double cropping is frequently found. This is especially true in the corn region of Cebu. Extension of the irrigation system is, therefore, one of the most important tasks in the reconstruction and development of Philippine agriculture.[16]

Irrigation works in the Islands are very limited. The Filipino farmer is still dependent on rainfall, and existing irrigation canals have only a supplementary effect. In the early 1930s no more than 300,000 ha. were irrigated by public or private systems. As late as 1938 the system operated by the Bureau of Public Works served only 75,000 ha. The census of 1939 mentions an irrigated area of 670,000 ha. of which 370,000 ha. were watered by primitive systems constructed by peasants.[17] In other words, almost 60 percent of the lowland rice area (around 1.5 million ha.) depends exclusively on rain for irrigation and only 20 percent has an adequate technical irrigation system.

The average yield of rice per hectare is 23 cavans,[18] almost one-third below that of Siam and Burma. Only Indo-China has a lower yield. This unfavorable output may be traced not so much to natural conditions but rather to the absence of crop rotation, the poor selection of seed, lack of irrigation, and the use of obsolete cultivating methods.[19] In some provinces, however, results have been somewhat better. In Nueva Ecija the average yield of lowland and upland rice was 38 cavans per ha. and in Bulacan 30 cavans.

15. James S. Allen, "Agrarian Tendencies in the Philippines," *Pacific Affairs,* XI (March, 1938), 55.
16. Pelzer, *Land Utilization,* p. 128, reports that in 1938, 44,000 ha. of rice, and 190,000 ha. of corn, out of 4.4 million ha., were planted more than once.
17. Pelzer, *Pioneer Settlement,* pp. 52–54.   18. One cavan equals about 44 kg.
19. Wickizer and Bennett, *op. cit.,* p. 62.

LAND TENURE   For centuries large estates have played an important role in Philippine economy and society. Spanish rule fostered and developed a powerful landowner class (*cacique*) which even today holds the whip hand over a dissatisfied class of dependent tenants (*taos*). The Spaniards intermarried with this upper class and in the course of time there developed a kind of feudal nobility, which still dominates the political life of the Islands.[20] Its members have been able to retain economic and political power even under American control, as they represented the only Filipino group which had administrative abilities based on education. Consequently, most of the advantages associated with the American regime have accrued to this group. As the landlords controlled the economic and political life of the Islands at the time of the coming of the Americans, their cooperation became one of the most important factors for the American administration; and in the course of time they have gradually replaced the American authorities.

Economic development under American control was on the whole favorable for the large estates,[21] although the American administration had liquidated the immense holdings of the Church and had encouraged the homesteading of public lands.[22] Indeed,

20. Pelzer, *Pioneer Settlement in the Asiatic Tropics*, pp. 88 ff., gives an excellent historical survey of the development of the upper class in the Philippines. The Spaniards governed the country from the beginning of the seventeenth century (after reorganization of the first colonial administration) by colonial government officials, who in the sphere of politics took the place of the *datos*, the village chiefs of the pre-Spanish days. The families from whom these officials were drawn constituted the aristocracy and enjoyed special political and social privileges. The Spaniards termed the *datos* or other leading families of the community "cacique" or chief, a term imported from Haiti. They favored these families, gave them the privileges of tax collecting, which included the opportunity of acquiring more and more land, and actually the capacity of changing freeholders into tenants.

21. *Ibid.*, p. 88.

22. The short-lived Malolos government of the Philippine revolution in 1898 had confiscated the estates of the Friars and actually established small independent farms which could not be contested without new bloodshed. When the Americans won control over the Islands they wanted to legalize this development and after long and difficult negotiations between Governor Taft and the Vatican (1902) succeeded in transfering the properties of the Friars to the Philippine administration; 165,000 ha. with more than 60,000 tenants were purchased for $7,239,000, which became part of the public debt of the Islands. The land was later divided and sold mostly to the previous tenants. However, the rate of interest was relatively high, 8 percent annually for 25 years, and certainly more than the poor beginners could pay without adequate credit facilities. Consequently, the land was gradually absorbed by large landowners, and partly again by the Church. This policy did not contribute to the solution of the agrarian problem as much as was expected, but only relieved

between 1903 and 1918, the number of farms in the Islands increased from 815,000 to 1,955,000,[23] a result of a vigorous campaign for the acquisition and settling of homesteads. The increase, however, proved to be only of temporary character. The Census of 1939 reports only 1,635,000 farms in 1938, showing a decrease of 320,000 or 16.4 percent of the 1918 number. The serious impact of this development becomes clear when one considers the large population increase of from 10 to 16 million during the same period. At the same time the number of farms operated by the owners decreased from 1,520,000 in 1918 to 805,000 in 1938, while the number operated by tenants increased from 435,000 to 575,000, not including the 255,000 part owners, whose social status does not differ greatly from that of the tenants.[24] The majority of former owner-cultivators were forced to join the agricultural workers or wage earners, a group totaling almost 3.5 million in 1939, of whom 3 million were male workers. As late as 1941, High Commissioner F. B. Sayre mentioned in an official report [25] that the number of landless families in the rural districts was increasing rapidly.

In the last decade the expansion of the large estates and their growing influence has been characteristic of the agricultural pattern of the Islands, especially in the sugar provinces, where capital was most concentrated. In Tarlac, an important sugar province on Luzon, the Luisita estate with 24,000 ha. owned by the Spanish company, Tabacalera, controls the Tarlac sugar central and through it the entire economy of the province. Small land ownership is decreasing much faster than the land register reveals. Tillers of small holdings, hopelessly indebted, become tenants in the economic sense, although they are still registered as proprietors. Large estate owners, control their land and pay the land tax.[26]

the political and social difficulties of the Church. In recent decades the Church and Friar orders have bought considerable estates and are again among the biggest landowners in the country. The Church estates actually provided the ground for recurring conflicts in Philippine agriculture. See James S. Allen, op. cit., pp. 52 ff.

23. Census of the Philippine Islands 1903 (Washington, 1905), Vol. IV; ibid., 1918 (Manila, 1921), Vol. III.

24. The part owner is unable to make a living out of his own land and is therefore forced to lease other land. 15 percent of all farms in the Islands are operated by part owners

25. Fifth Annual Report of the United States High Commissioner to the Philippine Islands to the President and Congress of the United States (Washington, 1941; covering the fiscal year ending June 30, 1941), p. 34.

26. Commonwealth of the Philippines, Labor Dept., Fact-Finding Survey Report

Land concentration is also advancing in other provinces. In 1936 approximately half of the cultivated land in the province of Nueva Ecija was controlled by only one-tenth of the owners. There were 15 estates of more than 1,000 ha., 50 comprising 500 to 999 ha., and almost 2,000 with 24 to 99 ha.[27] The trend to land concentration was everywhere favored by a taxation system much too heavy for the small owner to bear. In 1936 more than 9,000 small holdings in the province of Cavite ,originally parts of the Friar lands purchased by the Taft Commission and assessed at 2.8 million pesos, were confiscated because of tax delinquencies. A well-concealed system of "land grabbing" further contributed to the elimination of small ownership. Large owners in the course of a resurvey of their estates, frequently would claim adjacent parcels of land through the courts. More often than not, they won, chiefly because the legal costs were too high for the small farmer, but also because a deficient title system and incomplete surveys could easily be interpreted in their favor. Many Filipino peasants are inexperienced in the legal aspects of landholding, and still believe in the uncontested right to possess the soil which their forefathers had broken.

Generally speaking, large-scale cultivation of cash crops intensified the trend towards concentration of land ownership, which again resulted in an increased use of farm labor and tenant farming at the expense of small independent holdings. The opening of the American market for Philippine produce meant a breaking up of the ancient agricultural economy, adjusted over a number of centuries to domestic needs.[28] Large-scale agricultural production was superimposed upon an economic system still dominated by economic and technical mechanisms of Spanish feudal times. When the old system came to serve the commercial agriculture, its time-honored paternalistic features gradually disappeared and thousands of once independent self-sufficient farmers became tenants and farm hands. On the whole, agricultural development in the Philippines resembles the process of disintegration experienced by the Javanese

(unpublished manuscript, Manila, 1936); Report of an Investigation Commission appointed by President Quezon, 1935.

27. James S. Allen, op. cit., pp. 56–67.

28. Ibid., pp. 52 ff., 57. He sees in this development the basic reason for the conflicts which take place with increasing frequency in the countryside.

village economy, but involves, in addition, the loss of actually farmer-owned land by a large part of the peasant class.

In those provinces where large-scale sugar production has been established, the formation of sugar centrals, often with big landowners as shareholders, has run a parallel course with land concentration.

In the interwar years, private corporations and large estate owners, often connected with each other, succeeded the Church and the Friars in land-ownership.[29] The "sugar baron" is now the largest landowner in the Philippines, and has far greater economic and political power than the "rice baron." It is in the sugar provinces that the political history of the Islands has been written for the past twenty-fiive years, and from those provinces have come a considerable number of leading politicians.

By December 31, 1938, business corporations had about 350,000 ha. of land, mostly in the sugar provinces, of which about 120,000 ha. were Filipino, 110,000 American, and 70,000 Spanish-owned. The Filipino share appears greater than it actually is because companies controlled by naturalized Spaniards are registered as Filipino-owned. Aside from the corporations, Filipino and Mestizo landlords possess large holdings which are subdivided into small units and cultivated mostly by share tenants *(kasamas)* and to a lesser extent by cash tenants *(inquilinatos)* and farm managers. The farm manager is the typical representative of large-estate ownership (mostly absentee landlords) and is found most frequently in the sugar provinces.

The type of land tenure varies greatly in different parts of the Islands. As in other colonial or semicolonial countries, land concentration is strongest where capital concentration is most intensive. While 96 percent of the farms on the forest-covered island of Palawan were owner-operated, there were only 12 percent in Pampanga, the center for Luzon's sugar production.

The connection between highly capitalized cultivation and concentration of land becomes still more obvious when the relation between the type of farm and the tenure of the farm operator is considered (all figures are for the year 1939). Only a little over 20 percent of the farms specializing in sugar cane are operated by their

29. *Ibid.*, p. 55.

owners; more than 60 percent are operated by tenants, and 15 percent by part-owners. The situation is nearly as unfavorable on the tobacco farms; here about 35 percent are owner-operated, more than 40 percent tenant-operated, and the remainder operated by part-owners. Conditions are somewhat better in rice cultivation, where 40 percent of the farms are owner-cultivated. On the other hand, about 70 percent of the abaca (Manila hemp) and coconut farms are operated by the owners—the cultivation of these crops being less capitalized.

The Philippine Census of 1939 gives only a superficial picture of the tenure system. For example, it does not state exactly the extent to which the land is owned by the big estates nor how many of the so-called owner-operators are forced to work as wage laborers on the estates, their own plots being too small for complete sustenance. Further, it does not specify the size of farms with "20 ha. or more," thus concealing the actual share of the large estates in the farm area. However, it might be possible to obtain a clearer picture by combining certain statistical facts, as, for example, the number of tenants and farm managers in relation to the farm area, and the number of farms of 20 ha. or more in relation to the number of tenants. But the various bodies of information have to be weighed carefully. The type of production must be considered in relation to the size of the farm area; coconut plantations, for example, require a larger area for cultivation than sugar and rice fields. Statistics showing relatively few properties of "20 ha. or more" in a province indicate frequently the presence of large land ownership, particularly when, at the same time, the number of tenants is very high. The province of Bulacan is an excellent illustration of this. Only 25 properties are listed as being of "20 ha. or more," yet 23,000 tenants are reported on a farm area of only 55,000 ha.

The accompanying tabulation, compiled on the basis of the Census of 1939, coordinates some features characteristic of the tenure system in some of the main provinces.[30] Following are some of the more characteristic details:

30. *Census of the Philippines, 1939,* especially Vol. III: *Report by Provinces for the Census of Agriculture.* The Philippine census investigates and classifies the distribution of land as follows: 1) Farms operated by the owners themselves; 2) farms operated by part owners who also lease other lands; 3) farms operated by farm managers; 4) farms operated by tenants.

Pampanga (1940: 384,000 inhabitants), the large sugar province,[31] is notorious for its bad social conditions. The Census mentions 2,800 independent owners, 18 farm managers, 4,100 part owners, and 16,600 tenants. Together, the 2,800 owners and farm managers control almost 40,000 ha., as against a mere 80,000 ha. controlled by 21,000 tenants and part owners. It is characteristic of the position of the big landowners in this province that the 18 estate managers alone control more than 22,000 ha. or almost 20 percent of the total agricultural area.

More or less similar conditions prevail in the Negros provinces, the other two large sugar provinces. In Negros Occidentale (1940: 856,000 inhabitants), 10,400 owners and farm managers control almost 200,000 ha., while 25,500 tenants and part owners only have 98,000 ha. at their disposal. Almost half of the farms are smaller than 1.5 ha. As in Pampanga, the immense size of the estates is obvious; 700 estate managers, alone, control about 90,000 ha., that is, about 30 percent of the total agricultural area of the province. In Negros Orientale (1940: 404,000 inhabitants), 21,000 owners and managers control about 75,000 ha., while around 27,000 tenants and part owners operate only about 46,000 ha. In this province, 45 percent of the holdings are made up of less than one hectare, while only 29 farm managers control as much as 9,300 ha.

In Tarlac, the fourth sugar province, conditions resemble those in Negros Orientale.

Nueva Ecija (1940: 432,000 inhabitants) displays similar trends, although not as sharply as the sugar provinces: 18,000 owners and farm managers control 94,500 ha., whereas 60,000 part owners and tenants control only 195,000 ha. Although there are three times as many tenants and part owners, they have only a little more than double the area at their disposal. Sixty-nine farm managers control 11,500 ha., or 4 percent of the total agricultural area.

The Ilocos provinces, Ilocos Norte (1940: 238,000 inhabitants) and Ilocos Sur (1940: 272,000 inhabitants) show an entirely different picture. They are poor and economically backward. The number of tenants is insignificant, as there are but few large estates. On

31. The term "sugar province" is used for those provinces where sugar is produced on a large scale, even if it is only cultivated on a limited part of the total agricultural area.

	I	II	III	IV			V
			Number				
		Number	of Farms				
	Total	of Farms	Operated				
	Farm	of 20	by Owners	NUMBER OF FARMS			
	Area (In	Hectares	or	OPERATED BY			Numb
Province	Hectares)	or More	Managers	Tenants	Part Owners	Total	Mana
Pampanga	120,800	201	2,800	16,600	4,100	20,700	1
Negros Occidentale	298,100	1,904	10,400	24,400	1,100	25,500	70
Negros Orientale	121,900	342	20,900	20,800	5,800	26,600	2
Tarlac	111,400	107	7,100	15,200	6,300	21,500	3
Abra	25,700	18	7,100	1,500	4,700	6,200	
Albay	180,000	824	28,000	10,400	5,900	16,300	1
Batangas	134,900	122	14,500	22,600	13,200	35,800	1
Bohol	175,700	426	36,200	10,500	16,600	27,100	
Bulacan	91,000	25	7,700	23,200	5,200	28,400	
Cagayan	157,700	206	18,700	7,300	10,500	17,800	
Camarinas Norte	62,100	233	5,100	4,400	500	4,900	
Camarinas Sur	226,200	1,202	18,500	11,600	5,700	17,300	1
Cavite	67,400	91	6,200	12,700	3,800	16,500	
Cebu	199,000	239	50,500	50,400	20,700	71,100	2
Davao	328,900	1,496	19,000	6,800	300	7,100	6
Ilocos Norte	52,200	28	12,500	6,100	12,600	18,700	.
Ilocos Sur	44,700	7	10,600	6,600	10,000	16,600	
Iloilo	250,000	515	25,600	31,800	9,500	41,300	6
Isabella	185,800	894	17,000	9,500	6,200	15,700	1
La Union	55,200	4	13,500	4,600	7,600	12,200	
Laguna	100,000	344	5,600	10,300	5,800	16,100	
Mindoro	164,500	714	10,200	4,500	1,500	6,000	2
Mountain Province	76,200	95	34,500	700	1,000	1,700	
Nueva Ecija	289,200	458	18,200	52,000	8,100	60,100	6
Nueva Viscaya	29,300	19	5,600	2,800	1,600	4,400	.
Pangasinan	202,100	111	33,500	28,700	24,400	53,100	1
Rizal	48,100	73	5,200	5,200	3,800	9,000	1
Tayabas	326,700	920	27,800	19,200	5,900	25,100	3
Zambales	37,000	65	3,500	3,800	4,800	8,600	
Zamboanga	274,000	1,789	23,600	8,500	800	9,300	2

	VI		VII		VIII	
	A (IN HECTARES) OPERATED BY		Area Operated by Managers in Percent of Total Farm Area		SMALL FARMS	
...ers	Tenants and Part Owners	Managers		Main Productions	Number	Size (in Hectares)
,000	80,900	21,900	18.0	Sugar and rice	4,700	Less than 1.5
,700	98,300	88,100	30.0	Sugar and rice	15,600	Less than 1.5
,100	46,500	9,300	7.8	Sugar and rice	31,900	Less than 1.5
,100	72,100	11,200	10.0	Sugar and rice	14,000	From 1 to 2.9
,200	11,400	127	0.5	Rice	8,900	Less than 1.5 (5,400 from 0.6 to 1.49)
,600	67,900	4,500	2.5	Abaca, coconuts, and rice	17,400	Less than 1.5 (12,200 from 3 to 9.9 ha.)
,600	96,400	800	0.6	Rice, coconuts, and sugar	20,000	Less than 1.5
,800	64,100	7,800	7.0	Rice and coconuts		
,000	69,900	2,100	2.3	Rice	15,400	From 2 to 4.9 (8,400 from 1 to 1.49)
,600	50,500	17,600	11.0	Rice, corn, and tobacco	13,400	Less than 1.5
,800	30,100	135	0.2	Coconuts and rice		
,000	78,100	14,100	6.0	Rice, coconuts, and abaca		
,500	48,800	1,000	1.5	Rice	6,400	Less than 1.5 (9,600 from 2 to 3.9)
,000	95,500	2,600	1.3	Corn and coconuts	63,000	Less than 1
,000	53,000	45,900	14.0	Abaca	9,400	From 2 to 4.9 (6,400 from 5 to 9.9)
,600	29,600	..	..	Rice	14,900	Less than 1
,200	28,000	500	1.2	Rice	11,900	Less than 1
,300	125,600	11,200	4.5	Rice and sugar	38,100	From 1 to 2.9
,200	52,300	11,200	6.0	Rice and tobacco		
,400	22,300	500	0.9	Rice		
,200	66,000	1,800	1.8	Coconuts and rice	14,400	From 1 to 3.9
,800	33,200	14,500	9.0	Rice and coconuts	6,500	From 1 to 2.9 (only 1,000 less than 1)
,400	5,100	1,800	2.3	Rice and vegetables		
,000	194,700	11,500	4.0	Rice	39,700	From 1 to 2.9 (16,700 from 3 to 3.9)
,500	10,700	..	..	Rice		
,300	122,500	2,300	1.0	Rice		
,600	22,900	7,600	16.0	Rice	7,000	Less than 1.5
,000	136,700	10,000	3.0	Coconuts	28,700	From 1 to 3.9
,200	23,100	700	1.8	Rice		
,500	46,300	12,200	4.5	Coconuts, rice and corn	15,500	From 1 to 3.9

the other hand, the individual properties are very small, almost half of them less than one hectare. The result is that social conditions are very poor, in spite of the fact that relatively many farmers live on their own soil. The minute division of land means poverty, and every year thousands of Ilocanos are forced to look for seasonal work in Cagayan and other distant provinces.

Abra (1940: 89,000 inhabitants) contrasts favorably with the provinces mentioned above. In this comparatively small province, 7,000 owners and farm managers control 14,000 ha., while 6,200 tenants and part owners control as much as 11,400 ha.

The present level of land use in the Philippines is inadequate to the needs of the country and is partly the consequence of the management of the large estates. This can be proved by a comparison of the total farm area [32] with the total cultivated area within the different tenure groups. However, it must be admitted, in favor of the large estates, that they often include land unfit as crop area. Frequently, however, this land could be considerably improved by technical irrigation or by primitive methods of irrigation such as are usually carried out by tenant farmers.

RELATIONSHIP BETWEEN FARM AREA AND CULTIVATED AREA

CONTROLLERS OF FARM AREA (IN HECTARES)

PROVINCE	Owners	Managers	Part Owners	Tenants	Total
Pampanga	18,000	21,900	17,000	63,000	120,700
Nueva Ecija	83,000	11,500	29,000	165,700	289,200
Rizal	17,600	7,600	10,200	12,700	48,100
Cebu	100,900	2,600	37,200	58,300	199,000
Davao	230,000	45,900	5,800	47,300	329,000

CONTROLLERS OF CULTIVATED AREA (IN HECTARES)

PROVINCE	Owners	Managers	Part Owners	Tenants	Total
Pampanga	12,600	1,300	15,400	59,400	88,700
Nueva Ecija	43,600	3,200	24,700	150,600	222,100
Rizal	7,100	500	7,000	9,300	23,900
Cebu	64,400	1,700	27,600	45,500	139,200
Davao	99,000	12,700	2,800	36,900	151,400

The above survey shows that tenants and part owners cultivate their soil far more intensively than do the owner and manager groups. The contrast is greatest when comparing the area cultivated

32. The Census of the Philippines uses the term "farm area" for the entire area belonging to the farm, regardless of whether this is already cultivated or only fit for cultivation, and still used for grazing, lumber or wasteland. The term "cultivated area" is used only for those areas which, during 1938, were used as harvesting area, including the areas planted with coconut, fruit, and nut trees.

by tenants with that cultivated by farm managers, representing a discrepancy which could hardly be attributed solely to differing qualities of soil.

LANDLORD-TENANT RELATIONSHIP   The tenure system in the Philippines is not much different from that generally encountered in Southeast Asia. The landlords operate their big estates by dividing them into small farms which are cultivated by tenants. Under the *kasama* system (share-tenancy) most often used in the rice-growing regions, the landlord provides the land and seed, and the capital needed for cultivation, while the tenant supplies the labor and, frequently, the working animals. Generally, the tenant gets 50 percent of the crop after his half of the expenses for cultivation have been paid or deducted in kind.[33] Less common, although existing almost all over the Islands, is the *inquilinato* system (cash tenancy). In 1939, the number of actual cash tenants was below 20,000. The cash tenant has to pay a fixed amount of annual rent for the land, usually in cash. The system is highly speculative, as the tenant alone has the risk of failure and the chance for a bumper crop. On the other hand, he is more independent of the landlord and usually markets the crop himself. This system is particularly common in regions with heavy population pressure, where land is scarce and where the mere occupancy of the land is an asset highly in demand and often paid for in advance. Peltzer [34] reports that cash tenants often function as middlemen between big absentee landlords and share tenants, to whom they lease the land on a share-cropper basis, and that the landlords often prefer this system, as it saves them supervision and does not involve any risks.

Both systems cause serious friction between landlords and tenants. The share tenant, devoid of cash and credit, depends entirely on the landlord from the moment he enters the contract. He not only has to borrow cash but also rice to carry him and his family to the next harvest. The cash advances, seldom below 50 pesos or over 100 pesos, must be returned in kind or cash after the harvest (usually without interest). The rice rations, especially those granted

33. The share of the tenant may increase to two-thirds of the crop, provided he himself furnishes the cash needed for cultivation. This is, however, exceptional, as he generally has neither cash nor credit.
34. Pelzer, *Pioneer Settlement*, p. 92.

after the crop has been planted, are, however, frequently subject
to usurious rates of interest, which the tenant can seldom pay out of
his share in the crop but often only by the performance of additional
services to the landlord. The tenant usually remains indebted even
after the harvest and is thus bound to become a victim of usury
again and again. He is caught in a vicious circle which renders him
unable to develop the qualities of citizenship on which the Philippine Constitution is based.[35]

The conflicts with the less dependent cash tenants arise generally
from more normal economic calculations and demands by the landlord. The scarcity of land, due to increasing population pressure,
tempts the landlord to increase the cash rent and to expel the cash
tenant, when he refuses to meet the new demands, without any
compensation whatever for the improvements he may have made on
the land.[36]

Usury is endemic in the Philippines as in other countries in this
area. It is intimately related to the disintegration of the self-
sufficient village economy and to the lack of adequate credit facilities for the farming population. It contributes considerably to the
expansion of the large estates. The most common rate of interest
is the rigid *takipan* which claims two cavans of palay (unhusked
rice) for every cavan loaned. Failure to pay at the first harvest
doubles the debt at the next harvest.[37] As the loans are seasonal
loans, generally for about six months, the *takipan* means an interest
rate of 200 percent per annum.

In some provinces of central Luzon, the tenant is obliged to repay loan and interest in cash to the value of the rice borrowed. As
he is generally forced to borrow rice before harvest time, when the
old crop is consumed and the price of rice is consequently at its
highest, he often must sell up to three times as much of his new rice
in order to pay his debt and interest, the price of rice being, naturally, low when the new crop is harvested.[38] Aside from the usurious

35. The Fact-Finding Survey Report mentions, pp. 37, 226, a number of cases in
which the economically powerful landlord has abused the personal-liberty rights of
his dependent tenants and has expelled them if they ventured to protest.
36. Pelzer, *Pioneer Settlement*, pp. 92, 93.
37. Other rates of interest demand the return of 3 cavans for every 2 loaned, or
4 for every 3.
38. Allen, "Agrarian Tendencies," pp. 61 ff., mentions other forms of usury: In-
geniously arranged installments for repayment of petty loans, compulsory loans

rates of interest, a system of extra services and disproportionate fines for minor violations adds to the misery of the tenant. James S. Allen [39] reports that fines of about 2 to 5 cavans of rice are imposed for such petty violations of rules as permitting visitors from outside to the hacienda, fishing without permission, or cutting bamboo for personal use. From one hacienda in central Luzon, he reports a compulsory gift of a cavan of rice to the landowner on his birthday.

The Labor Department of the Commonwealth [40] reports 320 tenant disputes which came before the Department in 1940. In 86 percent of the cases, tenants complained of dishonest calculations of the crop or their debt to the landlord; 264 of the disputes were settled in favor of the tenants. More than one-third of these cases occurred in the sugar provinces, 73 alone in Pampanga. It may be safely assumed that only an insignificant percentage of such cases were reported to the Department of Labor.

THE SITUATION OF THE PEASANTS   The life of Filipino peasants is determined by the rigidity of the tenure system. The conditions under which they live are almost always the same, irrespective of the crop they raise. In the rice regions, where the average yield is 35 to 40 cavans per hectare, the average share of a tenant farmer with 2 ha. is only 31 to 36 cavans, providing he has paid his part of the costs. Based on prewar prices, this will correspond to an income of from 62 to 72 pesos per year for a 2 ha. farm. In most cases, however, he will not come into possession of his full share, because of the loans he must repay with interest after the harvest. Since the cultivation of one hectare of rice land requires about 300 hours of man labor in addition to 150 hours of animal labor, the tenant operating a farm of 2 ha. works an equivalent of only 75 eight-hour days a year, distributed over the planting and harvesting season.[41] The

from the landowner to the tenant, often in the form of merchandise and cheap jewelry, which he has to repay at harvest. In "Land Problems in Puerto Rico and the Philippine Islands," *Geographical Review*, XXIV (1934), 182, Theodore Roosevelt mentions that a peasant who had borrowed 300 pesos came to owe 3,000 pesos at the end of the 4th year. Whenever the time came to pay interest, the usurer offered remission if the peasant would sign a new document substituted for the original contract.

39. *Op. cit.*, pp. 62–63.
40. *Journal of Philippine Statistics*, I, No. 5 (Manila, November, 1941), 531.
41. Pelzer, *Pioneer Settlement*, pp. 96–97. The Fact-Finding Survey came to simi-

tenants with farms of less than 2 ha.—54 percent of all tenant farmers—are idle even during part of the planting and harvesting season.

The existing agricultural system in the Philippines is incapable of utilizing the abundant manpower, and, as a result, millions of working hours are wasted. The lack of a diversified economy forces tens of thousands of tenants to live on the produce of 600 hours or less of man labor during the year. It is extremely difficult for tenant families to find opportunities to make additional income in secondary industries during the off season.

The situation in the sugar regions is not much better. The average holding of the tenant is about 2 ha., usually rented from a lessee. Fifty piculs [42] per ha. is considered a good yield. As a rule the sugar central takes half the crop as its share for milling. Out of the portion left to the lessee and tenant, 7 percent of the total crop must be paid to the estate owner for rent. Based on the prewar price of 7 pesos per picul, the sale of the remaining 43 piculs will bring 301 pesos. The production costs usually amount to 120 pesos for 2 ha., leaving 181 pesos as net income, of which the tenant's share is 90.50 pesos.[43]

When the tenant sees no other possibility for additional income, and all sources for credit have been exhausted, he may pay his debt to the landlord by sending his minor children to the house of the landlord as servants, where they may possibly have to work for years without any pay. This form of child labor is mitigated under favorable circumstances by a patriarchal attitude on the part of the landlord. In the majority of cases, however, employment agencies in Manila take over the children (as a rule between 8 and 10 years of age) for a lump sum, pay their fare from the provinces, and support them until an employer is found. The latter then pays a fixed amount for the child (before the war 20 pesos) and repays the agency's expenses in small monthly installments, which are considered the debt of the children. Until the entire sum is repaid, the children do not receive one centavo in wages, though they have to work hard, as a rule without any education and often without adequate food and clothing.

---

lar results. It found, among 1,105 share croppers out of a total of around 10,000 on four monastic estates, an average income of 122 pesos for 2 crop harvests; 48.1% of tenant families had a net income (including all sources) of from 50 to 150 pesos. See Allen, *op. cit.*, pp. 58, 59.

42. One picul (in the Philippines) = 139 lbs.　　43. Allen, *op. cit.*, pp. 59 ff.

The distressing condition of the Philippine peasantry is almost a commonplace. It is emphasized frequently in official reports, but has not been fundamentally improved during the American control of the Islands, in spite of some noteworthy accomplishments, especially in the field of sanitation and public health. Francis B. Sayre, the last American High Commissioner before the war, stressed repeatedly the unrest in central Luzon: "The bulk of the newly created income went to the Government, to landlords, and to urban areas, and served but little to ameliorate living conditions among the almost feudal peasantry and tenantry." [44] "The gap between the mass population and the small governing class has broadened, and social unrest has reached serious proportions." [45]

AGRARIAN REBELLIONS   The Philippine peasantry rebelled in hundreds of bloody uprisings against the Spanish oppression. The final revolution against Spain, at the end of the last century, can be interpreted largely as an agrarian rebellion, fostered by the turbulent dissatisfaction of the tenants on the large estates of the Church.[46] Similarly, after the collapse of Spanish rule, they continued to protest against the maintenance of a tenure system which tied them to the lowest level of living. They rebelled in bloody uprisings, in strikes and demonstrations, and, in recent years, through the ballot.[47] The mystic power of the political slogan "Independence" was derived from the longing of the people for a basic economic change, i.e., agricultural reform, which they could not imagine without political independence, as they traditionally identified foreign rule with the power of the landlord.[48]

It would be beyond the scope of this study to mention all the rebellions and clashes during the last generation, particularly in the provinces of Pampanga, Nueva Ecija, Tarlac and Bulacan which were more serious than the usual incidents caused by a permanent

44. Francis B. Sayre, High Commissioner of the Philippine Islands, "Freedom Comes to the Philippines," *Atlantic Monthly*, March, 1945.
45. The *Fifth Annual Report of the United States High Commissioner to the Philippine Islands*, p. 34.
46. This was the actual reason for Governor General Taft's negotiations with the Vatican about the sale of the Friar estates.
47. In the 1940 elections, the Socialist Party had considerable success in Pampanga. It won the election in the capital, San Fernando, and in other towns.
48. Harlan R. Crippen, "Philippine Agrarian Unrest: Historical Background," *Science and Society*, V, No. 4 (1946), 337 ff., gives an excellent historical analysis.

agrarian dissatisfaction. Filipino officialdom was inclined to attribute the unrest to religious fanaticism, but J. R. Hayden states that American opinion in the Islands considered it as directed against "caciquism," agrarian oppression and Constabulary abuses.[49] Of more general interest are the Tayug incident, in 1931, and the Sakdalist Rebellion, in 1935. During the former incident,[50] armed peasants looted the City Hall of the town and destroyed the land records there on file, but still the official verdict was "religious fanaticism." Hayden quotes, in this connection, a contemporaneous account:

The reasons why the Filipino leaders did not wish the Tayug incident to be investigated by a body containing the appropriate members of the Governor-General's staff of advisers are obvious. Such an inquiry would inevitably be pushed into the whole realm of the oppression of the poor peasant by the local boss, the usurer, the Constabulary, and the local official. The fact that the machinery for the registration of land titles is years behind in its work and that the rich and influential "land grabber" is taking advantage of this situation to despoil the homesteader and small farmer would come up for consideration. The bitter and dangerous discontent of large numbers of peasants in many parts of the central plain of Luzon would be revealed. Here is a situation that many people believe would be extremely perilous should the support of American authority be withdrawn from the Government of the Philippines. Indeed, one of the highest officials in that Government, a Filipino, declared to the writer that the Tayug incident should not be called an agrarian uprising because the term might very well give rise to similar outbreaks elsewhere in the Islands.

The "Sakdal [51] uprising" of May 2 and 3, 1935,[52] occurred in the provinces surrounding Manila and was also based on the generally poor agrarian conditions. Particular circumstances gave it a more significant place, in that it revealed the real content of the word

49. Joseph Ralston Hayden, *The Philippines, a Study in National Development* (New York, 1942), pp. 379 ff.
50. *Ibid.*, pp. 380–81.
51. Sakdal is a Tagalog expression. It means to "accuse" or "strike."
52. Hayden, *op. cit.*, pp. 392 ff., gives an excellent description of the uprising and publishes a part of the Investigation Report of an American Investigation Committee. After pointing out the futility of the revolt and the suffering it had caused, Hayden asked a Filipino peasant involved in the rebellion. "Do you think it was worth it? Aren't you sorry that all this has happened?" "No, sir," he replied, "I am not sorry. We have shown that we have rights. We know that we have rights and are willing to die for them. We have shown America that the Filipinos want their independence.

"independence" for the peasants of central Luzon, though its leader, Benigno Ramos, was a political gangster. He was a discharged official who in an irresponsible way knew how to incite the hungry, deceived, and always disappointed peasants of central Luzon, and to organize them in a revolt against their masters. He accused Quezon of corruption and betrayal and of being a foe of the independence movement. He agitated against the already planned Philippine Commonwealth, which, he said, would never lead to independence but merely strengthen the cacique system and hand the resources of the country over to foreigners. Benigno Ramos, who later, during the Japanese occupation, fought on the side of the Japanese to the bitter end, pointed to Japan as the place from which final liberation would come. The bloody Sakdal rebellion, which involved 5,000 to 7,000 men and women, was brutally suppressed by the Commonwealth Police.

Hayden asserts that the Sakdal uprising was the revelation of the willingness of the Filipino *tao* to fight for what he conceived to be his country's welfare, for his political rights, or to avenge personal insults and injuries. He quotes (p. 393) from an American report, made by an investigation committee of disinterested members of the Malacanan Advisory Staff, as follows:

Fundamentally, the uprising of May 2 and 3, 1935, was due to political factors of long standing. . . . The Committee has been unable to find any evidence of Communism or radical socialism. The Sakdal leaders have taught their followers to believe that they have been betrayed by the Filipino political leaders and that the Filipino leaders who formerly advocated independence now support the Constitution and the Commonwealth. The rank and file of the radical wing of the Sakdal party now believe that the establishment of the Commonwealth Government is a move to establish and maintain in power a group of Filipino leaders who represent the upper classes and who will oppress the lower classes. They believe that immediate independence would enable the

I do not care if we go to Bilibid for a long time. I do not care if we were killed." (pp. 397 ff.).

Hayden's comment is as follows: "There was no bombast in this statement. No reporter was present to advertise the speaker as a patriot and a martyr. This Filipino Nathan Hale was not running for any office and had never been a 'politico.' He was representative of hundreds of thousands of his compatriots, however, the poor, unknown, individually inconsequential people who are as willing as was any Revolutionary American to die for their country, and who in the end will rise against oppressors, whether foreign or Filipino."

economically depressed classes to eliminate these leaders from politics. Economic and social factors did not operate to bring about the uprising, other than that the poor economic and social status of the people served to accentuate dissatisfaction with existing political conditions and opposition to the Constitution and the Commonwealth Government.

The investigation committee also listed a number of political and economic causes for the uprising: suppression of free speech,[53] lack of confidence in the Quezon adminisration, oppression and abuse by local caciques, poverty and misery. It also quotes statements by peasants involved in the Sakdal rebellion, most of whom associate independence with a better life, after many years of oppression and abuse under foreign control. A typical statement is the following: "I oppose the Constitution because we want independence. It is a good thing because living will be easy under independence." [54]

Governor John C. Early, who knew and understood the common Filipino people declared after the bloody uprising in Tayug: "Take away a man's land and he is desperate. This is an old condition in that region. Other parts of Pangasinan, Tarlac and Nueva Ecija are just as bad. The whole of central Luzon is ready for an uprising. It needs leadership only. Sandico has said that land troubles in central Luzon would not be settled as long as the Americans remain, but will soon be dealt with after they leave." [55]

The fight of the Hukbalahap [56] against the Japanese invaders

53. The Fact Finding Survey Report, quoted by Allen, *op cit.*, p. 64, states the same. "The hue and cry of the peasantry is for a radical change in the present scheme of their relations with the all-powerful landowning class. In all provinces surveyed it has been found that the average tenant does not enjoy his constitutional and inalienable civil and political rights. He cannot openly join in any movement organized for his betterment without courting the displeasure of the landowner and running the risk of being deprived of the piece of land he tills."

54. Hayden, *op. cit.*, p. 396. A plebiscite on the Constitution was scheduled for May 14, 1935, and the Sakdal uprising intended to prevent it.

55. Quoted from Hayden, p. 400. The quotation is a record of a conversation of Hayden's with Governor Early, dated Jan. 14, 1931. Teodore Sandico was officer in the revolution of 1899, leader of the farmers in Bulacan, and Vice President of the Constitutional Convention.

56. Hukbalahap, short for the Tagalog *Hukbo ng Bayan Laban sa Hapon* (United Front Against the Japanese) was a type of Popular Front of peasants in the central provinces of Luzon. It was organized immediately after the Japanese invasion and was supported by intellectual and middle-class groups in Manila which before the war partly had been organized in the Civil Liberties Union. During the occupation

and collaborating landlords must be understood on the basis of the economic and social development in central Luzon. From the beginning it was simultaneously a struggle for independence and social liberty. After the war, the peasants of central Luzon continued the fight against the landlords, with greater vigor and better arms than ever before but for the same ideas as in prewar times.

The Hukbalahap emerged as the natural leader in this fight. It was headed by Luis Taruc, leader of the General Union of Workers, and Dr. Vicente Lava, a graduate of Columbia University, and the most outstanding Filipino chemist. (He died in Manila in the summer of 1947). The Huk demanded the purge of former collaborators and a change of the land-tenure system. It became the main body of a new political party, the Democratic Alliance,[57] which included other peasant and guerrilla organizations. These groups drafted a political program urging an increase in the tenant's share, a minimum daily wage of 3 pesos for workers, and the purchase of large estates by the government for subdivision under conditions favorable to the tenants.

The attitude of the government of the new republic towards the well-armed and self-assured peasants of central Luzon hardly seems different from the traditional policy of Philippine administrations. Philippine history shows, however, that pacification by force will lead nowhere as long as it is not coordinated with an agrarian reform

it had about 100,000 armed members. See Barbara Entenberg, "Agrarian Reform and the Hukbalahap," *Far Eastern Survey*, XV, No. 16 (Aug. 14, 1946), 245, which tells the story of the Hukbalahap in its fight against the Japanese and the difficulties it encountered after the liberation, when it demanded agrarian reform and continued the fight against the landlords and the Roxas administration, which was supported by the United States Army. See also Bernard Seeman and Laurence Salisbury. *Cross-Currents in the Philippines* (Institute of Pacific Relations, American Council, Pamphlet No. 23, New York, 1946).

The Hukbalahap was officially outlawed on March 6, 1948, under a proclamation by President Roxas. A few days earlier the Philippine Congress had solved the collaboration problem, so strongly emphasized by the Hukbalahap, by extending amnesty to all political and economic collaborators. The amnesty even included José P. Laurel, President of the Japanese Puppet Government, and Jorge B. Vargas, President of the Executive Commission under the Japanese Military Administration.

After Manuel Roxas' death in April, 1948, his successor, President Elpidio Quirino proclaimed an amnesty for the members of the Hukbalahap and their leader, Luis Taruc. They were given a limited period in which to surrender their arms. Luis Taruc accepted the amnesty.

57. The Democratic Alliance was successful in the Philippine elections of April, 1946. In central Luzon, six of their candidates were elected to Congress, but the Roxas majority, after a fight over rules, refused to seat them.

which puts an end to the landlord rule. J. R. Hayden concludes his discussion of the cacique system with the following words: "But the victims of this system are increasingly determined to end it." [58]

REFORM LEGISLATION AND THE PUBLIC DOMAIN   From the very beginning, American authorities were aware of the difficulties they would face in the Philippines in endeavoring to change the semifeudal, precapitalistic structure of the Islands. They would have to battle the superior influence of traditional power and recklessness, which, in addition, was strengthened economically by the advantages gained in the free-trade relationship with the United States.

One of the most noteworthy efforts since the liquidation of the Friar estates was the Rice Share Tenancy Act of 1933, passed by the Philippine Legislature (No. 4054) under the administration of Governor-General Theodore Roosevelt, as "An Act to promote the well-being of tenants in agricultural lands devoted to the production of rice and to regulate the relations between them and the landlords of said lands, and for other purposes." [59] However, enforcement of the law was prevented because the landlords, dominating the legislature, succeeded in making its application dependent on petition to the Governor-General of a majority of the municipal councils of the provinces. These conditions were, naturally, never achieved, as the landlords also controlled the municipal councils.

The Act of 1933 was rewritten and amended in November, 1936, as Commonwealth Act No. 178. Under the new provisions, the President of the Philippines was empowered to put it into effect "when public interests so require." But even in a period of unrest, the tactics of the landlords prevented enforcement, until in January, 1937, a proclamation by President Quezon finally made the Act effective in the chief areas of disturbance, the provinces of central Luzon.[60] But it proved to offer no official protection against the powerful landlords, who reacted frequently with wholesale dismissals of tenants whenever they claimed the rights given them by the law.[61] Although laws against such dismissal (Act 461) and provisions

58. Hayden, *op. cit.*, p. 400.
59. See in this connection, Pelzer, *Pioneer Settlement*, pp. 98 ff.
60. It was later (February, 1941) extended to other endangered regions, among them, Iloilo, Capiz, and the tobacco province Isabella.
61. The most important ones were: written form of contract (local dialect); equal

for compulsory arbitration of all disputes (Act 608) were introduced later on, clashes and friction nevertheless increased. Once again it was proved that it is futile to attempt a peaceful adjustment of the landlord-tenant relation in central Luzon and the Visayas by mere procedural regulations.

Referring to eviction from the land without legal procedures and to landlords who ignored their duty to provide the tenant with the usual aids to farming, such as seed, High Commissioner Francis B. Sayre comments: "Although, in part, the increasing difficulty may have been the result of the activities of agitators among the tenants, in no small measure they appeared to be the result of intention on the part of landlords to rid themselves of tenants, legally or illegally, who demanded that the landlords live up to the existing laws." [62]

The tenancy legislation did not improve essentially the landlord-tenant relationship, yet it gave the tenants the opportunity to make a better-organized fight and the basis for publicity.[63] A powerful tenant union was organized under the capable leadership of Pedro Abad Santos, and President Quezon was forced to recognize the tenants and agricultural workers as an essential political factor.[64]

Unlike other countries in the area, the Philippines still have a great reserve of rich public lands which offer ample opportunity for an organized resettlement of the excess population from the central provinces of Luzon and Cebu.[65] The Islands owe this advantageous position to the American land policy which, as early as 1902, limited the area of public lands that could be acquired by in-

distribution of costs and crops; general one-year contract if not otherwise agreed; 10% limit for interest; guaranteed minimum share of 15% for the tenant, irrespective of his indebtedness. These regulations were largely evaded. For instance, the usurious rates were hidden by a simple IOU receipt or similar methods. Finally, the famous Pacto de Retro, based on old Spanish law, permits the sale of property to the creditor for the amount of the loan when the debtor fails to pay capital and interest at the fixed date. In this way, many part owners lost their small piece of land to the landlord.

62. *Fourth Annual Report of the United States High Commissioner to the Philippines to the President and Congress of the United States* (covering the fiscal year July 1, 1939 to June 30, 1940, Manila, Sept. 1, 1941; Washington, 1943), p. 50.

63. Pelzer, *Pioneer Settlement*, p. 101. The author probably overestimates the actual effect of the tenant organizations on the landlord-tenant relation.

64. Speech of President Quezon on "Amelioration of the Laboring Class," delivered July 16, 1939, at Cabanatuan (Messages of the President, Vol. V, Part I, Manila, 1941, pp. 147 ff.).

65. The *Census of 1918* estimated the public domains at 16.6 million acres, and later surveys showed it to be still larger.

dividuals and corporations to 16 ha. for the former and 1,024 ha. for the latter.[66] By this law, Congress prevented powerful corporations from monopolizing the public domain of the Islands, and the unfavorable effects thereof, a monopoly well-known in other countries of the area. Some students imply that these rigid restrictions against alienation of public land have prevented large-scale agricultural development.[67] But the successful sugar industry, both in the Philippines and in Java, proves that commercial agricultural production is not easily hampered by land restrictions and, generally, will adjust itself to legal requirements. It might be doubted whether the restrictive land laws, as is frequently asserted, actually were the main reason for keeping out American rubber capital from the Philippines (Mindanao). Most likely it was the lack of political stability in the Islands, where independence—contrary to the other rubber areas—has been an actual problem for decades and, therefore, a constant threat to large long-term investments. It can be stated, however, that the land laws, though they did not prevent the development of a large-scale sugar industry, nevertheless saved the Islands from becoming a mere plantation colony and thus secured space and opportunity for a future constructive resettlement policy in an independent Philippine republic.[68]

The Public Land Act of October 7, 1903, issued by the American controlled Philippine administration, established the homestead system in the Islands, regulated transactions concerning public lands, and made provisions for authorized titles. While this law contained no restrictions in regard to nationality, Act. No. 2874 (1919), passed by the Philippine legislature, practically limited the exploitation and utilization of public land to citizens of the Phil-

66. U.S. Public Act, No. 235, July 1, 1902, Sec. 12.
67. Catherine Porter, "The Philippines as an American Investment," *Far Eastern Survey*, IX (Sept. 24, 1940), 219 ff.
68. The so-called Quirino-Recto Colonization Act of 1935 initiated an organized colonization and resettlement plan for Mindanao. The Commonwealth began a large-scale road construction in Mindanao (Commonwealth Act No. 18) and finally, in 1939, the National Land Settlement Administration was established (Commonwealth Act No. 441) with a capital of 20 million pesos and with offices in Manila and Lagao (Mindanao). The first settlement district was in the Koronadal Valley (Cotabato). By February, 1941, 2,500 families had settled there on farms of 6 to 12 ha. While the Visayans were strongly represented among the settlers, there were but relatively few from the overpopulated provinces of central Luzon. So far, the resettlement project has been kept on a rather limited scale. See Pelzer, *Pioneer Settlement*, pp. 127 ff.

ippines and the United States and to corporations of which at least 61 percent of the capital stock belonged to Filipinos or American citizens.[69] The law of 1919 raised the limits for homesteads to 24 ha. and for general purchase of public land by individuals to 100 ha. (later, changed to 144 ha.) But the Philippine legislature defended emphatically the original limit set for the purchase of public land by corporations, in spite of official and private recommendations to raise it.[70] In contrast to most other dependent territories, the Philippines were thus able to maintain their reserve of public land as a national inheritance, after Congress, by the Act of 1902, had established the foundation for a wise land policy.

However, the Homestead program was, on the whole, a disappointment.[71] From its inception down to the establishment of the Commonwealth, a period of one generation (1904 to 1935), only 55,000 homestead applications out of 212,000 were approved, and less than 35,000 were patented. Almost 50 percent were rejected or canceled, partly because of lack of surveys, but largely because the margin for a progressive land policy is extremely limited in an almost feudal environment. The influential landlords, generally well-informed, would get ahead of the prospective homesteader and, for speculative purposes, take up the land nearest to the road, thus leaving the remote plots to the settlers, who, consequently, were discouraged by the immense difficulties in settling and disposing of their produce.[72]

Theodore Roosevelt [73] confirmed that the system failed to reach all those who wished to procure homesteads and that it failed to protect the settler by granting him title to his claim when it had been approved by the government. The cadastral survey had fallen

69. These regulations were largely evaded by the help of Filipino "dummies," especially for Japanese planters and corporations. Land was also frequently registered in favor of the Filipino wives of Japanese or Chinese citizens.

70. *Annual Report of the Governor General of the Philippine Islands, 1928* (Washington, 1930), p. 4.

71. *Fifth Annual Report of the U.S. High Commissioner to the Philippines*, p. 34: "The processes for Homesteading on the public domain, never highly efficient, appear to have deteriorated."

72. Theodore Roosevelt, "Land Problems in Puerto Rico and the Philippine Islands," pp. 182 ff., 199, 202, tried to fight this abuse by an executive order limiting the occupancy of the land along the road to public domain, but he was unable to eliminate the speculation. See also Karl J. Pelzer, *Pioneer Settlement*, pp. 111 ff.

73. *Op. cit.*, p. 198.

behind, and the cost of proving title was so burdensome that many small farmers never took out a title to the land they cultivated. It therefore frequently happened that homesteaders unwittingly took up land on a tract belonging to, or at least claimed by, a large estate owner. Roosevelt asserts that "the holder might be perfectly aware of this but, saying nothing, would let the little man clear and improve the property for a number of years and then turn him off without remedy." In addition, there were no adequate credit facilities for homesteaders.

The feeble response to homestead legislation indicates the difficulties of a resettlement policy in a country like the Philippines. The administration was not inefficient, yet it was unable to uphold the law under a social order which traditionally considers the public domain and the labor of the *tao* as rightly belonging to the privileged class.

Based on the constitutional provision (Article XII, Section 4) which authorized the National Assembly to expropriate lands for just compensation, the Philippine Legislature in 1936 passed Commonwealth Act No. 20, and No. 378 in 1938. The former authorized the President to prepare the expropriation of those portions of large estates which were subdivided to tenants, and the latter enabled the government to lease large estates for 25 years. In order to carry out this policy, the Rural Progress Administration was established by the government, with a capital of 1.5 million pesos. By 1940, the organization had taken over the homesite sections of a number of estates in central Luzon and had leased the large Buena Vista Estate of 27,000 ha. Contrary to expectations, however, conflicts with the peasant population continued. The government experienced the futility of a land program that did not increase the quantity and quality of the land, and, consequently, was of no use to the distressed tenant. The relation between government and tenant was hardly better than between landlord and tenant and the government was confronted by a hostile tenant class, which identified it with the hated landlords.

THE SUGAR INDUSTRY Cultivation of sugar cane was known in the Philippines long before Magellan discovered the Islands (1521). Large-scale production, however, was first introduced when the

Payne-Aldrich Act of 1909 opened the American market for Philippine imports. From then on, production rose rapidly; between 1920 and 1934, it increased from 410,000 to 1,400,000 long tons. Before the war, it was the dominating industry, so much so that the Philippines were frequently referred to as a sugar economy. Between 10 percent and 15 percent of the population depends, essentially or completely, on sugar production for its sustenance. More than 40 percent of the freight revenues of the government-owned railroad was derived from sugar cargo, while taxes paid by the industry financed the administration in five leading provinces and constituted an important item in the budget of the central government.

The two principal factors in the industry are the individual planters who produce the cane and the sugar mills or "centrals" that mill it. This particular division arose because the land laws prevented individuals and corporations from acquiring large tracts of public land. The planters and the centrals entered into a contract, usually for thirty years, according to which the sugar was equally divided between them, with the central in charge of the transportation and the entire milling procedure.

The Philippine sugar industry is located in four main regions: (1) the islands of Negros and Panay; (2) the provinces of Pampanga, Tarlac, and Bataan, located in central Luzon; (3) the provinces of Batangas and Laguna, south of Manila; and (4) the island of Cebu. These four districts, with about 250,000 ha. of sugar land, accounted for more than 90 percent of the total production, 50 percent of it in Negros Occidentale alone.[74]

The degree of dependence on the sugar industry varies from province to province. In Pampanga and Negros Occidentale, it is estimated at 90 percent; in Tarlac, at 60 percent; in Batangas and Iloilo (on Panay), at 50 percent; and in Cebu, at 10 percent. Production is technically most advanced in the Negros provinces, where the large plantations apply modern machinery and generally prefer the more efficient wage labor to tenant cultivation such as is still prevalent in the sugar areas of Luzon.

74. See Joint Preparatory Committee on Philippine Affairs, Report of May 20, 1938 (Washington, 1938), I, 38 ff. U.S. Tariff Commission Report No. 118 (2d ser.): *United States–Philippine Trade* (Washington, 1937), pp. 48 ff.

Before the war, there were 24,000 sugar planters and 46 sugar centrals on the Islands. The capacity of the centrals, based on a normal milling season of 150 days, was about 12 million tons of cane, or 1.5 million tons of sugar. In addition, four sugar refineries were in operation.

The last reliable appraisal of the investments in the sugar industry from 1935 estimates the capital investment at 84 million dollars and the investment in land and improvements at 181 million dollars.[75] While most of the investments in cane lands and improvements were made by Filipinos, the investments in sugar centrals were largely foreign. Thirty-three percent of the capital invested in centrals was controlled by Americans, 16 percent by Spaniards and the remainder by Filipinos.[76] The American-controlled centrals were the most modern and efficient in the Islands. Since 1936, production has been based on an export quota to the United States of 850,000 long tons per year. This quota is retained in the Philippine Trade Act of 1946.[77] Before the war, more than 99 percent of the total Philippine sugar exports went to the United States.

The comparison between the cost of production per pound for sugar in the Philippines and in competing sugar-producing areas is not entirely in favor of the Islands. According to the figures for 1931–32 in the report of the U.S. Tariff Commission,[78] the average cumulative cost of production per pound of Philippine raw sugar, f.o.b. Philippine Islands, including imputed interest, was 2.14 U.S. cents (2.41 cents when the cost of transportation was included, to

75. *Philippine Statistical Review* (1935), II, p. 310. However, the estimates of the Philippine Sugar Association are considerably lower. It evaluates the investments in land and improvements at only $105 million.

76. A considerable part of the Filipino investments belonged to naturalized Spaniards or Chinese.

77. The Philippine Trade Act of 1946, Sec. 211.

78. U.S. Tariff Commission, *Report to the President on Sugar*, with Appendix (Report No. 73, 2d ser., Washington, 1934), especially pp. 14, 117ff. Appendix 3, pp. 204 ff., is the latest official comparative cost rate report. It reveals that the cost rate of 1931–32 was already considerably lower than that of 1930–31, on account of the depression. See also Francis Maxwell, *Economic Aspects of Cane Sugar Production* (London, 1927), pp. 95–96.

Report on Philippine–U.S. Trade Relations (Prepared for the Interdepartmental Committtee on the Philippines by Members of the Staff of the Tariff Commission with the Cooperation of the Depts. of State, War, Commerce, and Agriculture Washington, 1935), I, pp. 115 ff., indicates, however, that it may be assumed that the costs of Philippine sugar in 1935 are likely to be somewhat lower because of improved cultural practices in the Philippines since 1932.

the Atlantic ports of the United States). The corresponding figures for Cuba, the greatest competitor, were only 1.61 and 1.73 cents per pound. At the same time, however, the average costs, f.o.b. Hawaii and Puerto Rico, were considerably higher, at 2.86 and 2.82 U.S. cents, respectively; but it may be assumed, that the increase in the average yield per ha. on the Hawaiian sugar plantations in recent years has brought the cost of production nearer to the level in the Philippines. For the three-year period 1929–30 to 1931–32, the total cost per pound (including imputed interests) at seaboard American continental refineries averaged 3.29 U.S. cents for Hawaii; 3.28 for Puerto Rico; 2.72 for the Philippines; and only 1.92 for Cuba.

In 1934, Senator Millard E. Tydings, Chairman of the Committee on Territories and Insular Affairs of the United States Senate, stated that the costs, c.i.f. to New York, of Philippine sugar averaged 5.40 pesos per 100 lbs., compared with the Cuban cost of 3.80 pesos per 100 lbs., and the Javan cost of about 2 pesos per 100 lbs. He stressed that the higher cost of producing Philippine sugar is due partly to lower production per acre as compared with Java, partly to higher wages (again in relation to Java) and partly to other factors (overcapitalization).[79]

Though the average yield per hectare of cane land in the Philippines had increased considerably since 1926, particularly in the Negros provinces, in 1933–34, it was only about one-third of that on Java and Hawaii and somewhat lower than in Puerto Rico. It exceeded, however, the average yield in Cuba.[80]

Without its preferential position in the American market, Philippine sugar production would hardly be profitable. Cuba, in the American market, and Java, in the Asiatic market, are superior competitors. It is a fact that the Islands have never been able to ex-

79. Address delivered December 22, 1934, before the Philippine Constitutional Convention, reprinted in Hearings before the Committee on Ways and Means, House of Representatives, 79th Congress, 1st Session, on H.R. 4185, H.R. 4676, H.R. 5185 (Philippine Trade Act of 1945), p. 109.

80. *International Year-Book of Agricultural Statistics, 1938–39* (International Institute of Agriculture, Rome, 1939), Table 84: Sugar production in quintals per ha. for 1933–34; Cuba 359.6, Philippines 425.6, Puerto Rico 677.9, Hawaii 1,333.9, and Java 1,378.0. While no later figures are published for the Philippines, those published for Java and Puerto Rico show more or less a stabilization and those for Hawaii an increase to 1,635.3 quintals per ha. in 1936–37.

port any considerable quantity of sugar to countries other than the
United States, though the productive capacity largely exceeded the
quota on the American market. This weakness is partly due to natural conditions. The Philippine Sugar Association asserted (as defense for the low earnings of the sugar workers in the Islands),[81] that
the soil and climatic conditions in Cuba and Hawaii are more favorable to the employment of agricultural implements than in the
Philippines and that, consequently, Filipino labor is only a third
as efficient as labor in Cuba and Hawaii. Furthermore, the practice
of leaving the cane in the field to ratoon year after year, as is done
with success in Hawaii and Cuba, is seldom profitable in the Philippines.

Natural conditions, however, are not equally unfavorable in all
Philippine sugar areas. In the Negros provinces they are far better
than elsewhere in the Islands, and the cost of production, therefore,
is considerably lower. Producers in this area also enjoy comparatively low transportation costs through their ability to ship directly
by water, thus saving the charges for rail and terminal storage
which the producer on Luzon has to pay.[82] But, even though sugar
from the Negros provinces might be able to compete in the world
market, the outlook remains unfavorable for the Philippine sugar
industry in general.

It seems evident that it will not be able to achieve a strong market
position without considerable preferential treatment. But even
such a protected position could be maintained in the past only by
a wage level extremely low compared with that in other sugar producing countries (with the exception of Java). Underpaid laborers
made possible the successful competition with Hawaiian sugar production. The average individual expenditure for food was less than
one-fourth of the amount spent by the lowest paid Filipino laborers on Hawaii.[83] The social principles of the Commonwealth could
never be enforced in the sugar provinces.[84] I. T. Runes says:

81. *Facts and Statistics about the Philippine Sugar Industry* (Philippine Sugar
Assn., Manila, 1928), p. 51.

82. Joint Preparatory Committee on Philippine Affairs, *Report*, p. 40; *Report on
United States–Philippine Trade*, p. 49; *Facts and Statistics about the Philippine
Sugar Industry*, p. 49.

83. I. T. Runes, *General Standards of Living and Wages of Workers in the Philippine Sugar Industry*, (Manila, 1939), p. 21.

84. *Ibid.*, p. 29.

But, undoubtedly, because of sugar that has sweetened the life of a few thousand planters and mill owners, about two million people in the sugar areas of the country live the most miserable and deplorable existence, in comparison with those in regions where other agricultural crops are raised. So deplorable is their condition, that labor troubles center around plantations where wages of landless laborers are not only apparently, but also obviously, inadequate to cover living expenses.[85]

During recent decades, negotiations for Philippine independence have been focused on the fateful dependence of Philippine economy on the American market. The necessity of economic diversification and need for confinement of the sugar industry to the most suitable areas motivated the inclusion of the ten-year period of adjustment stipulated in the Tydings-MacDuffie Act of 1934. An unrestricted preservation of the Philippine sugar production was not even contemplated before the war. A recommendation of the Joint Preparatory Committee on Philippine Affairs to extend the transitional period until 1960 was rejected (1938).

The Japanese occupation changed the situation completely. The Japanese regarded the Philippine sugar industry as the most important bond between the Islands and the United States and, therefore, endeavored to carry out its destruction. They removed much of the equipment to Japan and tried to enforce the cultivation of cotton, particularly in the sugar areas. The experiment, however, was badly prepared and doomed to failure. The disintegrated sugar industry is now the principal economic problem in the Philippines. According to the Filipino Rehabilitation Commission,[86] a period of three to five years would be needed to reestablish the industry at its pre-war level.

While pre-war negotiations on independence were focused on the reorganization and partial liquidation of sugar production,[87]

85. *Ibid.*, p. 6.
86. It was created by the U.S. Congress, July, 1944, and was composed of 9 Filipino and 9 American members, under the chairmanship of Senator Millard E. Tydings. The Commission investigated the war damages in the Islands, May–June, 1945.
87. Senator Tydings said in his address of Dec. 22, 1934, before the Philippine Constitutional Convention, reprinted in Philippine Trade Act of 1945, (p. 109): "Anticipating the full consequence of complete and absolute independence, it will be necessary to make such cost-of-production adjustment of the things which you produce and sell as will permit the Philippines to compete successfully with other countries producing similar products for sale, not only in the U.S. market, but in all the markets of the world." After indicating the necessity for severely cutting down

postwar discussions were concerned with the rehabilitation of the Philippine economy as a whole. The Philippine Trade Act of 1946, approved in Washington and, after considerable opposition, in Manila, is based on the idea that rehabilitation of the Philippines is identical with the reconstruction of the very same sugar industry, the dependence of which on the American market was the basic pre-war problem. To this end, the Act stipulates a free-trade period of eight years and a preferential period of twenty years, which se-cures the American market for Philippine sugar.[88] In other words, the economic dependence on the United States has been extended for another generation, though the pre-war sugar industry had been rightly considered an obstacle to independence. During the Hearings before the Committee on Ways and Means, House of Representatives, on the Philippine Trade Act in February, 1946, for-mer High Commissioner Paul V. McNutt made the following sig-nificant statement:

. . . In the Philippines the national economy was geared before the war entirely and completely to export trade. And 95 percent of that export trade was with the United States. Except for rice and fish, which are locally consumed, 98 percent of all other production in the Philippines, amounting to $266,000,000 in 1941, is produced for export.

That, in a few words, is why this bill is vital to the great problem of economic recovery in the Philippines. When you say trade in the Philip-pines, you mean the national economy. It is a trading economy. And I might and should say here and now that we, the United States, managed it that way. We are responsible for the sole dependence of the Philip-pines on the American market. Our businessmen and our statesmen in past years allowed the Philippines to become a complete economic de-

capital investments, the Senator continued: "It is doubtful, however, whether this alone would permit Philippine sugar to compete with that of Cuba and Java after you are an independent nation. Indeed, some informed Filipino economists have stated it will be necessary to reduce wages by at least 50%."

88. According to the Philippine Trade Act of 1946 (the so-called Bell Bill), the tariff on sugar which will be imposed after the eight-year period of free trade is to become gradually higher year by year until the full level is reached in 1973. It pro-vides an absolute quota of 850,000 tons of Philippine sugar which will be allocated annually to the sugar producers of the year 1940 or their legal successors. Further-more, absolute quotas are stipulated for cordage, rice, cigars, tobacco, coconut oil, and buttons of pearl and shells, while no restrictions are imposed on American exports to the Islands. For detailed information about the Philippine Trade Act of 1946, see: Shirley Jenkins, "United States Economic Policy Toward the Philippine Re-public" (Institute of Pacific Relations, Paper for Tenth Conference, Stratford-upon-Avon, England, 1947, U.S. Document No. 1).

pendency of the United States to a greater degree than any single State of the Union is economically dependent on the rest of the United States. And when in 1934 we granted the Philippines their independence, effective on July 4, 1946, we still didn't do anything fundamental to change their economy. We expressed pious wishes, of course. Congress provided that beginning in 1941, Philippine exports to us would begin to pay a tax, to be gradually increased until 1946, and after that, sudden death. Of course, we realized at the time that it wouldn't work. We provided for the holding of a trade conference no less than 2 years before independence to recommend such measures for post-independence relations as might be found necessary and desirable. That was the extent of our recognition of the paradox in our policy—of granting the Philippines political independence while maintaining them as economic dependents.[89]

McNutt's statement gives an excellent survey of the past, but it might be assumed that the same statement may hold true for the situation in 1973, when the fully reconstructed Philippine sugar production will cease to have a protected position in the American market.

The expediency of rebuilding the prewar sugar industry is questioned in many quarters.[90] In March, 1945, when American troops again moved into Manila, former High Commissioner Francis B. Sayre wrote:

Since 1941, Filipinos have been able to ship no sugar or other products to the American markets. It is reported that sugar cultivation, except for home consumption and the manufacture of alcohol for fuel, has been practically stopped. . . . When liberation comes, presumably sugar cultivation in the Philippines will be on a home-consumption basis. If the new Philippine government after the war is wise enough and strong

89. Philippine Trade Act of 1945, p. 199.

90. Shirley Jenkins, "Our Ties with the Philippines," *Far Eastern Survey*, XIV, No. 10 (May 23, 1945), 121 ff., opposes "the perpetuation of the unhealthy prewar economy profitable to a small group of Filipinos, Americans, and Spaniards and detrimental to the bulk of the Filipino population."

Leonidas S. Virata, "New Philippine Horizons," *ibid.*, XIV, No. 4 (Feb. 28, 1945), pp. 43 ff., proposes a transitional continuation of the free trade relationship "long enough to allow the restoration of existing industries to the place properly assignable to them in a new and diversified economic setting, but not so long as to permit them to resume the preeminent position which they occupied in the prewar years."

Abraham Chapman, "American Policy in the Philippines," *ibid.*, XV, No. 11 (June 5, 1946), 164, calls the adoption of the policy embodied in the Trade Act of 1946 a departure from the orientation of the Roosevelt Administration against a prolonged period of free trade.

enough to prevent a return to prewar sugar production figures, one of the great milestones on the way to economic independence, will be passed.[91]

The future of American-Philippine trade relations was decided according to the conception of Mr. McNutt and contrary to the expectations of Mr. Sayre. The reconstruction of the sugar industry is far advanced. The duty-free and unrestricted admission of American goods to the Philippines, so intimately correlated to the preferential position of Philippine sugar in the American market, will paralyze any attempt to diversify Philippine economy for a long time to come. In other words, the reconstruction of the sugar industry has reestablished the pre-war economy and thus preserved the semicolonial status of the Islands.[92]

The sugar regions will in the future be marked by serious unrest, as they have been in the past. It is difficult to conceive how a reconstruction of the industry can do more than stabilize the poverty and misery of the people dependent on it for their livelihood, since it will be rebuilt at a time when prices are high and will not reach full working capacity until the sugar shortage has passed and sugar again has become one of the most problematical surpluses on the world market.

The basic economic conditions, unfavorable for the development of a competitive and sound industry, cannot be improved by prolonged preferential protection. On the contrary, economic experience proves that protection weakens the structure of industry. It is beyond the scope of this study, however, to venture a predic-

91. "Freedom Comes to the Philippines," *Atlantic Monthly*, March, 1945. Regarding the future Philippine economy, he says: "If and when independence shuts the Filipinos out of the protected American markets, they will be forced to sell in world markets in competition with other areas with lower standards of living and production costs. They will have to turn away from the production of surpluses like sugar, which are saleable only in the protected American market, and learn to produce goods which they can sell at a profit in world markets. To achieve this, Filipinos must improve and lower the cost of their products through increased skill and scientific knowledge, through labor-saving devices, through utilization of by-products, through inventive ingenuity along a thousand different lines.

The solution of their economic problem will be a thorny and difficult task. It is not insoluble. American ingenuity and technical skill will be at the call of the Filipinos to help in the solution."

92. Shirley Jenkins, "United States Economic Policy Towards the Philippine Republic," p. 21

tion of the eventual consequences of this development for the political independence of the Islands.[93]

THE MARKETING PROBLEM   The Filipinos are foreigners in the marketing sector of their country's economy, as are the other peoples in Southeast Asia. While Americans and Spaniards, and, to some extent, Chinese, dominate the export of the cash crops and control the import trade, the Chinese maintain an extremely strong, almost monopolistic position in the retail business [94] and in the important rice trade, in spite of government intervention in recent years. Until the early thirties, they were in complete control of the rice market. Rice produced in the Islands was almost exclusively polished in primitive Chinese rice mills, and the millers were not at all interested in grading the rice. The price was correspondingly low and was fixed on the Chinese-dominated rice exchange in Manila, where a handshake between great Chinese rice merchants concluded big transactions.

The Chinese is the middle man and most naturally, therefore, subject to violent attacks arising from Philippine nationalism. He is considered the enemy who exploits the toiling Filipino peasant and is easily recognizable and hence vulnerable to attacks. He is usually the principal buyer of the rice crop, often the only retailer in the *bario* (hamlet or village) and is always moneylender. Even today, the Chinese merchant generally trades the rice crop of the peasant and very largely controls the expenditures of the small native household. In both functions, he sets the terms arbitrarily, since he disposes of the cash and is the last resort of the small

93. See Francis B. Sayre, *op. cit.;* Abraham Chapman, *op. cit.;* Senator Tydings, in the Hearings on the Philippine Trade Act of 1945, *op. cit.* (pp. 90, 103), indicates that most of the people outside of the Islands favoring free trade relations are fundamentally opposed to Philippine independence, even High Commissioner McNutt: "Their whole philosophy is to keep the Philippines economically even though we lose them politically" (p. 90). "Will the Philippines be independent if they are forever hooked to our economy? If they get ingrained into our economic system we will hold the whip and they will not be free and independent, just as sure as you are born" (p. 103). Later, however, Senator Tydings supported the redrafted Trade Act, which represents a compromise, though also based on a prolonged period of free trade.

94. Small Chinese retail stores called "sari-sari" stores, with a capital of but a few hundred pesos and purchasing on a cooperative basis, dominate retail trade not only in Manila but also in every village and hamlet in the provinces. They have a remarkable assortment of everyday merchandise at the cheapest price.

peasant for credit. A report of the Rice Commission to the President of the Philippines asserted correctly that the rice industry is dominated by speculative activities at the expense of the peasant class, and that the margin of price evaluation is very wide, often more than 150 percent.[95] The small farmer is, therefore, at the mercy of powerful speculators. "Compelled by poverty to convert into ready cash his usually small share, he sells it at prices below production costs. . . . He goes deeper into debt with no hope for salvation."[96] Landlords and Chinese traders buy and stock rice in order to sell it shortly before the next harvest at excessive prices. Both as producer and consumer, the peasant is decidedly the loser.

In 1936, the Commonwealth established the National Rice and Corn Corporation (NARIC) in an effort to break the Chinese monopoly and prepare the Islands for the status of political independence. Its functions were twofold: 1) to operate large, well-equipped rice mills, like the NARIC mill in Nueva Ecija which should benefit the producer by grading the rice and paying a fair price; 2) to reduce the seasonal fluctuations in prices, which are the basis for rice speculation and are largely responsible for the indebtedness of the peasants. The aim of the NARIC was to satisfy the needs of both producer and consumer, a difficult problem for a government institution. By importing rice at reduced custom duties and selling directly to the consumer, the NARIC has undoubtedly been successful in preventing disastrous price increases in times of poor harvest, when a number of rice producers were turned into rice consumers. The technique applied here was the setting of a minimum price which would be fair to producer as well as consumer and maintaining it by market operations.

The period of five years in which NARIC operated before the war in the Pacific was too short to prove whether the Philippine method of government intervention can solve the manifold problems of the rice market. It proved successful in reducing seasonal price fluctuations, especially in years of short crops, and helped to prevent increased indebtedness through price stabilization. But, as Wick-

95. Quoted from Wickizer and Bennett, *The Rice Economy of Monsoon Asia*, p. 179.
96. Victor Buencamino, *Solving the Rice Problem* (Philippine National Rice and Corn Corporation, Manila, 1937), pp. 2–3. See also Wickizer and Bennett, *op, cit.*, pp. 178 ff.

izer and Bennett [97] rightly point out, the problems of overproduction are much more difficult to solve than those arising from temporary scarcity, and price regulations in the long run will be extremely difficult to carry out without control of production. For it can hardly be expected that NARIC can carry the losses connected with its stabilizing operations during consecutive years of oversupply.

To a certain extent, NARIC succeeded in breaking the Chinese monopoly on the rice market. And, though the Chinese rice dealer is still a highly important factor, he no longer unilaterally decides the price of rice. The position of the small producer, however, has not been substantially improved. As he still depends on cash advances which he cannot obtain from NARIC, and has no access to reasonable credit, he remains tied to the Chinese channels of business.[98]

The tobacco growers are hardly better off. Cash advances generally bind them to sell their entire produce to the moneylender, at terms set by him. The growers receive only 33–40 percent on an average of the wholesale price of leaf tobacco in Manila, the remainder accruing to the middle man.[99]

In the copra industry, a long chain of middle men connects the small farmer with the market. Price differentiations according to grades and standards are almost unknown.

The cooperative societies which were established with the purpose of alleviating the credit and marketing situation of the peasants proved to be a failure, partly because the cooperative idea was misconceived. By 1939, only 163 agricultural marketing associations were in operation. The volume of their total sales did not exceed 8 million pesos. In the last years before the war, several new associations were in the process of organization in the provinces of Abra, Tayabas, Laguna, Ilocos Sur, and some others.[100]

Cooperative credit societies were only in the beginning of devel-

97. *Op. cit.*, pp. 178 ff.

98. In 1941, the author was informed that Chinese rice traders largely took advantage of the NARIC mills by using Filipino "dummies."

99. Owen L. Dawson, "Philippine Agriculture, a Problem of Adjustment," *Foreign Agriculture* (Vol. IV, Washington, 1940), pp. 383 ff., pp. 423 ff.

100. *Annual Report of the Secretary of Agriculture and Commerce, 1938* (Manila, 1939), pp. 76 ff.; and the *Report of 1939* (Semi-Annual Report, Manila, 1939), p. 74.

opment before the war. In 1938, 166 agricultural credit societies were maintained by the Cooperative Fund. Only seven, however, paid their account in full during the year. The outstanding loans were only about 650,000 pesos; but not even these loans were accessible to the tenant farmer, since he had no land to give as security.

For the capital [101] and effort invested in the cooperative organizations, the results were extremely meager. The movement was used largely to favor limited but influential groups, who established overstaffed and well-equipped office organizations in Manila, while field work received very little attention. But what was worse, the system was frequently a cover for actual cartel agreements. For example, shortly before the war, a small group of Filipino salt producers organized a so-called salt cooperative under the Philippine Cooperative Administration. Their purpose was to break the monopoly of the Chinese salt dealers, but, at the same time, to maintain the exorbitant price on salt. Generally speaking, the cooperative movement was used as the official weapon in the fight against Chinese business [102] without establishing any real cooperative spirit. Cooperative institutions would sell commodities, largely produced with government support, to private stores at cheap prices, provided that these were owned by Filipinos and not by Chinese. The Chinese, however, operated through Filipino dummy firms, and the largest part of the government-supported commodities sooner or later were found for sale in the Chinese sari-sari stores.

Although the record of the cooperative organizations under the Quezon Administration certainly is discouraging, it does not exclude the possibility of future success for a well-organized movement in the Islands. On the contrary, if furnished with adequate capital and prepared to work at the level of greatest need, without landlord interference in the management, credit and marketing

101. For the further development of cooperative marketing and credit societies, the Cooperative Department of the National Trading Corp. was established by Commonwealth Act No. 565, June 7, 1940. A capital of 5 million pesos was approved for this purpose.

102. Fifth Annual Report of the President of the Philippines to the President and Congress of the United States, Covering the Period July 1, 1939 to June 30, 1940 (Washington, 1941), p. 28. The President, however, applies the term "alien" (not Chinese).

The PHILIPPINES

THE PHILIPPINES 213

cooperatives might well be a valuable contribution in raising the level of living of the Filipino peasant.

LABOR Most of the workers are engaged in agriculture. Of 5.3 million gainfully employed, 3.5 million (or 65 percent) are farm hands.

Labor conditions in the Islands are notoriously bad, and are, to a considerable extent, responsible for the permanent social unrest in the central provinces of Luzon.[103] The "Social Justice Program" of President Quezon was the official acknowledgement of a social emergency. In the section directly concerned with labor conditions, it provided laws for collective bargaining, eight-hour work days, minimum wages for common laborers in government employment, a National Security Administration, a Court of Industrial Relations, and a Workmen's Compensation Act.[104] In support of this program, President Quezon stated that the right of property is secondary to the greater and more important right to live, and that he believed "in recognizing human rights in preference to property rights," when there is a conflict between them.[105] But by the logic of the political structure of the Philippine Commonwealth, the government was forced to interfere again and again on the side of the property owners in cases of conflict [106] and support the vested interests by means of police and court orders. Positive achievements of Quezon's Social Justice Program, therefore, remained limited. An essential part of the laws was actually evaded or sabotaged by powerful vested interests, which proved to be stronger than the authorities in Manila. This was particularly true in the sugar industry. With certain limitations, it can be asserted that the main effect of the Program was to give official emphasis to the problems of labor, hereby strengthening the social consciousness of the population and hastening the development of a Philippine Trade Union movement.

103. Fourth and Fifth Annual Reports of the United States High Commissioner to the Philippine Islands, respectively, pp. 50 ff., and pp. 34 ff.
104. Kenneth K. Kurihara, *Labor in the Philippine Economy* (Palo Alto, Calif., 1945), pp. 51–52. The Workmen's Compensation Act was practically insufficient because it did not provide benefits according to loss of earning power. In addition, it exempted injuries involved because of "notorious negligence of the worker." In this way, it gave no efficient protection.
105. *Manila Bulletin*, Feb. 15, 1938.   106. Kurihara, *op. cit.*, pp. 23 ff.

In 1939, the daily earnings of an agricultural laborer ranged from 15 centavos to 2 pesos, while the average minimum was 42 centavos and the average maximum 1.05 pesos.[107] The *Yearbook of Philippine Statistics* reporting on the wages of 670,000 agricultural workers in 1939, states that 147,000 workers received a daily wage of only 20 to 29 centavos, 125,000 of 30 to 39 centavos, 98,000 of 40 to 49 centavos, 156,000 of 50 to 59 centavos, and only 12,000 persons received a daily wage of more than one peso. About 43,000 workers, mostly adolescents, earned less than 20 centavos a day.

The economic level of the agricultural worker was even lower than that of the tenant. Kurihara refers to the agricultural wage level as "starvation wages." [108]

Conditions were particularly bad in the sugar industry, the largest employer in the Islands. In 1939 I. T. Runes stated [109] that the average laborer is employed only 2 or 3 days a week during almost half the year and then has to live on a weekly income of only 2 pesos. The average annual income of a sugar worker's family was only 189.93 pesos, of which one-fifth was derived from supplementary earnings of the wife and children.[110] This wage scale suggests that the worker alone must pay for the unsteady character of the work, while the industry apparently calculates that plenty of labor is always available at rates of pay that are lower than in any other area of agricultural production in the Islands. This is directly related to the excess population in the sugar provinces and the absence of a normally functioning labor market in the Islands. If the opportunity were given for any considerable migration, the sugar industry would have to reorganize and improve the working conditions of its laborers if it wanted to have competent labor at its disposal the whole year round.

The regulation of working hours was one of the main points in Quezon's social legislation. In 1939, an eight-hour labor law was passed (Commonwealth Act No. 444), but this was limited to nonagricultural workers (except piece-workers and domestic servants).

107. *Labor Bulletin* (issued by the Division of Labor Statistics, Philippine Commonwealth, Department of Labor, Manila), May, 1939.
108. *Op. cit.*, p. 45.
109. I. T. Runes, *op. cit.*, p. 31; *Report on U.S. Philippine Trade*, pp. 50–51.
110. According to an investigation by Horatio Lava, *Levels of Living in the Ilocos Region*, Institute of Pacific Relations (Manila, 1938), p. 86, the average annual income of a tenant family in the Ilocos provinces was 280 pesos.

Resistance to the law was very strong among Filipino employers, who finally succeeded in striking out the provision which prohibited wage cuts when the work day was shortened. The law was evaded wherever possible, largely by introduction of piecework, and was of but little effect outside of Manila and in enterprises not controlled by Americans and other foreigners. For the agricultural laborers—the bulk of the working population—it meant no improvement. I. T. Runes reports that the laborer in the sugar industry works as much as 15 hours per day during more than half of the entire milling season. The system of contracting laborers on piecework basis drives them to work longer and more strenuously, "despite the resultant physical strain which lessens the vitality of an individual and renders him susceptible to fatal diseases." [111]

With the exception of the cigar workers, who began to organize during the first years of American rule, trade unions did not develop until after World War I. They gained in influence by their fight against wage cuts during the slump but suffered a setback in 1935. A few years later they reorganized to assume the rights and the tasks contained in the Social Justice Program.

By 1941 a part of the Filipino working class, mainly in central Luzon, was organized in unions. According to official statistics, 438 trade unions were registered in the Islands, with a total membership of only 101,000, of which 95 percent were industrial workers.[112] But, in the same year, 190,000 industrial and agricultural workers were organized in unregistered and independent unions.[113] Among them were the large unions in the central provinces of Luzon; the General Workers Union, with about 50,000 members (Socialists), the Philippine Confederation of Peasants, with 60,000, and the Kapisapan Ng Anak Pawis (Sons of Sweat), with 80,000, the two latter under Communist influence. These unregistered unions actually represented the politically active body of the Filipino working class. The recognized leader of the agrarian socialist movement before the war was Pedro Abad Santos, son of a leading family, an intellectual of rank and an able politician. Running for the governorship of Pampanga, he polled, in the 1940 election, 33,000

111. Runes, *op. cit.*, pp. 14, 29.
112. *Journal of Philippine Statistics* (October, 1941), p. 323. These unions were partly controlled by the Department of Labor.
113. Kurihara, *op. cit.*, p. 70.

votes against the 40,000 received by the official candidate of the government, although 50 percent of his followers were not qualified as voters because of illiteracy.

In 1938 (under the influence of the CIO movement in the United States), the radical and liberal labor unions in central Luzon established the Collective Labor Movement,[114] affecting 1,800,000 persons throughout the country, as a front against the conservative National Federation of Labor, which had the official support of the government. Quezon, however, harassed by the growing unrest in central Luzon, sponsored in 1939 the establishment of the National Commission of Labor, which unified the rival labor groups. A so-called Labor Pact was signed, which became the Charter of the National Commission of Labor. Later, a National Commission of Peasants was established out of the same reasons and based on the same principles.

The National Commission of Labor was held together more by government pressure than by the spirit of solidarity.[115] Internal differences disintegrated the new labor body. Moreover, in 1939 opponents of labor within the ruling Nacionalista party established a competing labor organization, The Knights of Peace (Cawal ng Capayan), which was fighting unionized labor in the provinces and had clear-cut fascistic tendencies. Its activity contributed highly to the agrarian unrest before the war. Its fight against tenant and labor groups became the pattern for the government supported organization which Manuel Roxas, the first President of the Republic of the Philippines, established in Pampanga and Nueva Ecija after the war in order to fight the Hukbalahap.

The tense political situation in the new republic prevents independent labor and peasant organizations from achieving the publicity which is the attribute of sound democracy. Their actual existence, however, cannot be denied, since repeatedly they are reported as responsible for the unrest in the plains of central Luzon.

LEVEL OF LIVING   The Philippines are an excellent example of the expediency to differentiate between standards and levels of living.[116] Though the standard of living in the Philippines is the high-

---

114. *Ibid.*, pp. 76 ff.   115. Harlan R. Crippen, *op. cit.*, p. 355.
116. Joseph S. Davis, "Standards and Content of Living," *American Economic Review*, Vol. XXXV, No. 1 (March, 1945).

est in the Far East with the exception of Japan, the actual level of living is not above the average in Southeast Asia. The high standard was an effect of the basic democratic attitude of the Americans, who (contrary to the Spaniards) propagandized the benefits of their way of living for everybody and did not claim it as an exclusive privilege of the "master race." [117] Consequently, the standard of living is unrealistically high. It decreases proportionately with the increasing distance from American life and business. The discrepancy between standard and actual level of living is no doubt one of the psychological reasons for social unrest and dissatisfaction.[118] It arises in the moment when the mother country discovers the capacity of the colony to become a highly qualified market for its industry and consequently makes an effort to introduce a higher level of consumption. This advanced development changes the traditional relation between mother country and colony and thus endangers the foundation of the colonial system.

The discrepancy was far more dynamic in the Islands than in other comparable areas. This is easily understood, when considering the forces which contributed to the economic and cultural penetration of the Philippines. Most active were American export interests, popularized by congenial propaganda which aimed at changing the Philippines into a "little America," furnished with the mechanics, mass luxury, and equipment of the Western world.

This high standard of living was unfortunately in contrast with actual conditions and contributed materially to the misinterpretation of the Philippine problem in large sectors of American public opinion.

In 1939, the annual per capita income in the Islands was estimated at 80 pesos.[119] Such an income, if based on the fiction of equal distribution, would place everyone merely a few points above the subsistence level.[120]

Surveys and investigations in the last years before the war confirm the extremely low level of living in the Islands. While Horatio

117. The influence of American advertising and American pictures can hardly be overestimated in this connection.
118. The influential Spanish groups in Manila did not hide their dissatisfaction with the American ways, which "spoiled" the people.
119. By Manuel Roxas, then Secretary of Finance; quoted from his Ateneo de Manila speech by Kurihara, *op. cit.*, p. 37.
120. *Ibid.*

Lava, in a study of the living conditions in the overpopulated Ilocos provinces in 1935, pointed to an average expenditure for the year of 257 pesos per family,[121] I. T. Runes, in 1938, found an average expense account of only 184.86 pesos among the sugar workers in central Luzon.[122] As much as 82 percent of their expenses were for food, leaving only 11 percent for clothing and 7 percent for "other" items.[123] The Ilocano peasant was somewhat better off, as he only had to spend 62 percent of his income for food.[124] An occasional survey in 1940 of the financial status of the worker families in Manila, by the Department of Health, stated that more than 30,000 were living on a "poverty level," 4,541 on a "health and efficiency level," and only 909 families on the "comfort level." [125]

In a discussion of domestic rice production in Asia and the absolute decline in net imports, Wickizer and Bennett [126] state that the per capita consumption of rice in the Philippines dropped 10 percent between the twenties and the thirties. It was probably replaced by an increased use of beans, sweet potatoes, and so on, but "On the whole, it seems probable that reduction of per capita rice consumption in the Philippines has involved some degree of quantitative deterioration of the diet, particularly among the rural population—an involuntary and unwelcome change, partly in response to economic pressure." The decrease is partly explained by the sharp decline in the real income of the Filipino working class, caused by a steady increase in the cost of living, independent of the considerable fluctuations of the nominal wage.[127]

The caloric content of the food eaten by the worker family is notoriously inadequate. Lava estimates the daily diet of the Ilocano peasants to be 1,400 calories per adult, 700 per child.[128] A corre-

---

121. Lava, *op. cit.*, pp. 21 ff.

122. Runes, *op. cit.*, p. 42. In this connection it might be mentioned that according to Runes, pp. 23, 24, the canteens and stores on the plantation frequently considerably overcharge. James S. Allen, "Agrarian Tendencies in the Philippines," compares, with some reservations, the Philippine sugar hand in Tarlac with the agricultural worker in Kuangtung.

123. Runes, pp. 19 ff.   124. Lava, p. 80.

125. *Journal of the Philippine Medical Association* (November, 1940), p. 690, quoted by Kurihara, pp. 38, 39. Kurihara points out that "the popular belief that the Filipino working class enjoyed a higher level of living under the American regime than under the Spanish regime does not square with the facts and figures."

126. *The Rice Economy of Monsoon Asia*, pp. 223, 224.   127. Kurihara, p. 39.

128. This estimation is particularly significant when compared with the diet of university students, notorious for being very poor. According to an investigation by

sponding investigation was not made for the sugar laborers, but Runes believes it to be below the Ilocano level, in view of the smaller variety of items in the diet.[129] Comparing the consumption level with that of China, Lava states that actual starvation does not exist in the Philippines, except in isolated cases. He continues: "In the Philippines, poverty is less gnawing. One does not die as the immediate result of starvation. Our deaths are from other causes. They are slow deaths—deaths from tuberculosis, anemia, debility. They are all deaths which can be brought about by undernourishment, by slow starvation." [130]

In his famous speech of October 18, 1937, before the first National Assembly, President Quezon gave a vivid picture of the level of living of the poor in the Islands.

. . . The poor still have to drink the same polluted water that his ancestors have drunk for ages. Malaria, dysentry and tuberculosis still threaten him and his family at every turn. His children cannot all go to school, or if they do they cannot even finish the whole primary instruction for one reason or another.

Roads from his bario or his little farm to the town there are none. Only trails are within reach of his bare feet and not because they have been constructed. As he works from sunrise to sundown, his employer gets richer, while he remains poor. He is the easy prey of the heartless usurer because usury is still rampant everywhere despite legislative enactments intended to suppress it.

That is, concisely speaking, the lot of the common man in our midst after America's long endeavor to give to all fair opportunity in the pursuit of happiness and enjoyment of life.

Quezon adds: "It was, of course, impossible for American administrators to see and reach the lowest strata of our population." [131]

Though Quezon made this speech in order to show the immense social tasks ahead of the Commonwealth, he did not mention the grave responsibility of the ruling Filipino group for the continued existence of these conditions.

Dr. Isabelo Concepcion, Univ. of the Philippines, published in the *P.I. Medical Assn. Journal*, V, No. 16 (1936), 152, the daily food intake of students having a money value of pesos 0.35 was 2,311 calories. Quoted by Lava, pp. 21 ff.

129. P. 30. 130. Lava, p. 81.

131. "Message on Improvement of Philippine Conditions, Philippine Independence and Relations with the American High Commissioner," *Messages of the President*, III, Part I (Manila, 1938), pp. 211 ff., 223.

PUBLIC HEALTH American efforts in the Philippines achieved the most remarkable results in the field of public health. By fighting superstition, religious fanaticism, and customs and habits dangerous to health, American doctors and health officials improved the drinking water, introduced vaccination and isolation and general education in hygiene.[132] Endemic malaria was battled by effective antilarval control and biological control methods. By tearing down whole sections of cities and bringing the water supply under control, cholera was finally eliminated, typhoid fever was on the decline, and Manila and its environs were freed of malaria. The Islands became the only country in the Far East with an effective food control. In the fight against infant beri-beri, the health service organized a mass production of tiki-tiki, a concentrate of rice polishings rich in vitamin B_1, which was distributed to all infants free of charge.

However, even in the Philippines, where the public health policy was relatively outstanding and most efficiently organized, the effects were limited by the general economic conditions. Without raising the level of living, for the bulk of the population, it proved impossible to control diseases caused by undernourishment and lowered resistance. An early aging and a short life is still the lot of the average man in the Islands.[133]

The death rate in the Islands is still among the highest in the world (19.40 per 1,000 in 1931), and tuberculosis is the main cause of death today, as it was twenty years ago. In 1940, 214.67 deaths per 100,000 inhabitants were caused by tuberculosis, as against 240.33 in 1926.[134] Nor has the mortality among children of less than one year shown any considerable decline. In 1926, it was 156.71 per 1,000 children born alive; in 1939, 145.19, and, in 1940, still as many as 135.76. In the years between 1936 and 1940, the average number of deaths per 100,000 inhabitants was 6.49 from typhoid, 14.40 from dysentery, 62.84 from malaria, 85.08 from infant beri-beri, and

132. Victor Heiser, *An American Doctor's Odyssey* (New York, 1936). Dr. Heiser was the organizer of the health service in the Islands. League of Nations Health Organization, Intergovernmental Conference of Far Eastern Countries on Rural Hygiene, Preparatory Papers: *Report of the Philippines* (Geneva, 1937).

133. *Ibid.*, pp. 20 ff.

134. *Yearbook of Philippine Statistics, 1940.* No reliable statistics are available prior to 1926, as the Epidemic Department first was established in 1920. *Report of the Philippines,* pp. 9, 11.

218.56 from pulmontary tuberculosis. One-fourth of the Filipino population is contaminated by tuberculosis, and one death out of every eight is caused by this disease.

The greatly lowered resistance of the Filipino population is not only reflected in the figures for tuberculosis and infant mortality; it also affects the working capacity and causes a certain phlegmatic attitude towards physical work. Lava asserts that the Filipino workers do not have the strength and efficiency with which to compete with foreign workers in men's work. In this connection, he mentions that most Filipino workers in the United States are engaged in domestic services, or as casual farm laborers picking fruits, or in Alaskan canneries. "The work in which most of them are engaged may sometimes require comparatively long hours, but the prerequisite in these types of work is patience rather than strength and endurance. They do work which women and children and the sick can and usually do perform." [135]

CONCLUSIONS The economic and social development in the Philippines was, and still is, in accordance with the general trend in Southeast Asia. Some deviations exist, but they can easily be traced back to the 400 years of exceptionally strong Western influence particular for the Islands. Intimate contact with the United States during the last generation has certainly marked the Filipinos both economically and mentally, but has not changed the fundamental features of the country: a precapitalist agrarian economy and a semifeudalist structure of society. The educational work conducted by the United States could hardly be expected, therefore, to create the cultural basis for political democracy within only one generation.[136] More than 60 percent of the population does not participate in the constitutional life of the nation, and it is difficult to imagine an honest democratic election under the prevailing circumstances. Considerable American efforts had but limited effect on the economic, social, and political development in the Islands, since these efforts were not coordinated with adequate agrarian reforms. The

135. P. 29.
136. The public school system was developed by the United States. In 1940, almost 1,950,000 children went to public schools. This remarkable success, however, is only relative, when considering that there were, in the same year, 6 million children under 14 years of age in the Islands.

traditional tenure system was maintained, though its rigid structure prevented the organic growth of Philippine economy.

For the spiritual development of the Filipinos, however, American influence and education became of decisive importance. The American creed of equality and liberty, and the confidence in progress and in a high standard of living for everybody, have changed the Filipino. He feels different from his ancestors and has accepted Western ideology and ways of thinking, not as an additional attribute, but almost as an inherited right. This process of mental assimilation cannot be emphasized too strongly. It explains the vigorous resistance of the Filipino peasants against the Japanese invaders and their "Asia for the Asiatics" propaganda. It was owing to the cultural contribution of American democracy that the tumultuous uprisings of generations developed into a national movement for land. It was Abraham Lincoln—and not Lenin—who became the prophet and hero for the oppressed and impoverished Filipino peasants, although some might say that it was a simplified Abraham Lincoln. It was the untiring American teacher who formed the psychology of the Filipino peasant at the same time when American economic policy stabilized the existing social order for another generation or two.

The course of history has been dark and complicated for the people on the 7,000 islands, once emotionally called "Orphans of the Pacific." [137] American rule did not establish social and economic equilibrium, and, therefore, neither a real democracy. But it finally granted the Islands a status of political liberty, and, as it had safeguarded the public domain, it also provided for the people the space for a more fortunate future in a sovereign republic of their own.

Large estates still dominate political and economic life, and agrarian unrest will smolder, and perhaps ignite, as long as the land problem is not solved. But the American ideal of democracy and justice has taken root in the life of every Filipino peasant and has made him conscious of his human rights, often before he can even read. This contribution will never be forgotten. It will still be gratefully remembered when export quotas and duty-free imports have passed into oblivion.

137. Florence Horn, *Orphans of the Pacific; the Philippines* (New York, 1941).

7

Siam

INTRODUCTION: POLITICAL INDEPENDENCE, ECONOMIC DEPENDENCE
Siam is the only country in Southeast Asia which has maintained its
political independence intact through the centuries. It has, therefore, a special place in this study. Despite considerable territorial
losses, and even in the age of modern imperialism, Siam has remained politically independent by balancing the political tensions
and frictions between France and Great Britain, which command
the neighboring areas of Indo-China and Malaya. In the years before
World War II, Siam continued the game of balance between Great
Britain and Japan, and thus maintained its precarious position as a
buffer state between empires.

But Siam's political sovereignty is not accompanied by economic
independence. Therefore, it differs from the neighboring areas only
politically, and can rightly be considered a "semicolonial" nation.
It is, in fact, an economic satellite of the British Empire.[1] Moreover,
the concessions made to foreign investors, especially to British companies, were in many instances part of the national policy. The
political leaders in Siam were wise enough to recognize that public
debt endangers political independence, and have, therefore, avoided
external public loans as far as possible. In 1937–38, the total outstanding debt was only £6.4 million, almost entirely in the hands
of British subjects. The per capita debt in 1938 was only $U.S. 2.50,
the lowest in Southeast Asia.[2] It was not increased even during the
great depression; on the contrary, the amortization continued. The

---

1. Kate L. Mitchell, *Industrialization of the Western Pacific* (New York, 1942),
p. 165.
2. Helmut G. Callis, *Foreign Capital in Southeast Asia* (New York, 1942). Callis
gives the per capita debt in Malaya as $12, Netherlands Indies $10, the Philippines,
$3.5, and Indo-China $3.3.

government of Siam thus avoided a financial policy which sooner or later would undoubtedly have resulted in the transfer of national revenues as security to foreign hands, but it encouraged direct foreign investments.

This policy differed from that of the Japanese, who, out of fear of foreign control preferred to avoid direct foreign investments. However, this difference in attitude to the problem of entrepeneur investments corresponds only to different stages of economic development. While Japan, with the help of foreign advisers, was able to manage the process of industrialization herself, Siam still needs foreign initiative and management; in other words, direct investments. Japan feared that direct foreign investments might result in interference in her economic life and create difficult relations between the investor and the government, the laborers, and the general population. But she welcomed rentier investments which did not involve any active control, since the well-balanced, self-controlled economy in Japan guaranteed regular service for the loans.[3] The Siamese, however, who already were economically controlled by direct foreign investors, wished at any price to avoid the danger of additional political control which might come as the result of public indebtedness.

This cautious financial attitude, born out of experience with Western colonial practices, is largely responsible for the backward economic, social, and cultural status of this country. Siam intentionally avoided the import of rentier capital and thereby blocked any progressive development in the fields of public health, education, and agriculture; in other words, in order to avoid foreign entanglement, she spurned such Western penetration as might have been of great social benefit to the country.

The economic structure of Siam is that of a primitive agricultural economy, with a few foreign-controlled, extractive industries producing raw materials for export,[4] in which neither native capital nor native labor participates to any considerable extent. Only the production of rice is in Siamese hands, while the milling and trading operations are monopolized by the Chinese. Rice production

3. Callis; *Foreign Investments in Southeast Asia,* "Introduction," by Carl F. Remer, p. 4.
4. Kate L. Mitchell, *op. cit.,* p. 166.

is the livelihood of 80 percent of the population, although the export of rice (about 2 million tons, second only to Burma) [5] is placed on the world market without the participation of native producers or native merchants.

In 1938, Western business investments amounted to $U.S. 90 million, of which 70–80 percent were British and Australian; the remainder, Danish, American, Swiss, Japanese and French. British and Australian capital was primarily invested in tin mining and in the exploitation of teak forests. Most of the tin-dredging companies are Australian, though three great British concerns are also operating. The timber industry is 88 percent in foreign hands; two-thirds are concentrated in four British companies. Furthermore, Danish and French capital is interested in teak holdings.

The Chinese influence [6] is also important. Chinese investments are estimated at $U.S. 100–120 million. Chinese capitalists control the rice mills and the fishing industry completely and part of the saw mills. They have large interests in tin and rubber production and dominate the internal retail trade. It is reported that Chinese rice dealers earn as much as 50 percent of the export value of the rice. Remittances from Chinese in Siam to Hongkong were estimated by Remer [7] in 1933 to average $H.K. 20 million (bahts 16 million).[8]

Siam has no manufacturing industries and is almost completely dependent upon imports for all manufactured consumer goods. In addition, Siam's trade is depending on the British ports of Singapore, Penang, and Hongkong while Bangkok's position as a trading port is relatively small. In the period between 1934 and 1939, 70.7 percent of Siam's total foreign trade was carried on with the British Empire as a whole.[9]

The position of Siam in the international balance of payments

5. V. D. Wickizer and M. K. Bennett, *The Rice Economy of Monsoon Asia* (Palo Alto, Calif., 1941), p. 98, Appendix, Table IV.
6. Mitchell, p. 166.
7. Carl F. Remer, *Foreign Investments in China* (New York, 1933), p. 185.
8. Siamese currency was linked, before the war, to sterling at the rate of approximately 11 bahts to the pound. In 1941, the baht-dollar exchange rate, consequently, averaged approximately 1 baht to U.S. $0.36. However, with regard to the valuation of old, long-term investments and earlier statistics, we have applied the old rate of exchange, 1 baht to U.S. $0.45.
9. Mitchell, *op. cit.*, p. 165.

is not favorable. Her active export balance based on movements in goods, services, and gold (averaging between bahts 50–60 million annually), is compensated by "invisible" imports for which no figures are available. The "invisible" imports are made up of the profits of foreign companies and individuals carrying on business in Siam, of payments for freight and insurance and of private remittances, mostly by Chinese immigrants to their families in China.[10]

The economic dependence of Siam can hardly be better described than it is in the official report of the Financial Adviser on the Budget for 1936–1937: "These facts show how little the national wealth can be growing and, as most of the country's commerce is in foreign hands, a larger favorable trade balance in practice simply means larger remittances abroad; little of the increased wealth stays at the country's disposal."[11]

This almost complete economic dependence has aroused a strong nationalist sentiment against Western and Chinese economic penetration. After the revolution of 1932, the new constitutional government designed a nationalistic economic program aiming at a higher degree of self-sufficiency and at a reduction of foreign economic control. This was to be done partly by government participation and control in trade and industry and partly by the encouragement of private native initiative.[12]

Though it may sound contradictory, the status of political independence increased the unfavorable effects of Siam's semicolonial economy, especially during the period of the depression in the thirties. Siam did not have the backing of strong empires and, consequently, she had no protected markets like her competitive neighbors Burma and Indo-China, which were both political dependencies.

Siam's bargaining power for the sale of her 2 million tons of rice

10. *Report of the Financial Adviser on the Budget of the Kingdom of Siam for the year 1933–34* (Ministry of Finance, Bangkok, 1934); *Balance of Payments, 1935* (Geneva, 1936), pp. 138–139, and *Balance of Payments, 1938* (Geneva, 1939), pp. 118–120.

11. *Report of the Financial Adviser on the Budget of the Kingdom of Siam, for the Year 1936–37* (Bangkok, 1937).

12. Virginia Thompson, *Thailand, the New Siam* (New York, 1941), p. 589. According to Kate L. Mitchell, *op. cit.*, p. 173, shortage of liquid capital prevents private native investments. In 1939 only 2,731 Siamese paid any income tax at all. Less than 3,000 individuals had an income of more than 2,400 bahts, and the largest single income was only 39,000 bahts.

for export was naturally poor, as her purchasing power was relatively small.[13] Growing economic nationalism in China, Japan, and Malaya resulted in increased rice cultivation and decreased imports of rice, a development which, ironically enough, was of greatest damage to the only politically independent country in Southeast Asia. Siam suffered like a colonial country, but lacked the protection of the colonial power.[14]

POPULATION AND LAND UTILIZATION   The population—14,500,000 in 1937—is concentrated in the areas suitable for the cultivation of wet rice, especially on the alluvial plains and in river valleys. The density is not considerable—only 57 persons per square mile on an average (including the Bangkok population); it is greatest in central Siam, on the plains of the Menam river, where, in some districts, it is 362 and the nutrition density 145 persons per square mile.[15] Between 1920 and 1930, almost 90 percent of the population lived in agricultural communities.

According to the official census of 1929, there was a Chinese minority of about 450,000, but according to Credner,[16] the actual number was almost twice as large. The Chinese in Siam are not only workers, middle men and traders, import and export merchants, but they represent, at the same time, one of the strongest capital-holding groups in the country. They control the rice trade and rice processing—virtually the entire economy.[17] They are the economically privileged group. The Chinese minority, powerful by means of its economic influence, has been, and continues to be, the subject of vehement public criticism and a good deal of administrative discrimination.

13. Virginia Thompson, *op. cit.*, p. 371. Indo-China was gaining on Siam as provisioner of the Chinese market, mainly because of a treaty that France had finally concluded with China in 1935.

14. Rupert Emerson, *Government and Nationalism in Southeast Asia* (New York, 1942), Part I, Introduction, p. 9: "In the realm of hard actualities, the economic life and movement of Thailand has frequently been almost as circumscribed as that of its colonial neighbors."

15. Karl J. Pelzer, *Population and Land Utilization*, p. 46; W. I. Ladejinsky, "Thailand's Agricultural Economy," in *Foreign Agriculture*, VI (Washington, 1942), 162. Further, *Statistical Yearbook of the Kingdom of Siam*, 1937–39 (Bangkok, 1941), is generally used.

16. Wilhelm Credner, *Siam das Land der Tai* (Stuttgart, 1935), p. 199.

17. *Economic Development in Siam* (Trade Information Bulletin No. 606, Dept. of Commerce, Washington, 1929), pp. 7 ff.

Carle C. Zimmerman,[18] considers underpopulation to be an out-standing factor in Siamese economy. He relates it directly to the backward situation of agriculture, asserting that "greater numbers are necessary to an improved agricultural technique in many of the areas." This underpopulation is, first of all, the result of a complete lack of medical care, marked by a very low standard of public health and an unchecked death rate.[19] The only exception is vaccination against smallpox. Western medicines are seldom applied, largely because the prohibitive costs are an obstacle to their extensive use by the people. The Report of Siam to the Health Organization of the League of Nations says: "Thus it will be seen that not only is the demand for modern medicine lacking, but that such medical care as exists is ineffective." [20] The total expenditures of the Department for Public Health were in 1936–37 baht 1.6 million and in 1937–38, baht 2.1 million—certainly a negligible amount compared with the need. Virginia Thompson [21] reports that less than one percent of the population has had access to Western medical treatment through missions and government facilities. The increase of population in later years may, however, indicate some improvement in public health, although this cannot be confirmed, as no statistics on the death rate exist.

Only 10 percent (around 5 million ha.) of Siam's total land area is cultivated or utilized. The largest area for cultivation is in central Siam, where the population density is greatest. Here, 15.8 percent of the land's surface is cultivated, while the percentages for north, northeast, and south Siam are only between 6.8 and 7.0.[22]

Approximately six percent of the total land area (3.2 million ha.) and 94 percent of the crop area are cultivated in rice, which is generally of the glutinous variety in northern Siam and non-glutinous in the central and southern part.[23] The remaining 6 percent of the crop area is used for the cultivation of tobacco, corn, rubber, cot-

18. Carle C. Zimmerman, *Siam, Rural Economic Survey, 1930–31* (Bangkok, 1931), pp. 225 ff.

19. *Ibid.*, p. 232.

20. League of Nations Health Organization, Intergovernmental Conference of Far Eastern Countries on Rural Hygiene, *Report of Siam* (Geneva, 1937), pp. 10, 15.

21. *Thailand, the New Siam*, p. 324.

22. Carle C. Zimmerman, "Some Phases of Land Utilization in Siam," *Geographical Review*, XXVII (1937), p. 386.

23. Cooked glutinous rice is a staple food in north and northeast Siam; non-glutinous rice is exported and is a staple food in the remainder of the country.

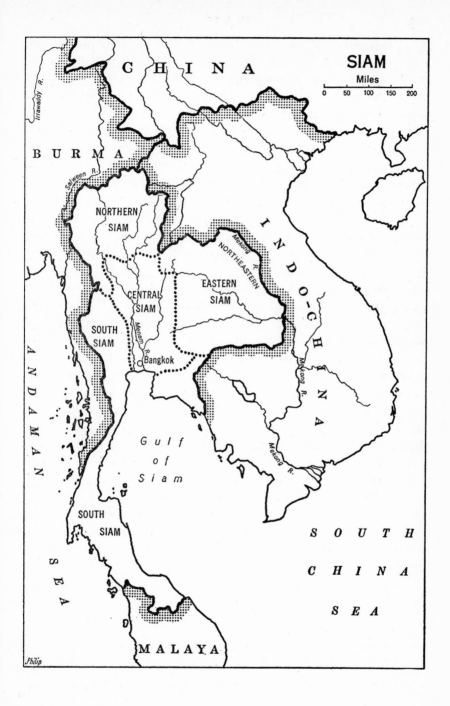

SIAM

Miles

0   50   100   150   200

CHINA

BURMA

Irrawaddy R.

Salween R.

NORTHERN
SIAM

CENTRAL
SIAM

Menam R.

SOUTH
SIAM

Bangkok

EASTERN
SIAM

NORTHEASTERN

Mekong R.

INDO-CHINA

Mekong R.

Mekong R.

A N D A M A N

S E A

Gulf
of
Siam

SOUTH
SIAM

S O U T H

C H I N A

S E A

Philip

MALAYA

ton, pepper and so on. Fifty-six percent of the rice production comes from the plains of the Menam River in central Siam,[24] as the Siamese, in general, prefer plains to hilly grounds, in accordance with their ancient primitive agricultural technique. Since time immemorial, they have been engaged in mere subsistence farming and did not begin to cultivate rice for export until 1855, after the treaties with the British representative Bowring, which brought about the development of an export trade. This caused a considerable increase of population in the enlarged areas of rice cultivation.

The average holding in the Menam valley is 24 rai (one rai is equal to 0.16 ha.), in the north it is 10 rai, and on the Karot plateau and penninsula, 6 to 7 rai. Virginia Thompson [25] explains that the size of the holdings in the various parts of the country is determined by the deep-rooted preference for plains and the dislike of the Siamese for terracing and more complicated irrigation. The utilized area belonging to one rural family differs in the various parts of Siam. While 650,000 rural families in central Siam (more than one-third of the total of rural families) use an average area of 4.25 ha., the average size in the north is 2.25 ha., and in the south and northeast, only 1.75 ha.[26]

According to the investigations of Andrews,[27] the Siamese farmer can generally meet the expenses of a normal year, especially in the villages with lively trade. But the expenditures for costs of agriculture approximate closely the cash receipts, especially in the northeast.

ESTIMATED AVERAGE PROFIT AND LOSS ON FARM OPERATIONS IN
SIAM 2476, APRIL 1, 1933 TO MARCH 31, 1934
(In bahts; 1 baht—U.S. $0.45).

Region	Total Annual Income	Total Expenditures	Operators' Profit
Northeast	30.16	29.58	0.58
South	73.89	58.59	15.30
North	65.20	51.93	13.27
Center	184.56	177.46	7.10

Source: Andrews, Siam, p. 217.

24. Virginia Thompson, Thailand, p. 125; Credner, Siam, p. 200.
25. Thailand, 326.
26. Zimmerman, "Some Phases of Land Utilization," pp. 386 ff.
27. J. Madison Andrews, Siam (2d Rural Economic Survey, 1934–35, Bangkok, 1935).

The level of living in central Siam is somewhat better than in the other districts on account of greater earnings, but, at the same time, the costs of living are much higher. As actual gains are very small, even in normal years, the situation becomes dismal when a crop fails, and indebtedness then increases very rapidly.

The degree of land utilization in Siam is a function of underpopulation. In contrast with overcrowded Java, where the forest area has dwindled to only 23 percent, already endangering the water supply of the island, underpopulated Siam can boast of an area of about 70 percent still covered by forests. Large areas of good rice land are still uncultivated, especially in the north,[28] and remnants of ancient dikes around the old ruined cities are reminders of periods of earlier cultivation. Secondary crops in supplement to rice production are almost unknown. The margin of both extensive and intensive cultivation could be increased, but stagnation characterizes agriculture everywhere in Siam. The statistics even indicate a decrease of the average unit yield between 1921–25 and 1931–35 from 36 to 32 bushels per acre (about 11 percent).[29]

Conditions in Siam prove that underpopulation is as detrimental as overpopulation; both must be considered with reference to the productive capacity of the country and in relation to the agricultural technique and levels of living. Zimmerman [30] writes:

With the exception of the fact that it is easier to make a living here than in most Oriental countries, and that the incomes are somewhat higher than for the rest of Asia, there is no reason to believe that the standard of living has gained anything from underpopulation in itself. The people have more land resources, but they are not used. Furthermore, the people are not sufficient in number to support many institutions, which might be done by community efforts in much poorer but more densely populated communities. Throughout the history of this country, there has been the same trouble of underpopulation. However, the chief defect of underpopulation is that there is no stimulus leading to economic progress or to improved methods of agriculture.

28. Credner, *Siam*, p. 201.

29. W. I. Ladejinsky, "Thailand's Agricultural Economy," p. 177. W. D. Wickizer and M. K. Bennett, *The Rice Economy of Monsoon Asia*, p. 200, assume that these figures are misleading and that the average unit yield has remained more or less the same.

30. Zimmerman, *Siam, Rural Economic Survey*, pp. 228 ff.

Though Siam has a different political status from the other countries of Southeast Asia, it suffers from the typical malady of colonial areas—lack of economic diversification and social stratification, here combined with the effects of underpopulation. The underpopulation, related to the low status of public health, is, ironically enough, to a great extent the result of uncompleted colonization.

LAND TENURE AND INDEBTEDNESS In general, the Siamese farmer works on his own soil, but no statistics are available to prove to what extent. While the farmer is almost always the landowner in the regions of subsistence farming,[31] in certain districts of central Siam, a class of poor and landless peasants working as tenants and laborers on big estates has developed.[32] This is especially the case around Bangkok and Klong Rangsit in the center of the intensively irrigated and highly commercialized area of central Siam. This development is intimately related to the increase of land values caused by the growing rice exports and superior transportation facilities. Where tenancy is found in north and northeast Siam, the land rent is generally paid in kind and usually amounts to half of the crop, while cash rent is predominant in central and southern Siam.[33]

The tenant problem is greatest around Dhanyabari and in the eastern irrigated district of central Siam, where 84 percent of the peasants are tenants. (In other districts of Siam, tenancy is usually between 5 and 30 percent.)[34] Consequently, there is considerable social tension in this district. The fact that the landlords, mostly absentees, receive the rentals in cash and not in produce proportionate to the size of the crop, contributes greatly to the large indebtedness. The situation is especially serious around Klong Rangsit[35] where the farms mostly belong to landlords in Bangkok and are managed by local rent collectors. The tenants are settled on large farms averaging about 100 rais, far away from the village and settled village life.

Tenure contracts are generally for one year only. One of the

31. Pelzer, *Population and Land Utilization*, p. 141.
32. According to *The Record*, April, 1922 (issued by the Ministry of Commerce and Communications, Bangkok), the largest estates are mostly owned by native landlords.
33. Zimmerman, *Siam, Rural Economic Survey*, pp. 18 ff.
34. Pelzer, *op. cit.*, p. 141.   35. Zimmerman, *op. cit.*, pp. 305 ff.

worst effects of this is the fact that the tenant is not interested in making improvements on his farm, since he is almost certain that he will get neither the benefits nor any compensation. Furthermore, the constant changing around makes him lose contact with his own village and he has but little possibility of settling down. As in Burma the tenant-farmer is rootless and without stable and lasting relations. Before the slump, the rent, mostly paid in cash, averaged about 4 bahts per rai, and the land tax was 1 baht. The average land tax of a family in central Siam was 20 bahts.[36] It is generally recognized [37] that the rentals are too high to be met in years of poor crops or low prices. The government was totally indifferent to the land problem and did not take any initiative until after the slump. It then set aside a capital fund of 3,000,000 bahts for loans to farmers, strengthened the position of cooperative organizations, and ordered in April, 1940, a 20 percent reduction in the rents of rice fields.

Land values in central Siam are obviously inflated by keeping the rentals high, in spite of decreased rice quotations, and by maintaining an obsolete land taxation system. This artificially high price level is detrimental to the rural population, and, more than any other factor, is the cause of their indebtedness. According to Zimmerman [38] the total agricultural debt in 1931 was estimated at about 143 million bahts (123.5 million in central Siam, alone). He refers to 78 million bahts of this amount as "harmful" because it is lent at an exorbitant rate of interest (generally 22 percent) by moneylenders who will claim the land if the interest is not paid.[39] These figures, however, are considered exaggerated by some authors. Andrews, who made his survey in 1934–35,[40] estimates the total agricultural debt to be only about 100 million bahts, a figure which Virginia Thompson [41] considers higher than the value of the land itself. About 80 percent of the total indebtedness was concentrated in the lower Menam valley, which has the most intensive irrigation system.

36. Ladejinsky, "Thailand's Agricultural Economy," p. 165.
37. Andrews, *op. cit.*, p. 109.
38. Zimmerman, *Siam, Rural Economic Survey*, p. 203.   39. *Ibid.*, p. 204.
40. Andrew, *op. cit.*, pp. 335-6. He is more optimistic, and believes that the majority of the creditors are relatives and friends.
41. Virginia Thompson, *Thailand*, p. 307.

The Zimmerman survey (1930–31) estimated the average indebtedness per famly as 190 bahts in central Siam, 30 bahts in the north, 10 in the south, and 14 in the northeast. The indebtedness was highest in the highly commercialized, fertile, central region, which also is the center of landlordism. Forty-nine families out of a hundred were in debt. The average rate of interest was between 23 and 32 percent, with an average of 23 percent in central Siam. However, in Klong Rangsit, the average rate of interest was 60 percent.[42]

At the time of the Andrews survey—in 1934–35, immediately after the slump—average indebtedness in central Siam had increased to 233.82 bahts per family, while it had decreased to a considerable extent in other regions. Central Siam seems to have only a limited capacity for economic recovery. This commercialized agricultural sector is the weakest in the country. The average indebtedness is about ten times greater than in the self-sufficient north, an exorbitant amount even when the fact is taken into consideration that debts are inseparable from commercialized agriculture. Certainly, abundant rice production for the world market has not enriched the peasants of central Siam. It is not unlikely that indebtedness will become still more serious in the future, on account of high rentals and concentrated ownership and because the lack of an efficient and reasonable credit mechanism will further hasten the process of land concentration.

The agricultural technique of the tenant is extremely poor. No machinery is used in cultivation, other than the wooden plough and harrow, and no artificial fertilizer is applied. Wherever modern machinery has been introduced, it has failed, largely because the tenant-cultivator, mechanically untrained, was unable to handle it. Although the rice area per family is relatively large, the general effect of the tenure system was to depress the level of living and create extremely poor economic and cultural conditions.[43] Indebtedness of the tenant to the Siamese landlord and Chinese merchant is high, and his diet is deficient. Just one poor crop or only a limited drop in prices may ruin him. He will lose the land and the crop and be forced to start the same poor existence all over again somewhere else.[44]

42. Zimmerman, *Siam, Rural Economic Survey*, p. 307.   43. *Ibid.* p. 306.
44. Pelzer, *Population and Land Utilization*, p. 141.

The tenant districts of Siam are marked by an atmosphere of hopelessness. This situation offers proof that stimulus to improvement is lacking under a system of landlordism, even where fertile lands are available. Conditions in some districts illustrate the fact that the mere existence of landlordism is detrimental to agricultural development in general and tends to lower the social and cultural standards of the people—a social factor far more influential than the political status of the area or the race of the landlord.

LEVEL OF AGRICULTURAL CULTIVATION   In the hills and mountain region of Siam, shifting cultivation is still practiced with the most primitive tools, such as the hoe or digging stick. While in some recently established rubber plantations in central Siam Western and Chinese managers have kept pace with more modern agricultural techniques, cultivation by primitive agricultural methods is still the predominant practice of native farmers in the fertile plains of central Siam.

The irrigation system is especially primitive, despite its position of importance in a country with practically a monoculture of rice, where only a limited section of the crop area receives the needed six feet of precipitation during the rice season. The systems of canals and ditches built by Siamese farmers to carry the floods of the river to their fields are inadequate, because there is no adjustment of their capacity to accord with the changing levels of the rivers. Siam's rice fields are flooded with excessive waters at times of high water level and lack water in dry years if there is no flooding of the river valleys. A well-balanced rice cultivation can be assured only if large irrigation works are provided for storing water from the great rivers in years of water abundance and for draining canals and dikes as a safeguard against devastating floods.[45]

In the north, the agricultural technique as a whole is still more primitive than in central Siam. Seed selection is still rudimentary. However, the northern farmer has learned that the mixing of glutinous with nonglutinous rice lowers the market price.[46]

The continued cultivation of rice, uninterrupted for generations, is exhausting the soil throughout much of Siam. As practically no manure is applied, nitrogen, phosphorous and potash are

45. Wilhelm Credner, *Siam*, p. 218.   46. Zimmerman, *op. cit.*, p. 144.

often deficient in the soil,[47] especially in central Siam, where the old rice fields on the plains of the Menam River give the smallest returns per acre. Nitrogen and phosphatic fertilizers would increase the yield considerably. The introduction of systematic fertilization is one of the most essential requirements in the reconstruction of Siamese agriculture. Any progress is hampered by the low level of education and the immense difficulties which agricultural training consequently encounters in a largely illiterate country. Progress is necessary in the use of implements,[48] methods of seed selection, and in preparation of the ground for planting. But, first of all, the Siamese peasant has to be trained to diversify his crops, because only through diversified agriculture can the badly needed new sources of cash income be created.

Zimmerman is of the opinion that commercialized agriculture should be extended, to a certain degree, to the nearly self-sufficient districts of the north, northeast, and south. This would increase the cash income in these regions. But the solution of the problem for central Siam lies in increased home production of food and other items of consumption, in order to reduce economic dependence on outside forces beyond their control. "The self-sufficient farmer in Siam can make more money without raising his cost of living, and the commercialized farmer can lower his cost of living and raise more food, etc., at home without lowering his rice production and cash income." [49]

THE MARKETING PROBLEM   The problem of rice standardization is intimately connected with the entire problem of agricultural production in Siam, as well as with the income level of the native producer. So far, this problem has not been solved. Although Siam grows the best quality of rice,[50] its market position is very poor. In 1941, Siamese rice was actually listed among the three lowest grades on the world market because of the lack of standardization. Virginia Thompson [51] gives, as one of the reasons, the speculative

47. Virginia Thompson, *Thailand*, p. 358.
48. *Ibid.*, p. 360, reports that the Siamese farmer still uses self-made crude ploughs, which break quite easily.
49. Zimmerman, *op. cit.*, p. 52.
50. Siam's rice won high awards at the Regina Exhibition in London in 1933.
51. *Thailand*, p. 364.

methods of the rice traders, but considers it still more important that Siam's most essential markets are tropical countries (75 percent) which are uninterested in standardized products. The poor appearance of Siamese rice, largely mixed with red grains, hampers any expanded transactions on the European market.

One of the weakest points in the economic structure is the lack of an efficient market organization. This phenomenon is typical all over the Far East, but is especially true of Siam. The Siamese are but little engaged in trading activities, and the market is not an integrating part of their national economic life. As a matter of fact, trade can be considered an unconquered sector in the economy, dominated by aliens and not by the Siamese, who never developed beyond the limits of simple agricultural production and, therefore, remained out of contact with world economy.

Almost a century ago, Chinese millers started the export of Siamese rice. Up to the present time, Chinese merchants have controlled this trade and, consequently, the entire economic life, since 80 percent of the Siamese population is directly engaged in rice production and about 70 percent of the government revenues are derived from rice. The Chinese merchant is the middle man in all economic relations of the Siamese peasant and functions as shopkeeper, moneylender, rice broker, and import and export merchant. Consequently, Siamese nationalism turns vehemently against him. Andrews [52] questioned the justification of this reaction and made an investigation about the influence of the Chinese moneylender and middle man. He draws the conclusion that the indebtedness of the Siamese peasants to Chinese moneylenders is highly exaggerated—indeed, that only a very limited percentage of debts (highest in the south, where it is 15.5 percent) was contracted with Chinese moneylenders, while the overwhelming majority was with Siamese creditors. We do not wish to criticize the methods and results of this investigation, which was made "because of the widespread conviction in Bangkok that most of the troubles of the Siamese farmer and debtor are to be ascribed to the hateful influence of Chinese moneylenders and middle men." But it may be doubted whether the investigation covered the real problem: the advance payment by the Chinese rice dealer

52. Andrews, *Siam, 2nd Rural Economic Survey*, pp. 311, 324, 333.

to the Siamese peasant, and the subsequent dictation of the final price. The combination of credit and purchase in the advance sale —often five months ahead of the harvest—is unfavorable to the distressed peasant producer, and presents the real problem of indebtedness. It is much more important than the isolated money-lender business.

If this very common transaction had been considered in the investigation, the result would have been entirely different. For the Chinese are, in general, the rice traders in Siam, and the cash advance is the normal way of business because of the farmers' lack of money. Although Andrews occasionally mentions the more than legitimate profits of the Chinese in connection with this kind of rice dealing, he does not extend his investigation to this point, making only a few defensive comments on it. But it is actually the effect of general conditions that forces the peasant to seek the highest possible advance, either in kind or in cash. This puts the rice dealers in a strong bargaining position, and it is not fair to regard the advantage they take as merely the result of the incompetence of the Siamese.

The marketing problem is intimately related to the cash problem. As long as the farmer is in urgent need of cash, and consequently indebted, he will be at the mercy of any middle man, regardless of nationality. The middle man, who in Siam happens to be a Chinese, is nothing but a function of the prevailing conditions, and his continued existence is favored by the very same conditions which—as is generally agreed—can scarcely be tolerated any longer. The farmer has no means of self-defense against the greed of the middle man [53] as long as he is unable to develop a cooperative spirit. Nor is he in a position to take advantage of competition among the middle men, and thus raise the selling price of rice, as long as the competition among the farmers for higher cash advances is greater than the competition among the rice buyers. Actually he is interested primarily in a higher cash advance, and only secondarily, in a higher price for his produce. Therefore, it

53. Zimmerman, *Siam, Rural Economic Survey*, p. 176. The literature on this problem is very contradictory. Zimmerman stresses, on one side, the impecuniosity of the farmers, who are compelled to sell their crops at any price, and emphasizes, on the other side, the difficulties of the rice broker. However, the racial tension in this area cannot be eliminated by a mere sympathetic explanation of the Chinese situation. It may be dangerous for the Chinese middle man, also, if the true situation is concealed and not clearly stated.

may be doubted whether Zimmerman's proposal of improving the competition among the rice buyers by better methods of measurement and general circulation of market-price knowledge among the farmers [54] would solve the marketing problem, as long as the credit problem of the Siamese farmer remains unchanged.

The small farmers do, indeed, generally lack any information about the current market price in Bangkok, and only the big estate owners have the necessary market contacts.[55] The price which the farmers are paid for their rice decreases rapidly with the distance from Bangkok, and this is only partly explained by the higher cost of transportation and the uncertainty of the price development during the time of shipment.

However, the greatest disadvantage brought about by the Chinese middle man is the practice of adulterating the rice, with the consequent poor rating on the world market.[56] A better-organized and less speculative marketing system would improve this situation, but it is difficult to conceive how this could be achieved without a simultaneous betterment in the economic position of the farmer by an increase of his cash income and a solution of his urgent credit problem. Government control of rice mills [57] may remedy the situation to a certain extent, but experience in other regions, as in the Philippines, proves that this has only a very limited effect unless combined with an expanded credit system. The distressed and indebted farmer will continue doing business with the Chinese as long as the Chinese is open-handed with advance payments.

In addition, the lack of modern equipment in rice mills lowers the quality and prevents a better classification of Siamese rice; [58] its position on the world market is endangered by the struggle for profits and market privileges, combined with racial and ethical differences between European export merchants and Chinese rice brokers.

Unlike other countries in Southeast Asia, the Siamese cooperative

54. *Ibid.*, pp. 182 ff. 55. *Ibid.*, p. 178.
56. Virginia Thompson, *Thailand*, p. 363.
57. The government controlled Thai Rice Company is supposed to free the Siamese growers from the Chinese middle man and exporter and to keep the grains of rice clean and pure. In 1939, the company had obtained export orders from Japan and Germany. In 1940, it operated eight large rice mills. See Kenneth Perry Landon, *The Chinese in Thailand* (London and New York, 1941), p. 245; see also Kate L. Mitchell, *The Industrialization of the Western Pacific*, p. 173.
58. Virginia Thompson, *Thailand*, p. 565.

societies, organized in areas of great agrarian difficulties, operated successfully to a certain extent. However, they have lacked the wholehearted backing of the government,[59] and, although this situation improved after the slump, the limited scale of the whole experiment prevented general success. As the farmers are not in a position to raise capital, the government has to make available the needed funds and therefore decides the rate of expansion. From their start in 1916–17, the cooperative societies were financed by the Siam Commercial Bank and controlled by the government. The funds were gradually increased to 1,800,000 bahts, equal to 790,000 dollars. Up until 1937, they borrowed money from the Bank at 6 percent and lent it to the members at 12 percent. Thereafter, the rate of interest was cut down to 4.5 percent, permitting the societies to give long-term loans to their members at 7.5 percent and short-term loans at 9 percent.[60]

By 1937, 11,000 members were organized in 922 societies. Already in 1926 official inspectors had noted marked improvement in the economic status of members—a more rational money economy, better housing, less gambling, and a stronger marketing position.[61] In 1934, in connection with an official study of the pressing rural debt problem, the cooperatives were designated by the government for the dual job of liquidating the farmers' debts and promoting progressive agricultural methods. Later, they were to operate in the field of cooperative marketing. After 1937, government support became far more intensive, and the farmers responded with rapidly increasing membership.

In 1938–39, government-owned savings banks granted cooperative societies a credit of 1,500,000 bahts. In these years, numerous new societies were established which drew about 1,150,000 bahts from the savings banks and about 120,000 bahts from the Siam Bank Limited. This made about 4,152 bahts per new society.[62]

59. The *Record*, July, 1932. The government gave as an excuse for not extending the work during the crisis the fact that the depression had so reduced farm income that the peasants were unable to repay their loans.

60. W. I. Ladejinsky, "Thailand's Agricultural Economy," p. 172.

61. The *Record*, October, 1926.

62. Kenneth Perry Landon, *The Chinese in Thailand*, pp. 248 ff. There existed further cooperative societies for land improvement, credit societies on an extremely limited scale for persons who own no land, cooperative stores, and five marketing societies for rice. Large programs were outlined for 1940, especially on credit societies for landless peasants.

The most important type of cooperative was the credit society. During 1938–39, 303 new credit societies were created, with 4,357 members, who borrowed an average of 324 bahts. Of every hundred bahts borrowed, 73.36 were used to pay off old debts, mostly to Chinese moneylenders. Loans were secured by land owned by the borrower and were in the proportion of 39.17 bahts for 100 bahts of land value.[63]

The scale of the cooperative operations must not be overestimated, even though they helped to reduce the debt burden of numerous farmers. By 1934, the cooperatives had taken over only 2 percent of the total farm debt, and the private capital market was still powerful; even the increase since then will not have changed the picture to any considerable extent. A really large-scale development of the cooperative organization is needed if the credit problem of the Siamese peasant is to be solved. No doubt, the movement is the most promising aspect of the Siamese economy. It might be concluded, though with some reservations in view of the limited scope of the experiment, that the atmosphere of political independence may have contributed favorably to the development of the cooperative spirit.

The marketing position of the Siamese in the rice trade of their country and the position of Siamese rice in the world market will be strengthened considerably when the projected port of Bangkok is created. As the entry to this port is obstructed by a bar, only shallow-draught vessels can pass, and before the war shipments had to be made through Hong Kong and Singapore. The Chinese, engaged in the lighterage business, carried the rice over the bar to vessels bound for those ports. After the opening of the port of Bangkok for deep-water ships, the rice can be exported under Siamese control.[64]

THE LEVEL OF LIVING The level of living of the Siamese population is a reflection of the agricultural economy in general. It can be said, as it has been by Zimmerman and Andrews, that it is simpler to make a living in Siam, with its privileged climate and soil, than in other oriental countries, and that the income there is somewhat

63. *Ibid.*, p. 249.
64. *Ibid.*, p. 252. The preparatory work for the port construction was started in 1939; an amount of 3.1 million bahts was raised in September of the same year.

higher and more stable. This is in contradiction to available statistical data, which, however, do not seem too reliable. According to these data, the relation between rice production and population increase has been very unfavorable since 1920–21. While the production of cleaned rice was more or less stable between 1920 and 1940 (7 to 7.7 billion lbs.), the population increased from 10.1 million to 14.9 million. The per capita production of the 1930s decreased by 22 percent from that of the 1920s, while the export increased by 29 percent. If these figures are correct, the per capita consumption would have been reduced by 34.5 percent.[65] But such a catastrophic decline of an already low level of living would have resulted in serious unrest and dissatisfaction if it really had occurred. V. D. Wickizer and M. K. Bennett [66] indicate correctly that this reported decline in per capita rice production undoubtedly misrepresents the facts; stability, or a modest decline, or a small increase in rice production seems the more reasonable assumption.

The level of living, however, is far from being in accord with the potentialities of the country.[67] Zimmerman [68] asserts that the people live well, though much can be done to improve their living conditions. Famines seldom occur and are of minor significance. The average cash income or the average value of the level of living (including cash and other income) is twice as great as the average for China or India. However, the low rural incomes ever since the slump, caused by the decrease in rice prices, have forced the farmers to cut their expenditures for clothing and food. In 1934 and 1935, the population of southern and central Siam was forced to cut food costs by almost one-third, while the north and northeast of Siam was obliged to revert to an almost complete self-sufficiency in food.[69] Nutrition deficiencies, however, are rare outside of the tenant population and are more often caused by lack of knowledge than by lack of food.[70]

65. W. I. Ladejinsky, "Thailand's Agricultural Economy," pp. 177–178.

66. *The Rice Economy of Monsoon Asia*, p. 200.

67. The rural economic surveys of Zimmerman, pp. 45 ff., pp. 107 ff., and Andrews, pp. 23, 193 ff., give the proportion of cash income and expenditures for living of the studied families in the four economic areas of the country. However, these figures do not give a clear picture, as they do not include the production for own consumption. Therefore, they are not interpreted here.

68. Zimmerman, *op. cit.,* pp. 112, 227.   69. Andrews, *op. cit.,* p. 199.

70. Zimmerman, *op. cit.,* p. 277.

The level of living of rural workers is reported to be very low. This is especially the case in the landlord-dominated area of Klong Rangsit. The seasonal wages of 80 to 120 bahts for six months' service (in prosperous times) are certainly no great attraction for the Siamese, who, like the Malays, do not like to work for others. No doubt, the low level of rural wages hampers the agricultural development of the vast uncultivated areas.[71]

CONCLUSIONS   Though the political status of Siam is different from that of other countries in Southeast Asia, typical colonial features are prevalent in the economic and social structure. The deficiencies of this semicolonial system were, in the past, aggravated by the lack of economic and political backing by a strong colonial power. The result was a complete stagnation in the fields of agriculture, public health, and education and serious drawbacks for the trade policy. While foreign loans to the politically dependent areas relieved the distress caused by the breakdown of the colonial industries during and after the slump, no such loans were contracted by Siam for fear of foreign penetration. The hardships which Siam suffers in order to protect its politically independent status may, in future, increase the social and racial frictions and bring about a bloody climax to a long-latent tension.

Siam does not have the capacity to use and develop her economic potentialities alone. That was her major difficulty in the past and is likely to be so in the future. Siam will never accept financial assistance from powers traditionally inclined to colonial expansion, but is likely to do so from institutions (United Nations) willing to grant assistance without imperial claims. Therefore, a new trend in the economic and social development of the country cannot be expected unless a general change takes place in the Western approach to the economic problems of the backward areas, especially in the field of credit.

The vehement fight against Chinese economic domination fits into the general pattern. Siamese nationalists, conscious of the semicolonial status of the country and resenting its economic dependence, look askance at the Chinese middle man. This reaction

71. Virginia Thompson, *Thailand,* pp. 608, 618. The nonagricultural laborers, mostly Chinese, do not enjoy any government protection; on the contrary, the government carries on a nationalistic labor policy against them.

corresponds to the resentment against the colonial power in the politically dependent countries. This naïve, but psychologically understandable, simplification of a subtle economic problem, reveals again the actual semicolonial status of Siam. Moreover, the desperate reaction against the Chinese as middle man between producer and world market demonstrates that nationalist unrest also in Siam has its origin in agricultural dissatisfaction. The people react instinctively against the Chinese merchants as the visible symbols of an economic and agricultural system which is unable to develop the resources of a rich country and gives an unfair share to the native producer. This reaction is more manifest than in other areas where the picture is distorted by general political ideologies.

The history of semicolonial Siam indicates that the future of the dependent areas is not less an economic problem than a political one. However, the status of political independence may eventually facilitate economic and social regeneration. There may be less difficulty in the diversification of agriculture and a better political and psychological atmosphere for the creation of a strong co-operative movement. The problem of independent Siam, however, is substantially the same as the problem of the other countries in this area and cannot be considered in isolation.

8

Agrarian Unrest
and National Movements

THE NATIONAL MOVEMENTS in Southeast Asia are deeply rooted in the realities of peasant life. They can be analyzed from different angles and can be related to various factors, but ought not be separated from the basic economic and social conditions.

It has been said that it is a mistake to seek the initial stage of a national idea. In the life of nations, vegetative periods, interrupted by occasional manifestations of awakening national impulses, precede the times of conscious national activity.[1] It might be more fruitful to look for the factors which force nations into periods of consciousness.

In the case of the people of Southeast Asia, these factors were the introduction of Western economic methods, the disintegration of the old village economy, and the disruption of the traditional uniformity of native life. All other experiences in the age-old history of Southeast Asia, brutal and merciless as they were, failed to shatter the citadel of native life. Indeed, they often strengthened it. Conquest and suppression, despotism and religious fanaticism may have shaken the people momentarily, but did not lead them beyond the threshold of national consciousness. Western penetration, however, did so.

It is always misleading to look for the release mechanism by simplifying the historic process, since it is always a plurality, a combination of factors, which leads to the final historic result. In the

1. Friedrich Meinecke, *Weltbuergertum und Nationalstaat* (Munich and Berlin, 1908), pp. 4 ff.

history of the Western world, the release mechanism was the industrial revolution in the beginning of the nineteenth century. Modern national ideology in Europe arose from it and from "the attitudes and achievements of modern scientific development which made the industrial revolution possible." [2] Rupert Emerson concludes that nationalism appears always to involve the notion of man's abilities to change and control both the material and social aspects of his environment. This is right when emphasis is laid exclusively on the factor of change. For, in the case of Southeast Asia and almost the entire Far East, the national idea was conceived by those who suffered the change but, at the same time, understood that others have the capacity of changing and controlling the conditions of existence. They saw how the foreigner had the power to disrupt the village life and, therefore, came to consider that they, themselves, should be capable of introducing a new and more fortunate change.

Developments all over the world prove the importance of basic economic changes and substantial ideas of progress for the establishment of national movements. The industrial revolution, so essential in the case of Europe, was not the deciding factor for the development of national movements in Southeast Asia.

Only if we abandon the belief that industrial development and nationalism are naturally coordinated can we evaluate rightly the importance of the peasantry as bearer of the national idea in Asia. The role of the industrialized areas is highly overestimated, though, in a number of cases, these areas have supplied the leaders of the national movements.

To speak in the terms of this study and deliberately simplify a complicated historical development, it may be stated that the national idea became a permanent force in Southeast Asia at the moment when the peasants were forced to give up subsistence farming for the cultivation of cash crops or when (as in highly colonized Java) subsistence farming ceased to yield a subsistence. The introduction of a money economy and the withering away of the village as the unit of life accompanied this development and finally established the period of economic dependence.

2. Rupert Emerson, "An Analysis of Nationalism in Southeast Asia," *Far Eastern Quarterly* (February, 1946), pp. 208 ff.

The first reactions were hardly more than the usual acts of dissatisfaction and desperation, frequently combined with religious fanaticism. They had mostly local color, and were, in general, determined by regional frictions and conflicts. Naturally, the colonial commanders and administrators saw nothing more in these disturbances of peace than the usual periodic uprisings.

In the course of time, however, Western penetration aroused more than occasional dissatisfaction. It brought about an economic and spiritual dislocation and a final disturbance of the native equilibrium. It forced the population into a completely new world, with totally different aspects and with rules and laws previously unknown. It eliminated the time-honored authority of the clan, widened the narrow circle of the village to an extent determined by the convenience of the colonial administration, and superseded the primitive ideas of the natives by new sensational experiences.

It can hardly be emphasized too strongly that the emergence of a national movement is primarily an emotional process, though capable of intellectual leadership and interpretation. Its foundation is the emotional experience of the masses of the people and their awareness of a common destiny in the present and the future. The social dislocation of the people in Southeast Asia established this consciousness, just as did the industrial revolution in the West.

It would, of course, be misleading to state that the peasants in Southeast Asia began with a revolt against the dependent economy as such. Naturally, they reacted against the most visible effects and conditions of the economic system which determined their lives to a steadily increasing extent. Little by little, they were forced into a common reaction. It was directed against the native landlord, as well as against the foreign plantation; against the Indian moneylender, as well as against the Chinese middle man; and seldom consciously against the authorities. It was stronger and more immediate against the Chinese and Indian partners of the dependent system, who interfered with the life of the peasants more directly than the Western authorities and the Western businessman.[3]

The development in British Malaya and even in Siam clearly shows the intimate relation between dependent economy and

3. In Burma, the first rebellion against the authorities was the result of the protection granted to the Indians.

national movement. The Malays, who are still mainly engaged in subsistence farming and, therefore, not directly involved in the dependent system, have developed only a relatively weak national movement.[4] It grows but slowly and is directed against the Indians and Chinese in Malaya, rather than against the British rule. On the other hand, in politically independent Siam, an exaggerated national movement against the Chinese middle man is prevailing, because the rural population is deeply entangled in the dependent economic system.

The Western penetration of Southeast Asia, however, added some particular features to the economic and spiritual dislocation of the native population, and these proved to be of the utmost importance in current developments. The dependent economic system needed an educated elite and a reliable native group which could furnish the clerks and technicians for the growing economic expansion and increased administration. This group of young people, seldom numerous, was brought into direct contact with the Western world and its ideas, partly at home and partly by studying abroad. Trying to understand its mechanism, they became aware of the weakness of the West during the first World War. They studied Western nationalism, Western ideologies and theories, and acquired knowledge enabling them to give a political interpretation to the developments in their home countries. Their zealous political nationalism was strengthened by a natural preference for absolute solutions and by their honest disappointment in the gap between the creed of democracy and reality, which certainly was nowhere wider than in the colonial environment. Thus, the colonial system itself created the weapons for its opponents.

The national movements in Southeast Asia are strongly influenced by the revolutions in China and India, partly indirectly, and partly directly through contact with the populous Indian and Chinese groups in the area. Some communistic influence doubtless also exists, but it is surely exaggerated to consider the social claims of the national movements, based as they are on the present social structure, as communistic activities. Communistic organizations are by no means dominant in any of the Southeast Asian coun-

4. P. T. Bauer, "Nationalism and Politics in Malaya," *Foreign Affairs*, XXV No. 3 (April, 1947), 503 ff.

tries, and their influence as such is based not on large membership, but on their often expedient representation of general national aims. Western education and example, the Western democratic creed, and contact with the great national revolutions in Asia have had far greater influence on the ideology of the national movements than has Communism.

National movements in Southeast Asia do not differ fundamentally from those in other parts of Asia. They are carried forward by a combination of racial and social resentments which can be explained only against the background of colonial dependence.

Awakened race consciousness is a collective reaction against the racial pride of the white man in his control of dependent economic systems. It is a natural reaction against the social stratification by race which can be maintained only by an openly recognized, or at least silently tolerated, superiority of the white man.[5] In *San Min Chu I,* Sun Yat Sen describes this psychological point as follows: "Now compare the Europeans and the Asiatics. Formerly the white people, assuming that they alone possessed intelligence and ability, monopolized everything. We Asiatics, since we could not in a moment learn the strong points of the West and the secret of building strong nations, lost heart—not only the Chinese but every Asiatic people." He then points out that Japan succeeded, having learned from Europe, though it once was as weak as Annam and Burma are today, and continues: "Although the races show variations of colors, there are no marked differences in intelligence and ability."

The national reaction takes its shape from the specific psychological and social conditions in the different countries of the area. It may take the form of supersensitiveness, as in the more remote islands of the Philippines, of very stubborn demonstrations, as among the Indian plantation workers in Malaya, of injustice against national minorities, as in Siam, or of advanced, aggressive policy, as in China, India, and now in Java.

In his political program, Sun Yat Sen emphasized and defended

5. Dr. Sun Yat Sen, *San Min Chu I, Three Principles of the People* (Shanghai, 1927), p. 15. See also K. M. Panikkar, *The Future of Southeast Asia, an Indian View* (London, 1943), p. 115. The author points out that the ideas of the Europeans are responsible for the ideas of the Asiatics.

the racial substance of Chinese nationalism.[6] He postulates that the principle of nationalism is equivalent to the "doctrine of the state" and adds that this doctrine is applicable in China, but not in the West. (He does not mention the other nations in Asia.) He justifies the principle of nationalism with the statement that only "China has been developing a single state out of a single race." [7] This argument is the more astonishing, as the Chinese people, in the course of their ancient history, never considered themselves a racial unity in competition and conflict with other equal or superior racial unities, but stressed, rather, their cultural unity.[8] Sun Yat Sen, like many other of his compatriots, became intensely conscious of belonging to the Chinese race because of the extraordinary race pride of the white man in China, and expressed his own race consciousness as Chinese solidarity.[9] This psychological interpretation is more convincing than Sun Yat Sen's own theory, and is of actual importance, also, for the people in Southeast Asia. The development of race consciousness was the last line of defense for the people in Asia who had become aware of the process of disintegration and had started to recognize the inferiority of their colonial status.

The rest of mankind is the carving knife and the serving dish while we are the fish and the meat. . . . Our position now is extremely perilous; if we do not earnestly promote nationalism and weld together our four hundred millions into a strong nation, we face a tragedy—the loss of our country and the destruction of our race. . . . From now on, the Chinese people will be feeling the pressure simultaneously of natural, political and economic forces. So you see what a critical time it is for our race.[10]

The racial ideology of Sun Yat Sen can be considered representative of the national ideologies in Southeast Asia during the last

6. Sun Yat Sen, op. cit., pp. 4–5.
7. This is more a Chinese tradition than a recognized scientific fact.
8. Paul Myron Anthony Linebarger, The Political Doctrine of Sun Yat Sen, an Exposition of the San Min Chu I (Baltimore 1937), p. 61.
9. Linebarger (ibid., pp. 61, 67) asserts that Sun Yat Sen's nationalism may represent a narrowing of the Confucian conception of humanity, for which he substitutes the modern Chinese race. See also Paul Myron Linebarger, The Life and Principles of Sun Chung-shan, p. 102. According to an anecdote, Sun Yat Sen encountered race hatred for the first time in 1880 in Ewa, Hawaii, where he just had arrived from China. A Westerner whom he met on the road called him "damned Chinaman." The boy of only 14 years was deeply impressed and always remembered this incident, which was certainly exceedingly disagreeable, but typical of the colonial atmosphere, especially at that time.
10. Sun Yat Sen, op. cit., pp. 12, 32.

decades. Everywhere, growing racial consciousness has succeeded the wish for assimilation.[11] The submissive approach to metropolitan ways of thinking and education is no longer the typical attitude; instead, the Western world has gained new importance for the native intellectual as an arsenal of the spiritual and technical weapons needed for the battle for national liberty. This very important change in attitude, coincident with the advance of Western economic penetration, can be encountered wherever a combined political and economic pressure is perceived by the dependent people.

Misery and poverty have always prevailed in the East and are not necessarily a product of Western penetration. But it became the lot of Western influence to open the eyes of the native population to the important factors deciding the material life of man. When they realized that their own life was misery, they related this fact to the presence of foreigners in their country, and the new national movement was born.

Sun Yat Sen gives a vivid interpretation of the economic background of Chinese nationalism and shows how economic oppression and the demand for reconstruction is the main content of national propaganda all over the area.[12] He mentions the disasters which threaten China.[13] His greatest concern is economic oppression, "the looting of China by the unfair economic measures of the great powers," which has to be met by a national economic program.[14] He speaks repeatedly of China's degraded position as a "hypo colony" [15] and recommends economic nationalism as a preliminary remedy. The formulation of the Third Principle, the principle of livelihood, which shows the way to economic reconstruction, is strongly influenced by Western ideas and theories,[16] especially by Marx, though Sun Yat Sen denies that the class struggle is the

11. José Rizal, martyr of Philippine liberty, has given a classical description of the self-abnegating attitude of the Filipino upper and middle classes, which only want to be considered Spaniards and not natives (Indians, as they are called in the novel). See José Rizal, *Social Cancer* (Eng. tr. of *Noli me tangere*), Manila, 1912.

12. "The Third Principle, the Principle of Livelihood (Min-Sheng)," *San Min Chu I*.

13. *Ibid.*, p. 103.

14. Paul Myron Anthony Linebarger, *op. cit.*, p. 176.

15. Sun Yat Sen, p. 39. The syllable "hypo," taken from chemical terminology, expresses the low degree of the Chinese status.

16. The Three Principles were written between 1895 and 1900 in Europe, where Sun Yat Sen studied social and political conditions.

method for solving the economic problem of his country. His argument that China's real problem is poverty and not unequal distribution brings him off the path of the Bolshevik revolution.[17] The problem of poverty, however, necessarily leads him to the importance of economic planning for the national movement. He considers the equalization of land ownership [18] as the basis for the realization of the Third Principle. He asserts (what, however, is wrong) that China no longer has any large landowners, since the feudal system was abolished 2,000 years ago, and he claims that the state should appropriate the unearned increment arising from the rise of land values caused by the industrial and commercial development following contact with the West. "The nationalization of the increase of land values is the true policy to effect the equal distribution of land; it is the basis of the Principle of the Peoples' Livelihood." [19] He proposes a law which shall entitle the government to buy back the land according to the amount of land tax reported by the owner, and considers such a regulation as a guarantee for honest self-assessment.[20] At the same time, provisions shall be made that later rises in value above the original assessment shall become a public fund "as reward to all those who had improved the community and who advanced industry and commerce around the land."

It is not essential in this connection whether Sun Yat Sen has analyzed the agrarian situation in China correctly or whether political expediency has influenced his formulations. Nor is it necessary to discover whether his propositions are of practical value and could be realized. But it is of importance to emphasize that Sun Yat Sen, who, more than anybody else, has given authority to the claims of the national movements in the whole of Asia, considers the land as basis for the existence of China as a nation, that he considers it

17. T'ang Leang-Li, *The Foundations of Modern China* (London, 1928), p. 136. See also Maurice William, *Sun Yat Sen versus Communism* (Baltimore, 1932); this book describes the influence on Sun Yat Sen of William's *The Social Interpretation of History, a Refutation of the Marxian Economic Interpretation of History* (New York, 1921). No doubt, William has given Sun Yat Sen an argument for refuting Marx, though it can be argued whether it actually was the deciding one. See Karl A. Wittfogel, *Sun Yat Sen,* pp. 117–118, 140, and Paul Myron Anthony Linebarger, *op. cit.,* pp. 141 ff.: "Sun Yat Sen regarded the class struggle as pathological in society."

18. Sun Yat Sen, pp. 409 ff., 430 ff., 434.

19. Quoted from T'ang Leang-Li, pp. 136–137.

20. Sun Yat Sen, pp. 409 ff., 430 ff., 434.

an actual problem formed by the Western economic penetration, and that he endeavors to solve it by an "equal distribution of land." Furthermore, it is significant that by confirming the original right of individual landownership this policy actually represents the most outspoken contrast to economic communism.

The central position of the land problem in the structure of native life in Asia raises it above the level of mere political doctrines. Political programs are adjusted to it. Political propaganda can use and abuse it. It has become the basis of the nationalist movements in all the countries of Southeast Asia, where, still, contrary to Sun Yat Sen's conception of China, a semifeudal system is prevalent. For the masses of the rural population, the movement for land has merged with the national movement.

It is hardly accidental that Rizal's great novel,[21] the national creed of the Filipino people, shows the peasant on Luzon fighting for his land against the foreign master, the Spanish friar, at the time of Rizal. The novel centers around a Filipino peasant, Tales, who has cleared and cultivated his land at the sacrifice of his wife and daughter. The land is taken away from him by the "land-grabbing" of a monastic community. He goes to court, but when he loses his case, he murders the friar administrator and the usurper of the land—significantly filling their mouths with earth—and he becomes an outlaw, a "tulisan," [22] a fighter for liberty.

Rizal generalizes this case by appealing to the inhabitants of the region, which is still today the center of permanent agrarian unrest:

Calm yourselves, peaceful inhabitants of Calamba! None of you are named Tales; none of you have committed any crime! You are called Luis Habaña, Matias Belarmino, Nicasio Eigasani. . . . Your name is the whole village of Calamba. You cleared your fields, on them you have spent the labor of your whole life, your savings, your vigils and privations, and you have been despoiled of them, driven from your homes, with the rest forbidden to show you hospitality! Not content with outraging justice, they have trampled upon the sacred traditions of your country! . . . . Any one of you has suffered more than Cabesang Tales, and yet none, not one of you, has received justice! . . . Weep or laugh,

21. *The Reign of Greed* (Eng. tr. of *El Filibusterimo*), Manila, 1912, pp. 30 ff., 86 ff. The novel is the continuation of *Social Cancer*, mentioned in note 11, above.
22. Bandit.

there in those lonely isles, where you wander vaguely, uncertain of the future!

The national movements differ in the various countries of Southeast Asia; [23] they are adjusted to the local environment and, often, to religion, but are always supported by the bulk of the farming population. Consequently, they all rally to the cry for land.[24]

In the Netherlands East Indies [25] the first considerable national movement was the Sarekat Islam,[26] which, at times, gathered two and a half million members. Its most important aim, the mutual economic support of the native population, was combined with the promotion of Islam. Its propaganda was directed against "sinful capitalism," officially explained as "foreign capitalism" (1917). After the first World War, Marxist ideas gained ground, chiefly under the influence of Dutch socialists but also under the impact of the successful Russian revolution. The socialist groups were especially active around Semarang and Soerabaja. The native movement turned more and more against the European plantation companies, which were considered as responsible for the intensive exploitation. Surjopranoto, a Javanese aristocrat, organized the workers on the sugar plantations into the Revolutionary Socialist Trade Union—later reorganized as the "Personeel Fabriek Bond." It fought the plantations over labor conditions and the lease of farm lands. Other similar organizations followed. The fight on the sugar plantations became the first serious test for the Indonesian national movement. From this time on, Indonesian nationalism remained conscious of the agrarian problem and its implications, although

23. Rupert Emerson, "An Analysis of Nationalism in Southeast Asia," *Far Eastern Quarterly* (February, 1946), pp. 208 ff. See also Rupert Emerson, *Government and Nationalism in Southeast Asia*, Part I: "Introduction" (New York, 1942); Virginia Thompson, *Government and Nationalism in Southeast Asia*, Part III: "Nationalism and Nationalist Movements in Southeast Asia" (New York, 1942); Kenneth Perry Landon, "Nationalism in Southeastern Asia," *Far Eastern Quarterly* (February, 1943), pp. 139 ff.

24. See also Chapter VI (the Philippines).

25. Raymond Kennedy, *The Ageless Indies* (New York, 1942), pp. 125 ff. Kennedy points out that there is little evidence of a direct connection between Indonesian nationalism and communism, as is often asserted in Dutch literature; Bernard H. M. Vlekke, *Nusantara* (Cambridge, Mass., 1943), pp. 337 ff., and *The Story of the Dutch East Indies* (Cambridge, Mass., 1945), pp. 178 ff.; Charles O. van der Plas, "Nationalism in the Netherlands Indies," 8th conference of I.P.R., Quebec, Canada, December, 1942, Netherlands–Netherlands Indies Paper No. 1; Amry Vandenbosch, The *Dutch East Indies* (3d ed., Berkley, Calif., 1942), pp. 311 ff., pp. 315 ff., pp. 323 ff.

26. Established in 1912.

a landlord class did not actually exist in Java. Nationalist-inspired cooperatives—Persatoean Cooperatie Indonesia—tried to fight the Chinese influence in the marketing of argicultural products and thus improve the position of the peasants. Within the Indonesian movement of today, Achmed Soekarno [27] has always represented the faction primarily interested in the economic needs of the peasantry.

In Burma the advance guard of the nationalist movement are the Thakins [28] who established their organization in 1930. They are led by a group of Rangoon University graduates and are primarily concerned with the serious problems of the Burma peasantry. The Thakins were the parent organization of the Anti-Fascist People's Freedom (AFPFL), which started as an underground movement in 1943 and organized the peasants in the fight against the Japanese.[29] Also in Burma, the war gave arms to the peasants in the villages and thereby created a still more dangerous aspect to the fight for land. The new national government in Burma considers itself primarily responsible for solving the land problem by radical reforms.[30]

Nationalism in Indo-China [31] is essentially an Annamite move-

27. Dr. Achmed Soekarno, together with other Western-educated intellectuals, founded in 1927 the National Indonesian Party—Perserikatan Nasional Indonesia. He is today the President of the Indonesian Republic.

28. The term "Thakin" is the Burmese word for prince or lord. Officially the organization is called Dobamma Asiayone.

29. J. Russell Andrus, "Burma; an Experiment in Self-Government," *Foreign Policy Reports*, Dec. 15, 1945, pp. 258 ff. Andrus mentions that during and after the war the Thakins have shown leanings towards communism. The AFPFL, however, under the leadership of General Aung San (assassinated July 17, 1947), represented after the war most of the prewar political parties. In November, 1946, it separated from the communist parties and is following a socialist democratic course. It dominates today the government in Burma. The Thakins are now split, but are still the outstanding political figures, both within the AFPFL and the Communist parties. While Burmese Communists were the first to organize the distressed peasantry under nationalist slogans and thereby dominated in the rural districts, the AFPEL has gained ground steadily since 1946 with a socialist democratic program which also promises to nationalize the land and abolish all large landholdings. The success of the AFPFL in its contest with the Communists will depend on the realization of its land program, since Burma's peasantry considers the solution of the land problem as being identical with the victory of the national movement. See Virginia Thompson, "The New Nation of Burma," *Far Eastern Survey*, XVII, No. 7 (April 7, 1948), and "Burma's Communists," in *ibid.*, XVII, No. 9 (May 5, 1948).

30. See Chapter III (Burma).

31. Virginia Thompson, "Nationalism and Nationalist Movements in Southeast Asia," pp. 203 ff. Lawrence K. Rosinger, "France and the Future of Indo-China," *Foreign Policy Reports* (May 15, 1945), p. 54.

ment. It is most powerful in the Tonkin area, where the high pressure of population and misery favored the rise of a peasant movement with strong nationalistic emotions under Western-educated leadership. After the first World War, Canton strongly influenced the revolutionary party of Young Annam, which was active especially in the north. Its activities together with those of other radical peasant organizations were symptomatic of the national and agrarian tension in the country. It is significant that the present national leader, Nguyen-ai-Quoc (often called Ho Chi-minh), though once a prominent communist, prefers a national course to a communist one. He is wisely in favor of a program which promises the peasants liberty with land. The alluvial lands and abandoned rice fields are to be divided among the peasants in need of land, and tax reductions are to be given in years of bad harvest.[32] Today all national groups consider agrarian reform as the most essential part of their economic program.[33]

The economic program of the national movement in independent Siam [34] does not differ fundamentally from the economic claims of the politically dependent people. The original program of the People's Party,[35] reaffirmed by the People's Assembly, demands emphatically that the government shall be the landlord of all productive land and banker for financing the projects of the peasants. It shall control the cultivation and marketing of rice, the main business of the nation, and shall thus eliminate the Chinese middle

32. The organization of Annamite nationalism is *Viet Minh*, the League for the Independence of Viet Nam. It was founded in 1939 and, besides political groups, it included from the beginning a number of large peasant organizations. It was broadened in 1943 to include all national organizations fighting in the resistance movement. Its program calls for fight against any political and economic foreign domination. See Robert Payne, *The Revolt of Asia* (New York, 1947), pp. 210 ff.

33. Lawrence K. Rosinger, *op. cit.*, p. 64.

34. A nationalist economic program, designed by Luang Pradist Manudharm, was presented in March 1933. It was based on the idea that the government should buy land from the landowners at a fair price and pay for it with bonds. The Siamese government, however, refused the program as "communistic," though it assures in Part V that the wealthy class must not be destroyed. Pradist went to Europe, but was, only one year later, officially cleared of the charge of being a communist. Though the program was banned from publication in Siam, it must be considered representative of the economic aims of Siamese nationalism. See Kenneth Perry Landon, *Siam in Transition* (Shanghai, 1939), Appendix III, A, pp. 260 ff.

35. See Landon, *Siam in Transition* and *The Chinese in Thailand* (London and New York, 1941); Virginia Thompson, "Siam and the Great Powers," *Foreign Policy Reports* (March 1, 1946), p. 322.

man. Luang Pradist, the brain of the revolution of 1933 and leader of the Siamese national movement,[36] is known as the author of the program.

Siamese nationalism fights the Chinese middle man just as vehemently as the dependent people in other parts of the area turn against the colonial power. Moreover, the national movement also covers the agrarian problem, since the Chinese middle man is part of the present agricultural system and the most visible reason for the misery and indebtedness of the peasantry.

It is frequently pointed out [37] that national movements in Southeast Asia are backed by only a few hundred thousands, but that the bulk of the people is still indifferent. Hereby, however, the fact is ignored that national movements are identical with the claim for land, and that, for this reason, the people are an integral part of it. The statements made by the partly illiterate participants in the Sakdalist uprising in Central Luzon (1935) clearly illustrate this fact. As a matter of course, the rebels associated the fight against landlordism and abuse with the fight for independence.[38]

If we want to apply the famous metaphor that a nation exists only as long as it is confirmed by a daily plebiscite [39] we can surely say: The people of Southeast Asia confirm their being a nation by a daily plebiscite for solution of the land problem.

The agrarian and national movements in the area were further emphasized by the war developments, which strengthened the national consciousness and, simultaneously, the class consciousness of the peasants. The ideas and example of the Chinese Revolution and its fight against the Japanese had a profound effect on the area and

36. Luang Pradist opposed capitulation to the Japanese and the subsequent declaration of war on Great Britain and the United States. He was the leader of the resistance movement, Seri Thai. After the war he became leader of the democratic faction and was honored by the title of Elder Statesman.

37. Virginia Thompson, "Government and Nationalism in Southeast Asia," p. 127. See also Rupert Emerson, "Government and Nationalism in Southeast Asia," Part I, Introduction, pp. 211 ff. Emerson agrees with Virginia Thompson that there are still relatively few convinced and conscious nationalists, but asserts that the nationalist movements do not couch their appeal solely in nationalist terms, but, naturally, seek to include different elements of the population.

38. See Chapter VI, above. The statements are reported by Joseph Ralson Hayden, *The Philippines, a Study in National Development* (New York, 1942), pp. 392 ff.

39. Ernest Renan, "What Is a Nation?" (Qu'est-ce qu-une nation?), a lecture delivered at the Sorbonne, March 11, 1882, published in the *Scott Library* (London and Felling-on-Tyne, 1896), p. 81.

proved to be of decisive importance when the countries in Southeast Asia became involved in the war in the Pacific. For most of them, this was the first opportunity to act as a nation, partly by guerrilla warfare against the Japanese invaders, and partly by a political attitude which they considered favorable for final liberty.

The national movements in Southeast Asia must be considered as an integral part of a continent-wide revolutionary process which affects all aspects of human relations. Like all great revolutions in history, it is at the same time spiritual and economic. Without underestimating other factors, it can be asserted that it was the land crisis which paved the way for the national idea. Though it is extremely difficult to prove such a statement satisfactorily, certain indications must be noted: even in politically independent countries, the national movement remains coordinated with the movement for land and skeptical towards the existing independence. The serious political crisis in central Luzon after independence had been granted to the Islands might suggest that the Philippine peasantry is unable to conceive national liberty without a solution of the land problem. Furthermore, Siamese nationalism claims a radical settlement of the land problem with all the pathos of a politically dependent people.

The reaction of the people in the Philippines and Siam reflects the emotional identity of the claims for land and liberty. It is difficult to separate agrarian unrest from national unrest, and it might even be dangerous to consider a status of autonomy, or political independence, as the final solution, if the economic and social emancipation of the people lags behind.

While in the first postwar years the national movements had noticeable success all over the area, colonial rule is now tightening its grasp again. Certainly, advanced positions like the Pihlippines, India, and Burma have been evacuated, but the colonial system is gaining new ground in the Netherlands East Indies, Indo-China, and Malaya. New terminologies poorly conceal a political technique in which indirect rule is cleverly applied in order to catch the imagination of the people, counteract the disintegration of the colonial system, and reconstruct an empire by securing economic positions within deliberately arranged political formations.

The political organizations of the national movements, inex-

perienced and lacking stability and credit, are time and again out-
witted by superior Western tactics and statesmanship. But even if
native political action is thus temporarily checked, still greater
disaster is bound to result. The enforced continuation of colonial
rule (whatever its shape or disguise) is multiplying the contradictions and increasing the tension, thus nurturing the forces destined
to succeed it.

The prospects for a peaceful bridging of the gap between dependence and independence will be equal to zero if a renewed
Western imperialism is allowed to exercise a power not in accordance with its economic basis and the ideology of the European
people. Economic shortcomings, combined with the lack of real
mastership, must ruin a political system which evidently has lost
its genuineness, especially when neighboring countries (like India
and Burma) are about to rid themselves of the colonial economy
and construct an economic home of their own, diversified and well-
balanced. The question remains, however, if there is still a way
out of a situation dangerous to peace and in contradiction to the
moral consciousness and actual well-being of the people—including the people of the colonial powers.

The mutual infiltration of political and racial, of social, economic, and humanitarian interests, is the main difficulty in any
solution of the colonial problem. It is, therefore, hardly to be expected that even the most humanitarian and broad-minded solution can achieve ideal results, without injustice and inequalities in
one or the other respect.

It is difficult, within the frame of this study, to give a definite an-
swer to the question of how the objective of political and economic
emancipation would be best furthered. There is much to be said for
the argument that economic emancipation presumes the long-over-
due industrialization,[40] coordinated with a far-reaching reorganiza-

40. Dr. P. C. Chang, Chinese Representative to the Economic and Social Council
of the United Nations, stressed, at a meeting of the Second Session of the Economic
and Social Council, the hunger for industrialization in the economically "low pressure" areas.

The promotion of industrialization has proved to be the only policy which so far
has been able to reduce the birth rate in Far Eastern countries. In this connection,
see Jacob Viner, "The American Interest in the Colonial Problem," published in
The United States in a Multinational Economy (Studies in American Foreign Relations No. 4, Council on Foreign Relations, New York, 1945), pp. 15, 16. Viner asserts
that it is very much to the interest of the United States that the governments of these

tion of the agricultural economy. The political setting for an economic development designed to lessen the political and racial frictions, however, must still be found. No solution, short of unrestricted political sovereignty, will be adequate for peoples that have conceived the national idea in all its aspects and are ready to develop the human and economic resources of their country in a liberal and democratic way. Certainly, the withholding of independence from those nations might involve the most dangerous political consequences.

Where a preparatory period is deemed appropriate, only a policy based on collective responsibility, that is, on the trusteeship institution of the United Nations, will be equal to the urgent needs of the dependent countries. The value of the trusteeship institution, however, will depend on the further stabilization of the United Nations.

The first and foremost duty of the power or powers in control of the trust territories must be the reconstruction of the agricultural system in all its economic and social aspects. A well-conceived agricultural rebuilding will lay the foundation for a democratic development in these territories and will, thus, become an earnest contribution to a peaceful development in an area where, so far, power policy has been the stronger and international law the weaker.

---

areas, whether autonomous or colonial, shall be such as to promote those educational measures and those changes in social habits and institutions that will most powerfully operate to foster the development of low birthrates.

Bibliography

Allen, James S. "Agrarian Tendencies in the Philippines." *Pacific Affairs,* Vol. XI, March, 1938.

Alsberg, Carl L. Land Utilization Investigations and Their Bearing in International Relations. New York, 1933.

Andrews, J. Madison. "Siam: 2nd Rural Economic Survey, 1934–35," Bangkok Times Press, Bangkok, 1935.

Andrus, J. Russell. Burmese Economic Life. Palo Alto, Calif., 1947.

—— "Burma; an Experiment in Self-Government." *Foreign Policy Reports,* Dec. 15, 1945.

—— "Three Economic Systems Clashed in Burma." *Review of Economic Studies* (London), February, 1936.

Bauer, P. T. "Nationalism and Politics in Malaya." *Foreign Affairs,* Vol. XXV, No. 3, April, 1947.

Bernard, Paul. Le Problème économique indochinois. Paris, 1934.

Bloom, Solomon F. The World of Nations. New York, 1941.

Boeke, J. H. The Structure of Netherlands Indian Economy. New York, 1942.

Bousquet, G. H. A French View of the Netherlands Indies. London, 1940.

Broek, Jan O. M. Economic Development of the Netherlands Indies. New York, 1942.

Buencamino, Victor. "Solving the Rice Problem." The Philippine National Rice and Corn Corporation, Manila, 1937.

Burma

Census of India. 1911, Vol. IX, Part I: Report on Burma.

—— 1931, Vol. XI, Part I: Report on Burma.

Department of Industries. Report on the Working of Cooperative Societies in Burma for the Year Ending June 30, 1940. Rangoon, 1940.

Department of Land Records and Agriculture. Land and Agriculture Committee, Report. Rangoon, 1938.

—— Markets Section Survey, No. 9: "Rice." Rangoon, 1941.

—— Season and Crop Report for the Year Ending June 30, 1941. Rangoon, 1941.

"Blue Print" for Burma. Conservative Imperial Affairs Committee, London, 1944.

Burma Provincial Banking Inquiry Committee. Report. Rangoon, 1930.

Report on Indian Immigration. By James Baxter. Rangoon, 1940.

Report on the Administration of Burma, 1935–36. Rangoon, 1936.

Report on the Rebellion in Burma up to May 3, 1931. CMD Papers 3900, Vol. XII. London, 1931.

—— Final Report of the Riot Inquiry Committee. Home Department, Rangoon, 1939.

Butler, Harold B. Problems of Industry in the East. International Labor Office, Studies and Research Reports, Series B, No. 29. Geneva, 1938.

Callis, Helmut G. "Capital Investment in Southeast Asia and the Philippines." *Annals of the American Academy of Political and Social Science,* March, 1943.

—— Foreign Capital in Southeast Asia. Institute of Pacific Relations, International Research Series. New York, 1942.

Census of India. 1911, Vol. IX, Part I: Report on Burma.

—— 1931, Vol. XI, Part I: Report on Burma.

Chapman, Abraham. "American Policy in the Philippines." *Far Eastern Survey,* Vol. XV, No. 11, June 5, 1946.

Christian, John Leroy. Burma and the Japanese Invader. Bombay, 1945.

Condliffe, J. B. China Today. Boston, 1932.

Credner, Wilhelm. Siam, das Land der Tai; eine Landeskunde auf Grund eigener Reisen und Forschungen. Stuttgart, 1935.

Crippen, Harlan R. "Philippine Agrarian Unrest: Historical Backgrounds." *Science and Society,* Vol. X, No. 4, 1946.

Davis, Joseph S. "Standards and Content of Living." *American Economic Review,* Vol. XXXV, No. 1, March, 1945.

Dawson, Owen L. "Philippine Agriculture, a Problem of Adjustment." *Foreign Agriculture,* Vol. IV. Washington, 1940.

Dobby, E. H. G. "Settlement Patterns in Malaya." *Geographical Review,* Vol. XXXII, 1942.

Doumer, Paul. Situation de l'Indochine. Hanoi, 1902.

Emerson, Rupert. "An Analysis of Nationalism in Southeast Asia." *Far Eastern Quarterly,* February, 1946.

—— "Introduction." Part I of *Government and Nationalism in Southeast Asia* (Institute of Pacific Relations, Inquiry Series). New York, 1942.

—— Malaysia, a Study in Direct and Indirect Rule. New York, 1937.

Entenberg, Barbara. "Agrarian Reform and the Hukbalahap." *Far Eastern Survey,* Vol. XV, No. 16, Aug. 14, 1946.

Furnivall, J. S. An Introduction to the Political Economy of Burma. Rangoon, 1931.

—— Netherlands India; a Study of Plural Economy. Cambridge, England, 1939.

——Studies in the Social and Economic Development of the Netherlands East Indies, Part III: State and Private Money Lending. Rangoon, 1935.

Gourdon, Henri. L'Indochine. Paris, 1931.

Gourou, Pierre. Land Utilization in French Indochina. Tr. of *L'utilization du sol en Indochine française*. New York, 1945.

Greenberg, Michael. "Malaya, Britain's Dollar Arsenal." *Amerasia*, June, 1941.

Grist, Donald H. An Outline of Malayan Agriculture. Straits Settlements and Federated Malay States Department of Agriculture, Malayan Planting Manual No. 2. Kuala Lumpur, 1936.

Hainsworth, Reginald G., and Raymond T. Moyer. Agricultural Geography of the Philippine Islands, a Graphic Summary. U.S. Dept. of Agriculture, Office of Foreign Agricultural Relations. Washington, 1945.

Hayden, Joseph Ralston. The Philippines, a Study in National Development. New York, 1942.

Haynes, A. S. "Industrialization as an Indispensable Means of Maintaining the Level of Prosperity in Tropical Regions; the Position of Malaya." *Comptes Rendus du Congrès International de Géographie*, Vol. II, Sec. III. Amsterdam, 1938.

Heiser, Victor. An American Doctor's Odyssey. New York, 1936.

Hendershot, Clarence. "Burma Compromise." *Far Eastern Survey*, Vol. XVI, No. 12, June 18, 1947.

Henry, Yves. "La Question agraire en Indochine." *La Dépêche Coloniale*, Dec. 16, 1936.

Horn, Florence. Orphans of the Pacific; the Philippines. New York, 1941.

Houser, Ernest O. "Britain's Economic Stake in Southeast Asia." *Far Eastern Survey*, Vol. VI, No. 25, Dec. 22, 1937.

Indo-China

Annuaire statistique de l'Indochine, 1936–37. Services de la Statistique Général, Hanoi, 1938.

Bulletin Économique de l'Indochine, 1938, Vol. II. Hanoi, 1938.

Institute of Pacific Relations, Eighth Conference, Quebec, December, 1942. Preliminary Report: "War and Peace in the Pacific." New York, 1943.

—— United Kingdom Paper: "Problems of the Post-War Settlement in the Far East." Quebec, 1943.

Institute of Pacific Relations, Ninth Conference, New York, 1945. Secretariat Paper: "Basic Problems of Relief, Rehabilitation and Reconstruction in Southeast Asia."

International Institute of Agriculture. International Yearbook of Agricultural Statistics, 1938–39, Rome, 1939.

International Labour Office. Labour Conditions in Indo-China, Studies and Reports, Series B, No. 26, Geneva, 1938.

Jain, L. C. Indigenous Banking in India. London, 1929.

Jenkins, Shirley. "Our Ties with the Philippines." Far Eastern Survey, Vol. XIV, No. 10, May 23, 1945.

——"United States Economic Policy towards the Philippine Republic." Document for the Tenth Conference of the Institute of Pacific Relations, Stratford-upon-Avon, England, Sept., 1947. United States Paper No. 1.

Kat Angelino, A. D. A. de. Colonial Policy. Abridged translation from the Dutch by G. J. Renier. 2 vols. The Hague, 1931.

Keller, A. S. "Netherlands India as a Paying Proposition." Far Eastern Survey, Jan. 17, 1940.

Kennedy, Raymond. The Ageless Indies. New York, 1942.

Kolff, G. H. van der. "Colonization and the Population of Java." The Far Eastern Review, 1938.

—— "European Influence on Native Agriculture." In B. Schrieke, ed., The Effect of Western Influence on Native Civilization in the Malay Archipelago. Batavia, 1929.

Kurihara, Kenneth K. Labor in the Philippine Economy. Palo Alto, Calif. 1945.

Ladejinsky, W. I. "Agriculture in British Malaya." Foreign Agriculture, Vol. V. Washington, 1941.

—— "Thailand's Agricultural Economy." Ibid, Vol. VI. Washington, 1942.

Landon, Kenneth Perry. The Chinese in Thailand. London and New York, 1941.

—— Siam in Transition. Shanghai and Chicago, 1939.

—— "Nationalism in Southeastern Asia." Far Eastern Quarterly, February, 1943.

Lasker, Bruno. "Southeast Asia Enters the Modern World." Southeast Asia Institute Paper, New York, 1947.

Lava, Horacio C. Levels of Living in the Ilocos Region. Institute of Pacific Relations, Philippine Council, Manila, 1938.

League of Nations. Balance of Payments, 1935, 1938. Geneva, 1936, 1939.

—— The Network of World Trade. Geneva, 1942.

League of Nations Health Organization, Intergovernmental Conference

of Far Eastern Countries on Rural Hygiene, Badoeng, Java, Aug. 3–13, 1937. Report. Geneva, 1937.
—— Report of French Indochina.
—— Report of the Malayan Delegation.
—— Report of the Netherlands Indies.
—— Report of the Philippines.
—— Report of Siam.
—— Report of Burma.
Linebarger, Paul Myron Wentworth. The Gospel of Chung shan. Paris, 1932.
Linebarger, Paul Myron Anthony. The Political Doctrines of Sun Yat Sen, an Exposition of the San Min Chu I. Baltimore, 1937.

Malaya
Federated Malay States, Department of Labor. Annual Reports, 1938, 1940. Kuala Lumpur, 1939, 1941.
Malayan Agricultural Statistics, 1940. Kuala Lumpur, 1941.
Malayan Year Book 1939. Singapore, 1939.
Straits Settlements and Federated Malay States, Department of Agriculture. Annual Report on Agriculture in Malaya for the Years 1933–37. Kuala Lumpur.
Maxwell, Francis. Economic Aspects of Cane Sugar Production. London, 1927.
Meinecke, Friedrich. Weltbuergertum und Nationalstaat. Munich and Berlin, 1908.
Mills, Lennox A. British Rule in Eastern Asia; a Study of Contemporary Government and Economic Development in British Malaya and Hong Kong, London, 1942.
Mitchell, Kate L. Industrialization of the Western Pacific. New York, 1942.

Netherlands East Indies
Berichten aan de leden der centrale organisaties van de suikerindustrie in Nederlandsch-Indië, No. 33, 1939.
Department van Landbouw, Nijverheid en Handel. Mededeelingen van het centraal kantoor voor de statistiek, No. 69. Weltevreden (Batavia), 1929.
Departement van economische zaken. Centraal kantoor voor de statistiek. Statistisch jaaroverzicht van Nederlandsch-Indië (Statistical Abstract for the Netherlands East Indies), 1928 and 1940. Batavia.
—— Statistisch zakboekje, 1940.
Encyclopaedie van Nederlandsch-Indië, 1917–39.
Pocket Edition of the Statistical Abstract of the Netherlands East Indies. Batavia, 1940.

Orde Browne, G. St. J. Labour Conditions in Ceylon, Mauritius, and Malaya. Published in Parliamentary Papers CMD 6423, London, 1943.

Ormsby-Gore, W. G. A. Report on a visit to Malaya, Ceylon, and Java. Published in Parliamentary Papers CMD 3235, London, 1928.

Panikkar, K. M. The Future of Southeast Asia, an Indian View. London, 1943.

Payne, Robert. The Revolt of Asia. New York, 1947.

Pelzer, Karl J. Pioneer Settlement in the Asiatic Tropics. New York, 1945.

—— Population and Land Utilization. Economic Survey of the Pacific Area, Part I. Institute of Pacific Relations, New York, 1941.

Philippines

Bureau of Census and Statistics. *Journal of Philippine Statistics,* October and November, 1941. Manila, 1941.

Philippine Statistical Review, Vol. II. Manila, 1935.

—— Yearbook of Philippine Statistics. Manila, 1941.

Census of the Philippine Islands, 1903, Vol. IV (Washington, 1905); 1918, Vol. III (Manila, 1921).

Census of the Philippines. Commission of the Census. (Manila 1940–41).

Department of Labor. "Fact-Finding Survey Report." Unpublished manuscript, Manila, 1936.

—— Division of Labor Statistics. *Labor Bulletin,* May, 1939.

Facts and Statistics about the Philippine Sugar Industry. Philippine Sugar Association, Manila, 1928.

Fifth Annual Report of the President of the Philippines to the President and Congress of the United States, Covering the Period July 1, 1939, to June 30, 1940. Washington, 1941.

Messages of the President. Vol. III, Part I (Manila, 1938); Vol. V, Part I (Manila, 1941).

Secretary of Agriculture and Commerce. Annual Report, 1938. Manila, 1939.

Semi-Annual Report of 1939. Manila, 1939.

Pim, Sir Allan. Colonial Agricultural Production. London, 1946.

Plas, Charles O. van der. "Nationalism in the Netherlands Indies." Netherlands-Netherlands Indies Paper No. 1, Eighth Conference of the Institute of Pacific Relations, Quebec, 1942.

Porter, Catherine. "The Philippines as an American Investment." *Far Eastern Survey,* Vol. IX, Sept. 24, 1940.

Ranneft, J. W. Meijer. "The Economic Structure of Java." In B. Schrieke, ed., *The Effect of Western Influence on Native Civilization in the Malay Archipelago.* Batavia, 1929.

Remer, Carl F. Foreign Investment in China. New York, 1933.

Renan, Ernest. "What Is a Nation?" (Qu'est-ce qu'une nation?). In the *Scott Library*. London and Felling-on-Tyne, 1896

Ringwood, Ona K. D. "Some Statistics on the Philippines." *Foreign Policy Reports*, Oct. 1, 1945.

Rizal, José. Social Cancer. Tr. of *Noli me tangere*. Manila, 1912.

—— The Reign of Greed. Tr. of *El Filibusterimo*. Manila, 1912.

Robequain, Charles. The Economic Development of French Indochina. Tr. by Isabel A. Ward. London and New York, 1944.

—— L'Indochine française. Paris, 1935.

Roche, Jean de la. "French Indochina's Prospective Economic Regime." Institute of Pacific Relations, French Paper No. 2. New York, 1945.

—— "A Program of Social and Cultural Activity in Indochina." Institute of Pacific Relations, French Paper No. 3. New York, 1945.

Roosevelt, Theodore. "Land Problems in Puerto Rico and the Philippine Islands." *Geographical Review*, Vol. XXIV, 1934.

Rosinger, Lawrence K. "France and the Future of Indo-China." *Foreign Policy Reports*, May 15, 1945.

Runes, I. T. General Standards of Living and Wages of Workers in the Philippine Sugar Industry. Institute of Pacific Relations, Philippine Council. Manila, 1939.

Sayre, Francis B. "Freedom Comes to the Philippines." *Atlantic Monthly*, March, 1945.

Schrieke, B. J. O., ed. The Effect of Western Influence on Native Civilization in the Malay Archipelago. Batavia, 1929.

Seeman, Bernard, and Laurence Salisbury. Cross-Currents in the Philippines. Institute of Pacific Relations, American Council, Pamphlet No. 23. New York, 1946.

Seitelman, Max. "Malaya in Transition." *Far Eastern Survey*, Vol. XVI, No. 10, May 21, 1947.

—— "Political Thought in Malaya." *Ibid.* Vol. XVI, No. 11, June 4, 1947.

Sheltema, A. M. P. A. The Food Consumption of the Native Inhabitants of Java and Madura. Batavia, 1936.

Siam

　Financial Adviser on the Budget of the Kingdom of Siam. Report for the years 1933–34, 1936–37. Ministry of Finance, Bangkok.

　"The Record," April, 1922 and October, 1926. Ministry of Commerce and Communications, Bangkok.

　Statistical Yearbook of the Kingdom of Siam, 1937–39. Bangkok, 1941.

Sitsen, Peter H. W. The Industrial Development of the Netherlands Indies. Institute of Pacific Relations, Netherlands–Netherlands Indies Paper No. 2, New York, 1943.

Spate, O. H. "Beginnings of Industrialization in Burma." *Economic Geography,* 1941–42.

Stockdale, Sir F. Report on a Visit to Malaya, Java, Sumatra, and Ceylon, 1938. London, 1939.

Sun Yat Sen. San Min Chu I, Three Principles of the People. Shanghai, 1927.

Taeuber, Irene B., and Edwin G. Beal. "The Demographic Heritage of the Japanese Empire." In "World Population in Transition," *Annals of the American Academy of Political and Social Science,* Vol. 237, January, 1945.

T'ang Leang-Li. The Foundation of Modern China. London, 1928.

Thompson, Virginia M. "Burma's Communists." *Far Eastern Survey,* Vol. XVII, No. 9, May 5, 1948.

—— French Indo-China, London, 1937.

—— "Nationalism and Nationalist Movements in Southeast Asia." Part III of *Government and Nationalism in Southeast Asia* (Institute of Pacific Relations Inquiry Series). New York, 1942.

—— "The New Nation of Burma." *Far Eastern Survey,* Vol. XVII, No. 7, April 7, 1948.

—— Notes on Labor Problems in Burma and Thailand. Institute of Pacific Relations, Secretariat Paper No. 8. New York, 1945.

—— Postmortem on Malaya. New York, 1943.

—— "Siam and the Great Powers." *Foreign Policy Reports,* March 1, 1946.

—— Thailand, the New Siam. New York, 1941.

Thompson, Warren S. "Population Prospects for China and Southeastern Asia." In "World Population in Transition," *Annals of the American Academy of Political and Social Science,* Vol. 237, January, 1945.

United States

Department of Commerce. American Direct Investments in Foreign Countries, 1936. Washington, 1938.

—— Economic Development in Siam (Trade Information Bulletin No. 606). Washington, 1929.

Interdepartmental Committee on the Philippines. Report on Philippine–United States Trade Relations. Washington, 1935.

Joint Preparatory Committee on Philippine Affairs. Report of May 20, 1938, Vols. I–III. Washington, 1938.

Tariff Commission. Report No. 73 (2d ser.): Report to the President on Sugar. Washington, 1934.

—— Report No. 118 (2d ser.): United States–Philippine Trade. Washington, 1937.

United States Congress

Annual Report of the Governor-General of the Philippine Islands, 1928. 71st Congress, 2d Session, H.D. 133. Washington, 1930.

Fourth Annual Report of the United States High Commissioner to the Philippine Islands to the President and Congress of the United States (Washington, 1940); Fifth Annual Report (Washington, 1941).

House of Representatives, Committee on Insular Affairs. Hearings on Philippine Independence. H.I. Res. 131, H.R. 3924, H.I. Res. 127, H.R. 2817. Washington, 1924.

—— Hearings on Philippine Local Autonomy. H.R. 8856. Washington, 1924.

—— Hearings on Independence for the Philippine Islands. H.R. 5182. Washington, 1930.

—— Hearings on S. 204, S. Res. 199, . . . To Investigate Feasibility of Tariff Autonomy of Philippine Islands. Washington, 1930.

—— Further Report to S. 3822. Submitted by Mr. Harry B. Hawes. Washington, 1930.

—— Hearings on Philippine Independence (H.R. 8573), and Report to Accompany H.R. 8573, . . . To Provide for Complete Independence of the Philippine Islands. Washington, 1934.

House of Representatives, Committee on Ways and Means. Hearings on the Philippine Trade Act of 1945. H.R. 4185, H. R. 4676, H.R. 5185. Washington, 1945.

Senate, Committee on Finance. Hearings on the Philippine Trade Act of 1946. H.R. 5856. Washington, 1946.

Senate, Committee on Territories and Insular Possessions (Insular Affairs). Hearings on Philippine Independence, a Bill to Provide for Withdrawal of the U.S. from the Philippine Islands. S. 912. Washington, 1924.

—— Hearings on Independence for Philippine Islands. S. 204, S. 3108, S.I. Res. 113, S. Res. 199, S. 3379, S. 3822. Washington, 1930.

—— Hearings on Independence for Philippine Islands. S. 3377, including H.R. 7233. Washington, 1932.

—— Complete Independence of Philippine Islands. S. 1028. Washington, 1939.

Vandenbosch, Amry. "The Netherlands Colonial Balance Sheet." *Southern Economic Journal*, 1937.

—— The Dutch East Indies, Its Government, Problems and Politics. 3d ed. Berkeley, Calif., 1942.

Van Gelderen, J. "Western Enterprise and the Density of Population in the Netherlands Indies." In B. Schrike, ed., *The Effect of Western Influence on Native Civilization in the Malay Archipelago*. Batavia, 1929.

Viner, Jacob. "The American Interest in the Colonial Problem." In *The United States in a Multinational Economy*. Council on Foreign Relations, Studies in American Foreign Relations, No. 4. New York, 1945.

Virata, Leonidas S. "New Philippine Horizons." *Far Eastern Survey,* Vol. XIV, No. 4, Feb. 28, 1945.

Vlekke, Bernard H. M. Nusantara, a History of the East Indian Archipelago. Cambridge, Mass., 1943.

—— The Story of the Dutch East Indies. Cambridge, Mass., 1945.

Wickizer, V. D., and M. K. Bennet. The Rice Economy of Monsoon Asia. Palo Alto, Calif., 1941.

William, Maurice. The Social Interpretation of History, a Refutation of the Marxian Economic Interpretation of History. New York, 1921.

—— Sun Yat Sen versus Communism. Baltimore, 1932.

Wittfogel, Karl A. Sun Yat Sen. Vienna, 1927.

Zimmerman, Carle C. Siam, Rural Economic Survey, 1930–31. Issued by the Thailand Ministry of Commerce and Communication. Bangkok, 1931.

—— "Some Phases of Land Utilization in Siam." *Geographical Review,* Vol. XXVII, 1937.

Index

Rice (*Continued*)

age: holdings, 145; farmers' indebtedness, 146; agricultural level and standards, 152, 155

—— Malaya: acreage: location of rice lands, 106, 110; production, 109, 110-13; formerly a Malay monopoly, 110, 112; present need for imports, 110, 130; sales methods, 111; price guarantee, 113*n*; per capita consumption: relation between price and earnings, 128

—— Java: peasant food supply, 55; imports to East Indies, 56

—— Philippines: the main crop, 174; level of cultivation, 177; tenure system in certain provinces, 184 f.; advances to share-tenant: repayment and interest, 188; marketing, 209-11

—— Siam: operations controlled by Chinese, 224, 227, 237 ff.; the leading industry, 225, 237; exports, 226, 227, 230; cultivation, 227, 228, 230, 235 f.; quality, 236; marketing, 236-41

Rice banks, 47, 48

Rice Commission, 210

Rice Share Tenancy Act, 196

Riots, *see* Rebellion

Rizal, José, 251; quoted, 253

Robequain, Charles, 145, 153, 154; quoted, 160

Rockefeller Foundation, 94

Roman Catholic Church, Philippine estates, 178, 180, 181, 190*n*; Taft-Vatican negotiations, 178*n*, 191*n*; agrarian rebellion against, 191; Rizal's novel based on the rebellion, 253

Roosevelt, Franklin D., on poverty, 4; Administration, 207*n*

Roosevelt, Theodore, 189*n*, 196, 199; quoted, 200

Roxas, Manuel, 195*n*, 216, 217*n*

Rubber, Southeast Asia main producer and exporter: U.S. main market, 4; Indo-China, 136, 137, 155 ff.; Netherlands East Indies, 114*n*, 115, 116, 118, 120; Philippines, 198

Rubber Research Institute, 115, 116

Runes, I. T., 214, 215, 218, 219; quoted, 204 f.

Rural Progress Administration, 200

—— Malaya: labor force, 103, 120 ff. (*see entries under* Labor); world's largest producer: record exports, 104; capital investment, 104 f., 106, 109; acreage used, 106, 108; land ownership, 109 f.;

regulation, 109, 114, 118 f.; effect upon rice production, 111; Stevenson plan: Ormsby-Gore recommendations, 114; rubber farming, 114-20; economic and social status of native producer, 116 ff., 119; competition of growers and synthetic producers: future aspects, 120; strikes, 125 ff.; resulting benefits, 126; threats to: alternative solution, 131

Saba-pe transaction, 87

Sakdalist Rebellion, 192 ff., 257

Salt monopoly, 162

Samar, *map*, 175; *see under* Philippine Islands

Sandico, Teodore, 194

San Min Chu I (Sun Yat Sen), excerpts, 249, 250

Santos, Pedro Abad, 197, 215

Sarekat Islam, 254

Saya San, revolt led by, 95

Sayre, Francis B., 179; quoted, 191, 197, 207, 208*n*

Selangor, 101, 106; *map*, 107; *see also* Malaya

Seri Thai, 257*n*

Settlement, land, *see* Land settlement

Shan states, *map*, 75

Share-cropping, 49, 140, 143, 145, 187, 190*n*; increase as result of excess population, 18

Share-tenancy, 176, 187

Siam, 223-44; *map*, 5, 229; lag in fields of public health and services, 11, 228; effects of political independence upon its semicolonial economy, 11, 226, 244; foreign trade figures, 13; population, 16, 17*n*, 227 ff.; rubber export restriction, 114*n*, 118; why politically independent through centuries, 223; avoidance of public indebtedness and foreign entanglement, 223, 224, 243; economic structure, 224 f.; financial attitude compared with Japan's, 224; foreign investments: raw materials: trading ports, 225; nationalist movement and its program, 226, 243, 247 f., 256, 258; land utilization, 227-32, 242; level of living, 231, 234, 241-43; land tenure and indebtedness, 232-35; level of agricultural cultivation, 235 f.; marketing problem, 236-41; trade an unconquered sector in economy of, 237; government-controlled banks, 240; conclusions re its problems and future, 243 f.

Tayug incident, 192, 194
Tenancy legislation, Burma, 82n; Philippines, 196 ff.
Tenant class in Burma, statistics, 84; migrating class, 86 ff.; *see also* Indians
Tenant problems, *see* Credit; Indebtedness; Land; Landlords
Tenant union, 197
Tenasserim, *map*, 75
Thai Rice Company, 239n
Thakin Association (Dobamma Asiayone), 97, 255
Thompson, Virginia, 155, 228, 230, 233, 236, 243n
Thompson, Warren S., estimate of future population of Southeast Asia, 16 f.
Three Principles of the People (Sun Yat Sen), 251n; excerpts, 249, 250
Tin, main producer and exporter: main market, 4; labor force, 103, 120 ff. (*see entries under* Labor); capital investment, 104, 106; smelter monopolies: export duty, 105
Tobacco growers, 211
Tonkin, 134, 164, 165; *map*, 139; *see also* Indo-China
Trade, *see* Foreign trade; Marketing; Middlemen
Trade union movement, Philippines, 197, 213, 215 f.; *see also* Labor
Trade Unions bill, 127
Trading companies, activities of: indirect rule, 30
Trengganu, 101; *map*, 107; *see also* Malaya
Tribes, primitive, in Indo-China, 141
Trusteeship institution of United Nations, 260
Tuberculosis, why prevalent in Philippines, 220, 221
Tydings, Millard E., 203; quoted, 205n, 209n
Tydings-MacDuffie Act, 205

Unemployment, 38, 56, 93, 123, 129, 190; a feature of agricultural problem, 9; technological, 20
Unfederated Malay States, 132; regions included, 101; *map*, 107
Unions, trade, *see* Labor
United Front Against the Japanese (Hukbalahap), 194n, 216
United Nations, 33n, 243, 259n; Netherlands-Indonesian truce agreement

mediated, 69; trusteeship institution of, 260
United States, Southeast Asian trade, 4; effect upon exchange situation of "mother countries," 6; Blaine Amendment to Tariff Law, 60n; recognition of Indonesian Republic, 68; products from, investments in, Malaya, 103, 104n, 105; Siamese declaration of war against Britain and, 257n
—— Philippine administration, 167-222; influence of educational and other efforts, 167, 221 f.; economic dependence, 168 f., 203, 205 ff.; investigations, hearings, committees to study trade relations and status of investments, 170, 206; capital investments, 171, 181, 202; number and influence of resident Americans, 173; condition of peasantry not improved under control by: resulting social unrest, 191; difficulties faced, and reforms accomplished, 196 ff.; land policy and its effects, 197 ff.; export quota of sugar to, 202; trade relations, 1946 and future, 206 ff.; extent of foreign trade control, 209; how responsible for high standard of living, 217; public health achievements, 220; *see also* Philippine Islands
United States of Indonesia, 69
United States Tariff Act (Payne-Aldrich), 168, 201
Usury, *see* Interest and usury

Vandenbosch, A., 41, 42; quoted, 49, 65
Van Gelderen, J., 68; quoted, 53, 57, 60
Vargas, Jorge B., 195n
Vellayan, A. M. M., 99
Viet Minh (League for the Independence of Viet Nam), 256n
Viet Nam, Annamite Republic, 165 f., 256n
Village economy, brought to slow death by money economy, 8, 21; Burma's early economy based on, 71; communal land, 71, 143, 145; loss of moral restraints following dissolution of, 87, 95; usury related to disintegration of, 188; disintegration as factor in national consciousness, 245, 246; *see also* Handicrafts
—— Java, 44; ways in which affected by Dutch colonial policy, 45 ff.; invasion by money: credit system, 46-50; effect upon land rights, 51 ff.; indirect influ-